The Public Library
of Nashville
and Davidson
County

KEEP DATE CARD IN BOOK

POCKET

HEMINGWAY'S ART OF NON-FICTION

Hemingway's Art of Non-Fiction

Ronald Weber

St. Martin's Press   New York

First published in the United States of America in 1990

Printed in Hong Kong

ISBN 0–312–03592–6

Library of Congress Cataloging-in-Publication Data

Weber, Ronald, 1934–
Hemingway's art of non-fiction/Ronald Weber.
p.   cm.
Includes bibliographical references.
ISBN 0–312–03592–6
1. Hemingway, Ernest, 1899–1961—Criticism and interpretation.
2. Reportage literature, American—History and criticism.
I. Title.
PS3515.E37Z935   1990
813'.52—dc20   89–38201
                                                                              CIP

For Edward Fischer and Thomas Stritch

Contents

Acknowledgements

Anyone writing about Ernest Hemingway builds upon the labor of many scholars. In thinking about Hemingway's non-fiction I have found especially helpful work by Susan Beegel, Gerry Brenner, Scott Donaldson, Charles Fenton, Allen Josephs, Robert W. Lewis, Kenneth S. Lynn, Jeffrey Meyers, Michael S. Reynolds, Robert O. Stephens, Jacqueline Tavernier-Courbin, Lionel Trilling, William White and Edmund Wilson. I must single out, as have many before me, a special debt to Carlos Baker for his biographical and critical work on Hemingway and particularly for his volume of Hemingway's letters, an invaluable mine of information and suggestion.

Anyone writing about Hemingway becomes beholden as well to the curators of the Ernest Hemingway Collection at the John Fitzgerald Kennedy Library in Boston. I want to thank Joan O'Connor and Megan Floyd Desnoyers for their help and courtesy while I was working in the library and for responding to telephone queries.

Initial work on the study was carried out during a fellowship year at the Gannett Center for Media Studies at Columbia University. I am grateful to the Gannett Foundation for its generous support and to Everette E. Dennis, the Executive Director of the Gannett Center, and Jane Coleman, the Associate Director for Administration, for providing an ideal environment for research and writing. The congenial company of my fellow Gannett Fellows and the opportunity to talk with them about the project added greatly to the pleasures of the year. Parts of Chapter 1 of the study were the basis of an occasional paper, *Journalism, Writing, and American Literature*, published by the Gannett Center (April 1987). Parts of Chapter 4 were drawn on in the article, 'Peddling Papa', which appeared in the *Chicago Times*, 1 (March–April 1988), pp. 50–6. Other parts of the study were treated in lectures at Columbia University, Hope College and Luther College.

Colleagues at the University of Notre Dame lent a sympathetic ear in conversations about the work. Pat helped as always. The dedication, to two teachers, colleagues and friends, recognizes many happy and instructive years in their company.

Hemingway's letters and unpublished manuscripts are quoted with the permission of The Ernest Hemingway Foundation.

Introduction: Permanent Records

*At Christmas I had written him that I wanted to come over and write
the truth, the absolute truth, about his work and his place in bullfighting so there would be a permanent record; something that would
last when we were both gone.*

This is a book about Ernest Hemingway as a writer of non-fiction. At
once, clarification is needed about the use of that uncertain term,
non-fiction, as applied to Hemingway's fact writing. He wrote five
non-fiction books – one left unfinished, and only two published in
his lifetime – and considered doing more, including a book about the
Gulf Stream and a second volume of his Paris memoirs, and he
produced a good deal of newspaper and magazine journalism. Yet
he was a non-fiction writer only in a special sense. Although he
began his writing career as a journalist and in later years liked to
refer to himself as an old newsman, and although he approached his
non-fiction as a form of fact writing, he was never devoted as a
writer to what Thoreau maintained was the rarest poetry, a true
account of the actual, or to what he himself called the absolute truth.
He frequently distinguished between the writer who describes and
the writer who makes, and always enlisted himself among the latter.
Even when he set himself to the task of describing – or, as he once
put it, to a kind of honest journalism based on reporting that wasn't
whoring – he shaped the material into a personal blend of fact and
fiction that rigorous practitioners of the discipline of fact would find,
to say the least, questionable.

Carlos Baker, commenting on one of the posthumous non-fiction
books, *A Moveable Feast*, said Hemingway worked in the gray area
between fact and fiction, and indeed he did. It was the inevitable
territory of all of his non-fiction books and much of his occasional
journalism. Yet just as it is clearly a mistake to take Hemingway's
non-fiction as a simple record of fact, it is equally mistaken to lump
it together with the fiction as similar excursions into imaginative

writing. When George Plimpton, questioning him in a *Paris Review* interview, referred to the *Green Hills of Africa, To Have and Have Not,* and *Across the River and Into the Trees* as novels, Hemingway promptly straightened him out:

> No, that is not true. The *Green Hills of Africa* is not a novel but was written in an attempt to write an absolutely true book to see whether the shape of a country and the pattern of a month's action could, if truly presented, compete with a work of the imagination.

After repeating the exact language he had used in the foreword to *Green Hills of Africa*, he re-emphasized the point. The two stories that had come from the African material, 'The Snows of Kilimanjaro' and 'The Short Happy Life of Francis Macomber', had been 'invented from the knowledge and experience acquired on the same long hunting trip', but the book about one month of the adventure was something different, a 'truthful account'.[1]

Hemingway's non-fiction wasn't fiction by another name, yet neither was it non-fiction free of the play of invention. In the preface to *A Moveable Feast* he cheerfully acknowledged (with one eye perhaps to fending off threats of libel) that the book might be regarded as fiction if the reader preferred. Nonetheless, the governing impulse behind the non-fiction was fundamentally different from that of the fiction. The stories and novels were made up but the non-fiction, as Hemingway approached it, wasn't. It was true, meaning that it was more fact than fiction. Where the non-fiction books and the fiction most deeply joined was in the effort to create works of lasting value. Hemingway said he wanted to be judged not by the journalism he tossed off for money but the serious writing he did for keeps. He meant the enduring category to include his major efforts in non-fiction. They were intended as permanent records, books that would last after he was gone, standing side by side with the fiction in his complete works.[2]

Critics, however, have seldom accorded them this position. With the exception of *A Moveable Feast*, a special case given its subject, starting out in Paris in the glamorous twenties, and its place as the first posthumous book, the non-fiction books commonly have been taken as curious diversions or unfortunate lapses from the main business of his career – experiments at best – and as such have lived a twilight existence in the commanding shadow of the fiction. One reason is their odd publishing history. After the publication of *Death in the Afternoon* and *Green Hills of Africa* in the 1930s, Hemingway didn't again appear in print as a writer of extended non-fiction until *Life* magazine published an edited version of his manuscript of *The Dangerous Summer* in 1960. *Life* said the complete work would be published by Scribner's the following year, but a quarter of a century passed before it made its appearance – in another edited version of Hemingway's manuscript – in book form. *A Moveable Feast*, essentially finished before his death and given to his publisher to read but with instructions that it be returned to him, was published in an editorially altered form in 1964, three years after his death. An unfinished 200 000-word account of the second African safari has yet to appear in book form, though lengthy excerpts appeared in *Sports Illustrated* magazine in 1971 under the title 'African Journal'. Editions of the last three non-fiction books, published as Hemingway left them, is an obvious need.

A more important factor in the relative obscurity of the non-fiction is the critical tendency automatically to grant fiction primary status – to see fact restraining the free exercise of imagination whereas in fiction there is, in theory at least, no such limitation. Whether this attitude is warranted in Hemingway's case is not an issue here. The view set out in the following pages is that non-fiction – principally the five book-length efforts, the heart of his achievement as a fact writer – occupied a large part of his career and deserves more close and undivided attention than it has hitherto received. Although one of his biographers, Jeffrey Meyers, has claimed him as the most important American novelist of the century, Hemingway's finest work was done in the short story; it was, as has been frequently remarked, his suited genre. I would add that non-fiction writing in a vigorously personal vein and mingling fact and fiction was another. Few American fiction writers of major status also produced such a varied and enduring body of non-fiction. As Hemingway himself might have put it, against the competition – Henry James and Mark Twain at the turn of the century, John Dos Passos, James Agee, John Hersey, Joan Didion and Norman Mailer since – he more than holds his own.

This isn't to say that the non-fiction matches or surpasses the fiction in reader appeal or artistic quality. It is simply to say that Hemingway's fact work stands by itself both as a major part of his lasting achievement and as a significant body of American non-fiction. Once again, the merits of the non-fiction versus the fiction aren't the question. That approach invariably leads to second-class citizenship for the non-fiction – often to scarcely noticing it at all.

Accounts of Hemingway's journalistic origins unfailingly look to the effect of his early newspaper work on the fiction, bypassing the more obvious link with the later non-fiction. The biographies and major critical studies likewise lean heavily toward the fiction. Carlos Baker gives the non-fiction careful and revealing attention in *Hemingway, The Writer as Artist* but finally emphasizes the ways in which *Death in the Afternoon* illuminates *For Whom the Bell Tolls*, how *Green Hills of Africa* contrasts with the imaginative freedom of the two celebrated African stories of the same period. The single critical study devoted to the non-fiction, Robert O. Stephens' important 1968 book *Hemingway's Nonfiction*, holds that the 'best reason for studying the nonfiction is to better learn the fiction.'[3] The view at the center of this book is the reverse: the best reason for studying the non-fiction is to better learn *it*.

One of the most astute Hemingway commentators, taking note of the general neglect of the non-fiction, has said that 'if a writer is attempting to play the man-of-letters role, then we must judge his entire performance, not just the fiction.'[4] This book doesn't embrace the whole of Hemingway's performance, but it does try to redress an imbalance in thinking about his career through concentration on his major efforts in non-fiction. In so doing, it tries to add a greater measure of breadth to Hemingway's stature as a writer.

The opening chapter retraces his early career as a newspaper journalist, arguing that, as a fiction writer, the experience was useful to him chiefly in negative ways – that is, in providing him with a varied case against journalism that served in turn as an aesthetic program for fiction. Where his training in fact had the greatest positive carry-over was in his later magazine journalism and, most notably, in the book-length non-fiction. Yet here as well Hemingway brought to his work an essentially anti-journalistic outlook, one in which he sought to escape the inevitable death of topical writing by mingling fact with invention, observation with creation. It was, he believed, the only way to fashion the permanent records to stand with his permanent fictions. Subsequent chapters are devoted to each of the non-fiction books. I concentrate on the process of conception and writing, on the critical reception, and especially on matters of internal craft and design. With *The Dangerous Summer* and *A Moveable Feast* I take note of discrepancies between published versions and the manuscripts Hemingway left behind;

with the 'African Journal' I discuss the portion of the work that appeared in magazine form. At this writing, the full manuscript of the second African book has yet to be made available for examination.

As works of fact the five non-fiction books are remarkably different. Each has its roots in a conventional genre of non-fiction writing – handbook, travel book, journal, reportage, memoir – and each (with the exception of the unfinished African book) evolves into highly individual work marked by a good deal of technical ambition and imprinted with personality. The familiar genre was a starting point; the end was all Hemingway's own. Over the years his admirers have occasionally lamented the time given to the non-fiction and consequently diverted from the fiction – the years at the height of his career with *Death in the Afternoon* and *Green Hills of Africa*, the years at the end with *The Dangerous Summer* and *A Moveable Feast*. If there is cause for regret, as I hope the following pages show, it is only that he didn't turn his hand to non-fiction more often.

1

In Spite of It

It is only by never writing the way I write in a newspaper office . . .
that I make you believe that I can write.

Early in 1951, Charles A. Fenton, a young English instructor at Yale, began corresponding with Hemingway about the doctoral dissertation he was writing on the author's early years in journalism. He had a central idea and eventually, in an exchange of letters over the next three years, set it out directly:

> My thesis is that journalism was a lot more important than the critics have recognized, as a training not only in technique, but in the treatment of material, and, indeed, in the very choice of material. The critics have conventionally presented you as one part Pound, two parts Gertrude Stein. This has never made complete sense to me.[1]

For Fenton, it wasn't the literary hothouse of Paris in the 1920s that had shaped Hemingway so much as fledgling high school journalism in Oak Park, Illinois, and the newsrooms of Kansas City and Toronto. He repeated the idea in a letter to Hemingway's first wife, Hadley Richardson, soliciting information about her husband:

> . . . the more I investigate these various areas the more convinced I become that the standard literary commentary on Mr. Hemingway, which has assigned the bulk of the credit for his early success to the teachings of Gertrude Stein and Ezra Pound, has been vastly over-rated. I believe the city rooms of the Kansas City Star and the Toronto papers must be a more prominent role.[2]

To prove his thesis, Fenton cast a wide net of letters to those who had known and worked with the young Hemingway, asking for recollections; but he also needed confirmation from Hemingway himself on several matters. Could he, for instance, recall particular stories he had written for the *Kansas City Star*? Had he kept any copies of the *Co-operative Commonwealth*, the monthly house organ he had worked on in Chicago in 1920–21? Why had he used the byline 'John Hadley' on some of his Toronto dispatches?

At first, Hemingway was a congenial correspondent. Always restive in the company of his Paris contemporaries, maybe he thought that as influences go his early journalism was harmless enough; certainly it didn't touch as acutely on the sensitive matter of his memories of former friends and literary rivals. Maybe there was even some appeal in an Ivy League professor asking his help, especially one who made a strenuous effort to establish his credentials as a passable Hemingway character. Fenton noted that he had served in the Royal Canadian Air Force during World War II and had written fiction, and he adopted an epistolary style meant to be disarming. In one letter he brought up the critical battering of *Across the River and Into the Trees*, brashly instructing Hemingway to pay attention only to the views of genuine professionals:

> The rest are all either tiresome little fags or embittered scholars, and I'm sure I'm not revealing any scoop to you when I say they'll do the same to everything you write, unless you turn phony, since the line right now is God and America. Most of the people in the literary and academic worlds, I find, in fact, are all slobs, and sometimes I even find myself thinking nostalgically of all the illiterate bastards I soldiered with.[3]

The approach worked. Hemingway grumbled about taking time from his own work, but he provided information, corrected mistakes, and generally encouraged Fenton by addressing him as 'My dear Air Marshall' and telling him 'if you want the true gen on anything else let me know.'[4]

The era of good feeling was, of course, short lived. Hemingway already had his back up over Philip Young's psychobiographical study of his fiction, written as a doctoral dissertation in 1948 and under revision for book publication, and he was engaged in a testy correspondence about that work while he was dealing with Fenton. 'Criticism', he growled in a letter, 'is getting all mixed up with a combination of the Junior F.B.I.-men, discards from from Freud and Jung and a sort of Columnist peep-hole and missing laundry list school.'[5] Carlos Baker had just written him about a critical study he was beginning, and Hemingway still bore scars from Lillian Ross' profile in *The New Yorker* that he said he had read with horror. His irritation with all the poking around in his life carried over to Fenton. Soon he was charging the Yale instructor with invading his privacy by writing biography in the guise of criticism and ruining material from his early life that he meant to employ in his fiction.

Hemingway's second thoughts about the project were also aroused by Fenton's informants, their views communicated to him by Fenton, who put forward various newspaper colleagues and editors as guiding lights, always a prickly issue. Lionel Moise, a flamboyant, itinerant reporter Hemingway had known in Kansas City, was a case in point. Hemingway had praise for Moise as a facile journalist but bridled at the suggestion that the older man taught him anything about writing; he told Fenton it simply wasn't so. He added that the Moise business was a trap, just the sort he saw no way of keeping Fenton out of short of taking on an endless job of correction. The heart of the problem was Fenton's reliance on the shaky memories of survivors – survivors, moreover, who had been newspapermen. Hemingway pointed out that it was in the nature of newspaper work to destroy memory since the journalist always had to forget what had taken place the day before; as a result, the recollections of newspapermen were the least dependable of scholarly materials.

There was doubt as well about the shaping effect of journalism in his development as a writer. He didn't confront Fenton's thesis directly but declared that the 'only thing of any importance to you except as back-ground is that the discipline started on the K.C. Star and when I got to where I had something to write about I had some idea of what discipline should be when self applied.'[6] That, the carry-over into fiction of the discipline of regular writing for a newspaper, was a far cry from the grander sort of journalistic influence Fenton had in mind; but, with the addition of journalism's early usefulness to him as a way of earning a living, it was all Hemingway himself would allow. In the letter to Hadley Richardson, Fenton quoted Hemingway as telling him that 'I never considered journalism as of any permanent value or in any way connected with my serious writing except as an apprenticeship. It was a way to earn a living while I learned to write and, later, to make a living while I wrote.' Fenton must have hoped Hadley would counter with a larger claim for journalism's influence, but she sidestepped the matter entirely, saying only that her husband had been profoundly occupied with the theories of Gertrude Stein, Ezra Pound and Sherwood Anderson – the very view Fenton hoped to correct.

As the Hemingway–Fenton correspondence wore on, Hemingway's irritation turned to anger, and finally he demanded that Fenton break off the study. Surprisingly, Fenton responded with equal heat, defending himself as serious and knowledgeable, lecturing Hemingway that a book on his apprenticeship would be done sooner or later and that he was 'better off having it done by a guy who's a writer, who admires your work immensely, who's in the Ivy League and not the sticks.'[7] Hemingway held his ground. He told Fenton the project was getting out of hand and to 'lay off the words that provoke with guys like ourselves.'[8] But his own language escalated; Fenton was soon tagged as a failed writer and Hemingway was offering him two hundred dollars to come to Cuba and say in person what he was saying in his letters. There was also a threat to alert Yale to his bad behavior. A more serious threat, one used before against Young, was to withhold permission to quote from his published work.

In the end, both sides calmed down. Hemingway either wearied of the correspondence or satisfied himself that Fenton was more interested in his work than his life. He continued to read sections of the dissertation and correct Fenton's information; in a letter written in the summer of 1953, shortly after threatening to withhold permission to quote, he graciously told Fenton: 'I think you did a wonderful job on the journalism and I am very grateful for your recalling so many things I wrote and forgot.'[9] After the dissertation was accepted at Yale in 1953 with the title *Ernest Hemingway's Literary Apprenticeship, 1916–1923*, Fenton cut the manuscript in half and readied it for book publication. 'I think this is now a good book,' he wrote to Hemingway. 'I know it is. It is fair to you and it's fair to me, and what it says is worth saying and worth having read.' He also asked if Hemingway wanted to contribute a preface 'saying whatever you think about it, me, scholarship, the Ivy League, etc.'[10] Hemingway declined on the grounds that he hadn't the time or disposition for more squabbling over questions of fact or taste, and offered good luck with the book.

But if that was his final word to Fenton, to others he expressed less congenial sentiments. In 1955, he told a professor named Fraser Drew who was visiting him in Cuba that Fenton's book was overdone and Fenton himself was a disappointed fiction writer and FBI stories and he wanted to see if anything had been compromised by Fenton's identification of real people. In a letter to Carlos Baker from the Mayo Clinic three weeks earlier he had referred with his best leaden sarcasm to news that Fenton had leaped to his death from a hotel window:

> Hope that won't set an example to my other biographers. Wonder what he thought about on the way down. Understand he had started to go down once and then decided to climb up and started all over again . . . Never met him but feel very sorry for him although his school of biography and criticism was that type of F.B.I. treatment which I did not care for . . . Hope this levity is not out of order.[11]

As one of the earliest critical and biographical studies of Hemingway, Fenton's book, published in 1954 as *The Apprenticeship of Ernest Hemingway*, attracted wide attention. The *Atlantic Monthly* serialized three sections, the opening installment featured on the magazine's cover, and there were reviews in the major journals. Mark Schorer in the *New Republic* had praise for Fenton's methods, finding his interviewing and correspondence as scrupulous as that of a sociologist. John Aldridge in the *New York Times Book Review* agreed that the book was conscientious but found it lifeless and dull, Hemingway still safe from plodding intrusions of scholarship.

Neither critic took up the main idea announced in the book's preface – that the 'principal instrument' of a literary apprenticeship that, as Fenton said, turned a conventional talent into an artistic skill 'was journalism'[12] Aldridge even declared the main weakness of the book was the failure to document adequately the influence of Stein and Anderson on Hemingway, the notion Fenton was trying to set straight. Part of the failure to confront his central idea can be laid to the reviewers; but part belongs to Fenton as well. Although he announced his view clearly enough, the book frequently drifted from concentration on Hemingway's journalism, especially in sections dealing with war experiences in Italy and literary associations in Paris in the 1920s. More important, the argument for the central importance of journalism was simply unconvincing. Fenton performed an invaluable service in recreating Hemingway's early years in journalism; subsequent students of Hemingway have remained in his debt. But he seriously overstated the importance of the period for the fiction to come. About the influence on the extended non-fiction, the more apparent area of carry-over from Hemingway's newspaper days into his serious writing, he said nothing.

*   *   *

The apprenticeship began on the Oak Park high school weekly newspaper the *Trapeze* where Hemingway's byline appeared with regularity in his final two years, usually on sports stories and satirical columns, the latter in the boisterous manner of Ring Lardner's popular work in the *Chicago Tribune*. High school news-writing settled Hemingway on a career in journalism despite his father's wish that he follow him into medicine; even if he went to the University of Illinois, he told classmates, he meant to major in journalism. But the next step wasn't college but a cub reporter's job on a newspaper arranged by one of his father's brothers, a Kansas City businessman.

The *Kansas City Star*, when Hemingway joined it in the fall of 1917 for a brief stay of six months before leaving for Italy and the war, was one of the country's better papers. It promoted fresh, plain writing and took pride in hiring young men without experience and bend-ing them to the *Star* way. A central training device was a style sheet with 110 rules governing the newspaper's prose, most of them mechanical matters of spelling and punctuation but a few directed to style. 'They gave you this to study when you went to work,' Hemingway told Fenton, 'and after that you were just as responsible for having learned it as after you've had the articles of war read to you.'[13] The first rule of the style sheet bore obvious consequence for Hemingway's early literary style:

> Use short sentences. Use short first paragraphs. Use vigorous English. Be positive, not negative.

Rule 21, of equal bearing, was insisted upon by Pete Wellington, the assistant city editor in 1917, who exercised strong influence on young *Star* reporters:

> Avoid the use of adjectives, especially such extravagant ones as splendid, gorgeous, grand, magnificent, etc.

Hemingway apparently had such injunctions in mind when he said in an interview published in the *Kansas City Times* in 1940 that 'those were the best rules I ever learned for the business of writing. I've never forgotten them. No man with any talent, who feels and writes truly about the thing he is trying to say, can fail to write well if he abides with them.'[14]

Besides landing on a newspaper that valued good writing, Hemingway found himself in a setting in which literary interest on the part of reporters was taken for granted. Everyone on the paper seemed to be writing a novel on the side. The *Star* also had a literary department that reprinted examples of modern and classical literature, and the newsroom provided veteran journalists like Moise who had a storehouse of colorful experiences and strong opinions about fiction writing. To his young disciples Moise preached the virtues of objective storytelling, cautioning them against all mannered forms of narration, including stream of consciousness.

Fenton found it impossible to overvalue the importance of the *Star* for a fledgling writer. The newspaper taught all the right things, and taught them in a thoughtful if demanding setting of long days and six-day weeks. 'A young man who worked on the *Star*', he concluded, 'learned to write declarative sentences, and to avoid hackneyed adjectives, and to tell an interesting narrative; and, because of the literary department, he learned to do these things in a school which was interested in a more complex aspect of writing that the mere coverage of the day's events.'[15] It seems pointed evidence of the newspaper's importance that when Hemingway was working on the prose miniatures of *in our time* in Paris in 1923 he followed the techniques of the *Star* style book as well as its spelling rules for place names, and in two instances he drew on material first turned up during his newspaper days.

Back from the war, he resumed his journalistic career after months of working on short stories that he couldn't get published. The *Toronto Star Weekly*, when he joined it in the winter of 1920, paid only for work actually printed in its columns, was the polar opposite of the *Kansas City Star*, a Saturday edition of the parent *Toronto Star* that offered a steady fare of features and humor and had few standards beyond the entertainment of readers. Had the jobs been reversed, Toronto before Kansas City, Hemingway might not have lingered in newspaper journalism as long as he did, but following sound formal training on the *Star*, the glitter and especially the freedom of the *Star Weekly* was just right.

Hemingway was now able to pick his subjects and experiment with methods. The *Star Weekly* encouraged his gifts for satire and ironic compression, for stories based on action and dialogue as well as lengthy pieces of knowledgeable exposition, and it required that he think of his writing in terms of appealing to a broad audience. Although much of his Toronto journalism was hasty and overdrawn, there were passages that prefigured the precise economy of the short fiction to come. One such appeared in a report on the impact of Canadian liquor laws on American prohibition:

> In the cities you see the evidences that there is a liquor traffic between Canada and the States. I saw a slack-lipped, white-faced kid being supported on either side by two scared looking-boys of his own age in an alley outside a theater in Detroit. His face was pasty and his eyes stared unseeingly. He was deathly sick, his arms hanging loosely.
>
> 'Where'd he get it?' I asked one of the scared kids.
>
> 'Blew in his week's pay for a quart of Canuck bootlegged.' The two boys hauled him up the alley. 'Come on, we got to get him out of here before the cops see him.'
>
> If the people who talk about 'good liquor' could see a kid drunk – but this isn't a sermon. It is merely a few facts on the way liquor is coming into the United States from Canada.[16]

Setting his own work habits and selling his work to the *Star Weekly* also allowed Hemingway the satisfaction of considering himself, at age twenty, a professional writer. He made little money at space-rate work – an editor recalled that his biggest check was for ten dollars – but enough partially to support himself by writing.

There was an interlude in 1920–1 when he returned to Chicago to work as assistant editor of a monthly house organ, the *Co-operative Commonwealth*, a modestly useful time in that it kept him writing in a feature vein and on a schedule he largely set for himself – and in that it marked the beginning of his friendship with Sherwood Anderson. The next large step in his journalistic career was going abroad in the winter of 1921 as a roving correspondent for both the Toronto papers with headquarters in Paris. Essentially, the job was an extension of the freelance feature work he had done for the *Star Weekly*, giving him broad freedom of movement and choice of material, with the newspaper paying expenses and space rates for stories it printed together with $75 a week and expenses while on specific assignments.

If Hemingway had gone on a full-time basis to the European

bureau of an American newspaper, he would have followed the familiar routines and time pressures of straight reporting. The *Star* used wire services for such coverage; what it wanted from Hemingway were entertaining features and some interpretative articles that could be mailed in and printed when space allowed. One of his first pieces, published in the *Star Weekly* in February 1922, was typical, opening with a quick, impressionistic account of the harbor of Vigo, Spain, where he and Hadley had arrived two months before. It was the kind of free-wheeling personal journalism that came easily to the hand of an aspiring fiction writer:

> Vigo is a pasteboard-looking village, cobble-streeted, white and orange-plastered, set up on one side of a big, almost landlocked harbor that is large enough to hold the entire British navy. Sun-baked brown mountains slump down to the sea like tired old dinosaurs, and the color of the water is as blue as a chromo of the bay at Naples.
>
> A gray pasteboard church with twin towers and a flat, sullen fort that tops the hills where the town is set up look out on the blue bay, where the good fishermen will go when snow drifts along the northern streams and trout lie nose to nose in deep pools under a scum of ice. For the bright, blue chromo of a bay is alive with fish.[17]

Given the stylistic freedom allowed by the work, Hemingway was also able to indulge his developing skill with dialogue and a taste for comic effects. The lead of a story published in the *Star Weekly* in the same year played with the entrepreneurial spirit of a Spanish mailman:

> The postman comes in sight down the street waving a letter. 'A letter for the Senor,' he shouts. He hands it to you.
>
> 'A splendid letter, is it not, Senor? I, the postman, brought it to you. Surely the good postman will be well rewarded for the delivery of such a splendid letter?'
>
> You tip the postman. It is a little more than he had expected. He is quite overcome.
>
> 'Senor,' says the postman, 'I am an honest man. Your generosity has touched my heart. Here is another letter. I had intended to save it for tomorrow to insure another reward from the always generous Senor. But here it is. Let us hope that it will be as splendid a letter as the first!'[18]

Most of Hemingway's European journalism was neither so bright nor so controlled, nor was it of much aid to a fiction writer trying to learn his craft. It was conventional, make-do work that seemed only a drain on the time he preferred to spend on his real writing. Three months after he arrived in Europe he was grumbling to Sherwood Anderson that 'this goddamn newspaper stuff is gradually ruining me' and making plans to 'cut it all loose pretty soon and work for about three months.'[19] Newspaper work became more demanding when the *Star* sent him off to the Genoa Economic Conference in 1922 and then to Asia Minor for material on the war between Greece and Turkey. With no great regard for journalistic ethics, Hemingway cabled virtually identical dispatches from the war to Hearst's International News Service under the byline John Hadley despite the *Star's* exclusive right to his material. In 1923 he was in Lausanne covering the Greco-Turkish peace talks and sending material to Hearst's Universal News Service as well as the INS – a three-ring circus, he later called it, in which he ran 'a twenty-four hour wire service for an afternoon and morning news service under two different names.'[20] In both Genoa and Lausanne, Hemingway, for one of the few times in his news career, was in the harness of something akin to ordinary journalism, covering some breaking news as well as churning out his features and associating with veteran foreign correspondents like Lincoln Steffens, Guy Hickok and George Seldes.

He was particularly struck by a young South African journalist on the European circuit, William Bolitho Ryall (who later used the name William Bolitho), then a correspondent for the *Manchester Guardian*, admiring his strong personality and easy professionalism. Bolitho, who liked to say that newspaper work was a stepping-stone rather than a career, also played into Hemingway's growing restlessness with journalism. 'Exchange the newspaper game', he told another young journalist at the time, 'for the thing we are trained to do, namely, writing. Book or plays, or what have you . . .' Bolitho had only disdain for writers who lingered too long in journalism, urging them to turn to more important work. 'I don't care whether it's fact or fiction,' he said, 'but it's got to be done somehow unless you want to end up like old "whiskers" – you know who I mean – as a burnt-out reporter cadging drinks and dead-dog assignments from his younger friends.'[21]

Bolitho's cynicism, directed to politicians as well as journalists, was a likely influence on several effective pieces Hemingway sent from Lausanne that gleefully portrayed the flaws of world leaders. In one, he sketched a hard-eyed portrait of Mussolini as 'the biggest bluff in Europe':

> If Mussolini would have me taken out and shot tomorrow morning I would still regard him as a bluff. The shooting would be a bluff. Get hold of a good photo of Signor Mussolini sometime and study it. You will see the weakness in his mouth which forces him to scowl the famous Mussolini scowl that is imitated by every 19-year-old Fascisto in Italy. Study his past record . . . Study his propensity for clothing small ideas in big words. Study his propensity for dueling. Really brave men do not have to fight duels, and many cowards duel constantly to make themselves believe they are brave. And then look at his black shirt and his white spats. There is something wrong, even histrionically, with a man who wears white spats with a black shirt.[22]

But however deftly he handled it now and then, journalism wasn't the kind of writing he wanted to do. Shortly after the end of the Lausanne conference he and Hadley traveled down to see Ezra Pound, now living in Rapallo, a visit that had two practical consequences for his real writing career. He met Edward J. O'Brien, a Bostonian who edited an annual anthology of short stories, and O'Brien accepted 'My Old Man' for the 1923 volume. It would be Hemingway's first publication between hard covers. Another visitor in Rapallo was Robert McAlmon, a poet, short-story writer and independent publisher. When Hemingway told him about Hadley losing most of his early manuscripts in a Paris railway station, McAlmon wanted to see what was left. Later in 1923 McAlmon's Contact Publishing Co. would bring out *Three Stories & Ten Poems*, Hemingway's first collection of imaginative work.

The same year, the *Star* sent Hemingway to the Ruhr for a series of interpretative articles on French occupation of the region. It was his most demanding assignment as a journalist, resulting in some 20 000 words; six of the ten articles he produced appeared on page one of the newspaper. The *Star* heavily promoted the series, drawing as much attention to the young reporter as the material. One blurb declared that 'Hemingway has not only a genius for newspaper work, but for the short story as well. He is an extraordinarily gifted and picturesque writer. Besides his dispatches for the *Star*, he writes very little else, only two or three stories a year.'[23] There was a nice irony about the final remark, for with the money brought in by the Ruhr series Hemingway was close to abandoning journalism for the full-time pursuit of fiction.

In the fall of 1923 he was back in Toronto with the *Star* due to Hadley's pregnancy and the need for steady income. To this point, his journalistic work had been graced with good fortune; now it turned sour, offering only the advantage, from Hemingway's point of view, of leading to a final break with newspapering. In Paris he had possessed a roving correspondent's freedom; in Toronto he was under the thick-handed discipline of Harry Hindmarsh, the assistant managing editor of the *Star*, and subjected to a heavy load of routine assignments and dull travel designed to bring a star reporter down to journalistic earth. By his own account, the work kept him exhausted, draining away – or so he claimed to a colleague – ten years of his literary life. He said working for Hindmarsh was like being in the German army with a poor commander. To Gertrude Stein he complained that the 'free time that I imagined in front of a typewriter in a newspaper office has not been.'[24] When Hindmarsh kept up the pressure, Hemingway promptly resigned effective 1 January 1924, a planned two-year stay with the paper reduced to four months, and returned to Paris with Hadley and their infant son. He never went back to Toronto, though a *Star* legend had it that he returned in triumph to the newsroom to distribute copies of his first novel.

*   *   *

The newspaper world Hemingway entered in Kansas City in 1917 had changed drastically for aspiring writers. When Whitman and Twain were working on newspapers a half-century before, it was still the heyday of a casual style of personal journalism. Reporters spent their days tramping around after local news and wrote it up in forms meant to entertain as well as inform and often at rambling lengths; invention here and there to brighten or expand a story wasn't unknown. Sketches, color pieces and letters from distant places were as common as accounts of events. Whitman turned out long sketches thick with the sights and sounds of the urban landscape for the *New York Aurora* that bore some resemblance to 'Song of Myself' (leading to Emerson's remark that *Leaves of Grass* was a mixture of the Bhagavad Gita and the *New York Tribune*). Twain's letters to newspapers as a traveling correspondent prefigured the loose narrative form of his fiction. There were few requirements for a reporter's job save some flair with words and a capacity to endure long hours at low pay. When Twain took his first reporting job on the *Virginia Daily Territorial Enterprise* he was simply told to 'go all over town and ask all sorts of people all sorts of questions, make notes of the information gained, and write them out for publication.' After a day on the job he got the hang of it and decided he was 'peculiarly endowed' with newspaper ability, having found his 'legitimate occupation at last'.[25]

If newspapering could be casually entered, it could be as easily put aside. Young men of literary ambition soon learned that reporting was a demanding grind that left little time or energy for private work; Twain discovered that his legitimate occupation brought no 'rest or respite' and before long he was 'unspeakably tired of it'.[26] The trick was to get the benefit reporting offered – regular writing and the need to interest readers, plus some experience of the world that might be mined in stories and novels – and then move on before being overtaken by superficial observations and story formulas.

By the turn of the century, journalism, especially in its metropolitan dress, offered a more complicated apprenticeship to young writers. Beginners now were frequently legmen who followed regular beats and turned in their material to desk-bound writers (the literary castrati, Mencken quipped, who never left the office) who in turn produced impersonal copy. Personal modes of writing were reserved for sports writers and columnists and feature writers, the newspaper stars who now functioned as the magnets drawing the young to journalism. For those who succeeded as regular reporters, usually through a lucky break with a big story, journalism placed even heavier demands on their time and subjected them to stiff editing that often removed color elements from stories in favor of plain information. And there was increasing danger that, insofar as young writers mastered the new professional demands of newspapering, the material they turned up for their literary work would be cast in the same ready-made structures as their journalism. It was a harder world to break into now – and for that reason a harder world to escape. The idea for young writers was still to get their schooling in journalism, then get out before turning into dreary lifers, but the education took longer now and the trickling away of talent and ambition was harder to avoid.

Hemingway's apprenticeship in journalism was exceptional in that he experienced little of the new harm for a writer and reaped whatever literary benefits journalism still had to offer. With the exception of the final months on the *Toronto Star*, he was in the right places at the right times, and never for too long. He had the good luck to start on a serious newspaper and to write under the direction of competent editors who stressed the prose virtues of clarity and simplicity; after this brief exposure to journalistic discipline his work was mostly free-lance feature writing in an atmosphere of unusual editorial freedom, allowing him to tell stories more than report events, encouraging his gifts for narrative. All this, Fenton concluded, indicated that 'journalism had been the most important single factor' in Hemingway's literary development; all else – the travel, the shocks of war and peace, and personal and literary associations – were merely supplementary matters. He 'had been a newspaper-man,' Fenton put it in his book's final line, 'but he had become a writer.'[27] The implication, directly stated in the preface, was that journalism was the tool of change.

What seems closer to the truth is that newspaper work had some useful bearing on Hemingway's development as a fiction writer but was far from central. Fenton noted that Hemingway always acknowledged his debt to journalism, and he did – yet always in carefully guarded terms. When asked late in life if his training on the *Kansas City Star* had been helpful to him as a writer, he said simply: 'On the Star you were forced to learn to write a simple declarative sentence. That is useful to anyone.'[28] There was also, as he had told Fenton in a letter, the writing discipline he first learned in journalism. The matter of discipline had been brought up more than thirty years before in a letter to his friend Bill Horne from Italy during his first war. He noted that newspaper work had taught him the discipline of writing every day with or without inspiration; yet in the same letter he said that newspaper work was to real literature what a snowman was to the Pietà, and that he meant to return to it only to make a living.[29]

The importance of Fenton's book was that it called attention to Hemingway's early work in journalism and to some of the likely effects of the work on his fiction, the weakness that in pursuing a thesis it overvalued it. In addition to cautions from Hemingway, there were significant cautions from some of Fenton's informants, particularly about Kansas City days, that remained tucked away in the scholar's files. For example, the *Kansas City Star* style sheet, seemingly so instructive for a young writer, was hardly noticed by some *Star* reporters of the time. One told Fenton: 'I never heard of or saw a Star style book. I know they did not call married negro women "Mrs" and they frowned on adjectives.'[30] Another said: 'I never knew The Star had a style book . . . As to peculiarities of style, it didn't have any. The only rule I ever saw posted in The Star office was simply "Be accurate"'.[31] And another: 'I don't believe our style sheets of 1917–18 were widely distributed. As I recall it a few of the copy desks had the galley sheets containing the admonitions on style.'[32]

Opinions differed, too, about the possible influence of Moise on Hemingway. Some of Fenton's informants thought him a fraud and a third-rate reporter and couldn't recall that he had any theories about writing. John Selby, who became editor-in-chief of Rinehart Publishers, told Fenton that the Kansas City newsroom in Hemingway's time was a literate place and bristled with novels being written, but he thought 'this had little or no influence on Hemingway, who wrote rather badly at the time, and was forever disappearing into the receiving ward of the city hospital or onto the tail of an ambulance. I never felt that he was much interested in newspaper work, or that he had much aptitude for it.'[33] Fenton quoted Selby on the nature of the newsroom and Hemingway's ambulance riding but passed over the rest of his letter. In his notes to the book, Fenton thanked Marcel Wallenstein for help in reconstructing Hemingway's Kansas City days, but he didn't mention that Wallenstein had held that 'The Star taught Hemingway nothing about writing,' nor that the former journalist took issue with the book's central idea:

> . . . I feel that Hemingway would have done his great work as well if he had never seen The Star or been in a newspaper office. I do not believe that the profession of letters and the journeyman's trade of obtaining news and writing it have a great deal in common. I believe that Gertrude Stein influenced H. to a greater extent than any newspaper in his years of development.[34]

One of Fenton's correspondents even casts doubt on the merit of the *Star's* prose style. J. N. Darling told him: '. . . remembering the stodgy, almost stuffy texts which characterized the so called "K. C. Star style" in those days I can't believe that the pungent diction of Hemingway had its source in the Star News Room.'[35]

Carlos Baker wisely concludes that Hemingway's brief stay on the

Kansas City Star was a 'useful beginning' for his future work, and Jeffrey Meyers adds that the more extensive and professional work as a European reporter 'influenced but did not entirely account for' the development of his distinctive literary manner.[36] Journalism didn't turn Hemingway into a writer of unique power but it was a step in that complex and ultimately mysterious direction, as no one knew better than Hemingway himself. It was what he had tried to tell Fenton at the beginning of their embattled correspondence. Two years after Fenton's book was published Hemingway brought up the correspondence in a letter to Harvey Breit, boasting that he had kept some 'Hemingstein gen' hidden from the prying scholar. One thing was that 'there was something behind my writing besides the Kansas City Star which I always thought was a step in education.' He then added: 'But all these guys have theories and try to fit you into the theory.'[37]

*   *   *

Hemingway didn't abandon journalism when he left the Toronto newspapers behind. He continued to write it for the rest of his life – magazine journalism for mass-circulation publications that paid handsomely and demanded little, newspaper and magazine journalism during the Spanish Civil War and World War II. In a foreword to *By-Line: Ernest Hemingway*, a collection of his newspaper and magazine pieces, Philip Young offers the observation that Hemingway would have ranked among the best there ever were had he spent a career in reporting. There are, to be sure, moments of able reporting in Hemingway's journalism early and late, but the bulk of it was slapdash and some, especially during the Spanish war, notoriously bad. His credentials as a reporter covering the ordinary fare of ordinary journalism were limited; what he covered as a journalist after he left Kansas City and cub reporting behind was largely himself – his life, his interests. His journalism was nearly always unfettered personal journalism.

Some of that work bore marks of the distinctive qualities of his fiction – sharp compression; a detached, ironic point of view; dialogue that suggested more than it said; spare, exact description – though never all of these qualities altogether. At its best, parts of his magazine journalism even had something of the careful finish of the fiction – the opening section of 'A Paris Letter', for example, written for *Esquire* in 1934. Hemingway's editor at Scribner's, Max Perkins, properly admired another *Esquire* article, 'Wings Always Over Africa', a grim look at the Italian war in Ethiopia, telling him that there wasn't 'a living man who can write about things like that or can do that kind of writing (which really is only minor writing for you) who can be compared with you.'[38] William White also has pointed out material that was first published as journalism and later recycled as fiction.[39] Nonetheless, Hemingway brought to journalism hardly any of the hard effort and serious intent of his fiction or his extended non-fiction. At first it was a way of making a living, and later it was easy money; he gave it as little time and energy as he possibly could, and sometimes less, as he wryly acknowledged in the disarming opening of a magazine piece for *Esquire*:

> To write this sort of thing you need a typewriter. To describe, to narrate, to make funny cracks you need a typewriter. To fake along, to stall, to make light reading, to write a good piece, you need luck, two or more drinks and a typewriter. Gentlemen, there is no typewriter.[40]

Given Hemingway's early years on newspapers and his subsequent journalistic work, the natural temptation is to hunt out carry-overs into the fiction, to search out positive influences.[41] But the most striking legacy of his journalistic labors on his fiction is an insistently negative one – an elaborate case constructed over the years against journalism. Before he could emerge as as writer of serious fiction, Hemingway, like most writers who pursued journalism into the literary life, had to unlearn most of journalism's lessons. He had to discover, with the aid of Sherwood Anderson in Chicago and Pound and Stein in Paris, the difference between journalism and writing. He would learn that central lesson so well and articulate it so often that, finally, he would come to embody for writers of his own generation and since the literary argument against journalism. The journalist Russell Baker recalls first rejecting journalism as a career because his 'passion was to become the new Hemingway, not a newspaperman. The new Hemingway, after all, would be a great artist; what could a newspaperman ever be but a hack?'[42] The existence of an unbridgeable gulf between the artist and the newspaperman was one many another young writer would absorb from Hemingway.

'You ruined me as a journalist last winter,' he wrote to Gertrude Stein from Toronto in 1923. 'Have been no good since.'[43] The reference was to advice Stein had given him about the difference between reporting and creating, and about the conventions of newswriting that destroyed freshness. 'If you keep on doing newspaper work,' she had told him, 'you will never see things, you will only see words and that will not do, that is of course if you intend to be a writer.'[44] As early as 1924 he was declaring his own aesthetic aims in similar terms, writing in the 'Pamplona Letter' in *the transatlantic review* that 'it is only by never writing the way I write in a newspaper office . . . that I make you believe that I can write.'[45] In later life he invariably returned to the same negative contrast with journalism to make the case for his serious work. He granted that journalism had its early uses for a writer, but beyond this it was the opposition with journalism that marked his fiction. Fiction was simply everything journalism was not.

Fiction began with memory – with the reservoir of personal experience. Part of his running argument with Fenton was that in writing a biography of his early years, naming real people and real places, Fenton was ruining material he meant to employ in fiction. But newspaper work had the effect of destroying a writer's memory since, as Hemingway put it, 'you have to learn to forget every day what happened the day before'; the value of newspaper work stopped at 'the point that it forcibly begins to destroy your memory. A writer must leave it before that point. But he will always have scars from it.'[46] Although a writer started with the recollected facts of experience, if the work was to last it had to be intensified through invention into a new and independent reality. It was here that Hemingway the fiction writer separated himself most forcefully from the journalist. Journalism was writing for the moment; as such, it was doomed to the death of topicality. But the fiction writer, by adding invention to experience, gave his work the possibility of enduring life. Through invention, he said in the *Paris Review* interview, the writer makes 'a whole new thing truer than anything true and alive, and you make it alive, and if you make it well enough, you give it immortality.'[47]

Twenty-five years earlier he had made the same point in an *Esquire* article, explicitly marking out the difference between journalism and fiction:

> If it was reporting they would not remember it. When you describe something that has happened that day the timeliness makes people see it in their own imaginations. A month later that

element of time is gone and your account would be flat and they would not see it in their minds nor remember it. But if you make it up instead of describe it you can make it round and whole and solid and give it life. You create it, for good or bad. It is made; not described. It is just as true as the extent of your ability to make it and the knowledge you put into it.[48]

And before that, in *Death in the Afternoon*, he had described his early struggle to write serious fiction by noting the contrasting ease of 'writing for a newspaper' in which

> . . . you told what happened and, with one trick and another, you communicated the emotion aided by the element of timeliness which gives a certain emotion to any account of something that has happened on that day; but the real thing, the sequence of motion and fact which made the emotion and which would be as valid in a year or in ten years or, with luck and if you stated it purely enough, always, was beyond me and I was working very hard to try to get it.[49]

The passage suggests another element of Hemingway's case against journalism. In *A Child of the Century* Ben Hecht remembered his early newspaper work as a carefree world offering no discipline and requiring little of him beyond enthusiasm; Hemingway had the same sense of the undemanding nature of journalism. In *A Moveable Feast* he maintained that he could turn out journalism anywhere and under any circumstance. With serious fiction, on the other hand, he always stressed the difficulty. It was the roughest trade of all. The writer had only a pencil and a blank sheet of paper and the need to invent a world that was true and understandable, a task difficult to the point of impossibility, which was why good fiction was so highly valued. What was required was stern discipline and complete mental focus. After she read some of his early work Gertrude Stein had wisely told him to begin over and this time to concentrate; as against the 'one trick and another' of journalism, it was, he later acknowledged, the only way to capture the 'real thing' he was after in fiction.

Stephen Crane once said 'a reporter is no hero for a novel', and with the notable exception of the journalist from Kansas City, Jake Barnes, Hemingway agreed.[50] He rarely dealt with journalists in his work; when he did they were usually treated with broad satirical strokes. In *Death in the Afternoon* he relates a story about two homosexuals told to him by an uncomprehending journalist who is described as 'a poor newspaperman, a fool, a friend of mine, and a garrulous and dull companion' who held his job only because the 'circumstances which were later to demonstrate how poor a newspaperman he was had not yet arisen.'[51] Jake's dashing, knowledgeable life in *The Sun Also Rises* is set against the dull journalists Woolsey and Krum who talk wistfully about good bars in the Latin Quarter and getting out into the countryside. Morrow Alford, a veteran reporter-sleuth in an early unpublished mystery story, is insistently dull. 'Morrow Alford', Hemingway begins the story, 'wore suspenders, habitually lunched on a roast beef sandwich and a glass of milk, believed that Francois Villon was a greater poet than Robert W. Service, and every afternoon at 5:45 caught the Prospect Avenue car enroute for Mrs. Alford and the three young Alfords.' He adds that Alford, known as 'Punk' to his editor, is the sort of journalist 'who writes the stuff in the paper that you glance at and don't read all the way through.'[52]

In a sketch probably meant for *A Moveable Feast*, foreign correspondents that Hemingway knew from meetings of the Anglo-American Press Club on the Right Bank come 'slumming' in the Latin Quarter and pompously advise him about the length of his hair. '"You mustn't let yourself go, Hem,"' one of them tells him. '"It's none of my business, of course. But you can't go native this way. For God's sake straighten out and get a proper haircut at least."' The moral of the sketch, Hemingway pointed out at the end, was that such interfering types wanted 'you to conform completely and never differ from some accepted surface standard and then dissipate the way traveling salesmen would at a convention in every stupid and boring way there was.'[53] In another manuscript fragment, a reporter's work is said to be nothing more than mechanical action of a

> . . . photographic plate – when exposed to a fight he automatically registers an impression that will be conveyed through his typewriter to the people who buy the paper. Great feature men are constructed like color photographing plates – humorous writers are cameras with a crooked, comically distorting lens. When a reporter ceases to register when exposed, he goes on the copy desk. There he edits the work of other men who haven't been exposed so many times as to cease to register.[54]

In his unflattering comments about journalists, Hemingway was putting distance between his labors as a writer and their circumscribed, workaday worlds. He acknowledged the existence, as he said in a *Ken* article, of 'hard-working, non-political, straight-shooting correspondents', but it wasn't among their number that he wished to be counted.[55] Even though he occasionally trotted out his credentials as a correspondent, it clearly was a trade that had little bearing on his real work. He was a writer, not a journalist. In his bleak remarks about journalism he also was echoing the way the trade generally has been treated by imaginative writers who once spent some newspaper days. Like Hemingway, Whitman emphasized the transitory nature of writing for the press. 'The newspaper is so fleeting,' he said, 'is so like a thing gone as quick as come: has no life, so to speak: its birth and death almost coterminous.'[56] In his story 'Claude Emerson, Reporter', John O'Hara underscored the conventions of newswriting that reduce events to the fog of cliché rather than bring them to life: 'Claude Emerson had never pretended to be a writer. He learned early that there was a set journalese phrase for nearly every detail of every event that made a news item, and when he had acquired them all he saw no reason to originate another batch.'[57] Saul Bellow's hero in *The Dean's December*, a journalist turned writer, wonders about the usefulness of his earlier work as a newspaperman: 'A man of words? Yes, but words of the wrong kind. For some years, to cure himself of bad habits, bad usage, he had been mostly silent.'[58] Such passages, easily multiplied, suggest an overall view. In a study of forty years of fiction about newspapermen written by former newspapermen, Howard Good found the work significantly at odds with cultural pieties about the uses, literary and otherwise, of journalism. The theme of disillusionment was strong, and a central message was that journalism was a trade to be mastered and then set aside as swiftly as possible.[59]

*   *   *

In a 1935 *Esquire* article called 'Monologue to the Maestro:A High Seas Letter', Hemingway told of a young man named Arnold Samuelson who hitchhiked from Minnesota to Key West for advice about writing and stayed on to work as night-watchman and deckhand on his fishing boat. The advice included the remark about the short-lived nature of reporting ('If it was reporting they would not remember it'), but beyond this Hemingway had little to say about journalism. When Samuelson pressed him about the best early training for a writer, Hemingway told him it was an unhappy childhood. As Samuelson remembered it in a memoir he wrote about the year spent in Hemingway's employ, when journalism came into the advice sessions it was only as the 'antithesis' of real writing. Hemingway granted it was okay to begin in journalism 'because that limbers you up and gives you a command of the language'; it was 'good practice'. But he was sternly opposed to any thought of a career in journalism while trying to do serious writing at the same time:

> 'Forget about newspaper work. Do anything else to make a living, but not that. Newspaper work is the antithesis of writing and it keeps writers pooped out so they can't write; besides, there's no future in it. The only ones who can possibly do newspaper work and write are supermen who have such brilliant minds the newspaper work isn't anything at all for them, but you're not that type . . . The most fortunate thing that ever happened to you is that the editor of the Minneapolis *Tribune* refused to give you a job.'

Samuelson, who had already done some newspapering, offered a mild protest. 'But you used to be a newspaper man,' he said, 'and you became a writer.' Hemingway replied: 'In spite of it.'[60]

The remark neatly condensed the distinction Hemingway insisted upon between journalism and writing. At the same time, it obscured his lifelong mingling of journalism and writing – and, of more importance, the mingling within his serious work of fact writing and fiction writing. In 1956, after complaining that he had given up three or four months of work on his account of a second African safari for involvement in the filming of *The Old Man and the Sea*, he readily accepted $5000 from *Look* magazine for 3 000 words to accompany a flattering picture story on his domestic life in Cuba. He cranked out 'A Situation Report' in a day and a half, beginning it with a quotation from Cyril Connolly's *The Unquiet Grave* about the fleeting nature of journalism and other ephemeral activities:

> All excursions into journalism, broadcasting, propaganda, and writing for the films, however grandiose, are doomed to disappointment. To put of our best into these forms is another folly, since thereby we condemn good ideas, as well as bad, to oblivion.

It is in the nature of such work not to last, so it should never be undertaken . . .

The *mea culpa* tendered via the quotation wasn't directed to his present hack work for *Look* but to the time he had squandered on the film production. There would be, he promised, no more picture work ever. Then he turned to the nature of the task at hand:

> As for journalism, that writing of something that happens day by day, in which I was trained when young, and which is not whoring when done honestly with exact reporting; there is no more of that until this book is finished.

There would be no more of it, that is, until 'A Situation Report', a piece presumably dashed off with exact if hurried reporting, was finished and 'we go back to work tomorrow on the long book.'[61]

The comment to Samuelson that he had become a writer in spite of his early days in journalism was later echoed in what he told Fenton, that newspaper work was at best a step in his artistic development. Both remarks captured one side of his characteristic response to journalism, one that firmly distinguished journalism from writing – indeed, defined writing by its opposition to journalism. The grudging admission that at least the honest journalism of exact reporting wasn't whoring – together with the fact that the long book he was going back to after 'A Situation Report' wasn't fiction but a non-fiction account of his second African safari – suggested another side. Exact reporting, broadly understood to mean fact writing undertaken with full concentration and serious purpose, occupied a considerable part of his literary endeavor. Here, in ambitious and extended non-fiction, was the clearest carry-over of his early days in journalism into his career as a writer – the carry-over from fact to fact rather than from fact to fiction. Yet in serious non-fiction as much as in serious fiction his work was meant to be set against the transitory world of ordinary journalism. It was work undertaken as exacting excursions into fact writing as against journalism's flimsy whoring, and so it was meant to be free of the ultimate disappointment of work that would not last.

Even in his fiction Hemingway was willing to grant reporting an honorable place. Although few critical assaults irritated him more than the claim that his fiction was *only* reporting, he freely acknow-ledged the uses he made of it in his true fictions as against his made-up ones. 'A fool like Canby', he fumed to Max Perkins about a review of *Winner Take Nothing* by Henry Seidel Canby, 'thinks I'm a reporter. I'm a reporter *and an imaginative writer* and I can still imagine plenty and there will be stories to write *as they happened* as long as I live.' He added that some of his stories were simply literary reporting, stories written 'absolutely as they happen', and singled out one from the book as an example: 'The Wine of Wyoming' was nothing but 'straight reporting of what heard and saw when was finishing A Farewell to Arms out in Sheridan and Big Horn.'[62] All the same, he knew that the way to the permanence of art wasn't through separating reporting and imagination but combining them; it was his usual formula for fiction. The same was true for his serious efforts in non-fiction, with the central difference that in non-fiction the stress was meant to come down on a different activity, on the role of fact gatherer and creator of permanent records, while still giving broad rein to the shaping instincts of an imaginative writer. Ordinarily, he was exactly what he said he was, a reporter *and* an imaginative writer, and in his major works of non-fiction as much as in his fiction.

2

All the Dope

I think a really true book if it were fairly well written about the one thing that has, with the exception of the ritual of the church, come down to us intact from the old days would have a certain permanent value.

He was thirty-three years old, his reputation established as a fiction writer, when he produced something very different – a work of non-fiction that he described as a 'rather technical book'.[1] A common complaint addressed to the fiction, then as now, is that it remains within familiar grooves, unable to escape the prison of the Hemingway manner. With his first venture into extended non-fiction he was making it new with a vengeance while at the same time returning to his beginnings as a writer of fact. *Death in the Afternoon* was a former journalist's book, but a journalist who had become a writer, one grown comfortable with the ways of fiction and with considerable experience of the ways of the world. His earlier fact work for newspapers and magazines had frequently been heightened with the play of imagination and the confident voice of his own experience; now, with his non-fiction book, fact writing was turned in startling fashion into an inventive and deeply personal creation.

With the book he began the rash practice of taking on his detractors in print, and with it he experienced the first serious critical thumping of his career. Over the years opinion has mellowed yet the book remains one of Hemingway's least valued, and surely least read, works. When considered at all, it is usually for light shed on the two Spanish novels, *The Sun Also Rises* and *For Whom the Bell Tolls*; given rare attention on its own merits as a work of non-fiction, it draws, at best, guarded praise: 'a strange case from beginning to end'; Hemingway's 'most curious production'; a 'loose, baggy monster' of a book.[2] *Death in the Afternoon* ought properly to take its place as one of his most original and enduring books – and in American writing join company with *Walden* and *The American Scene* and *Let Us Now Praise Famous Men*, another in a tradition of idiosyncratic monuments of literary non-fiction.

*   *   *

In one sense the motivation behind the book is puzzling. Hemingway was at the critical peak of his reputation as a fiction writer with *In Our Time, The Sun Also Rises* and *A Farewell to Arms* behind him, published in a richly productive span of five years. The demand was for more fiction, capitalizing on his first commercial success with the novel of love and war in Italy, and Max Perkins at Scribner's did nothing – with one mild exception – to suggest otherwise. It hardly seemed the appropriate moment to launch into an esoteric handbook on tauromachy.

Green Hills of Africa and *The Dangerous Summer* began as shorter pieces, a short story and a magazine assignment, that developed into extended works of non-fiction. *A Moveable Feast* began as discrete pieces of recollection eventually ordered into a book. But *Death in the Afternoon* was conceived as a full-length work from the start. What may have been behind it was Hemingway's wish to enter the ranks of the wide-ranging men of letters, those consummate professionals who deftly turned from fiction to fact, from poems and plays to travel pieces and literary criticism, essays and memoirs. Hemingway was well acquainted with the tradition, having seen it practiced by, among others, Ford Madox Ford, Ezra Pound and D. H. Lawrence. Late in life, in remarks about his Nobel Prize, he would pay tribute to two American writers who failed to get the award, Mark Twain and Henry James, classic men of letters each. Although Perkins didn't encourage Hemingway in this enlarged conception of himself – discouraged him through silence, perhaps, since Hemingway didn't fit the editor's picture of the intellectual novelist with man-of-letters qualities – Hemingway may have launched upon it himself with *Death in the Afternoon*.[3] In the book, appropriately, he calls for the appearance of a bullfighter with the mastery of the ring's many skills, 'a complete bull-fighter who is at the same time an artist' as against matadors who narrowly specialize; what bullfighting needs, he adds, is 'a god to drive the half-gods out'.[4] During the decade of the thirties the book was followed with a flow of varied work – magazine articles, a play and a film, stories and novels, and another ambitious work of non-fiction. Hemingway even mentioned to Perkins during the period that he anticipated putting out a collection of his essays as well as his stories.

Whatever the larger motivation, it is clear that Hemingway had long wanted to do a big book about bullfighting even though it meant ushering the uninitiated into a secret society, breaking again Jake's unstated agreement with Montoya in *The Sun Also Rises* that 'it would not do to expose it to people who would not understand.'[5] He had already revealed his passion for bullfighting in the novel and in the powerful story 'The Undefeated', but in a non-fiction book he could tackle the subject directly, in his own voice, and with the *aficionado's* full delight in insider knowledge and exact detail. There was always an instructional, lecturing side to Hemingway's fact work, the master handing down his 'true gen' on any number of subjects. In his European journalism for the Toronto newspapers he had easily adopted the role of the expert, authoritatively informing readers about the ways of the Old World, and the impulse carried over into *Death in the Afternoon* and his other non-fiction.

He once said that the great delight of his early journalism was the privilege of writing profoundly about matters he knew little about. With bullfighting, however, his credentials were impressive. By his own count he had seen over 1 500 bulls killed, had enthusiastically involved himself in the world of bullfighters and promoters, and had read widely in the exotic literature of the sport. In the late fall of 1929, while *A Farewell to Arms* was on the bestseller lists, he had turned out an article on bullfighting for Henry Luce's new business magazine *Fortune* – $1 000 for 2 500 words. 'Bullfighting, Sport and Industry' appeared in the March 1930 issue, lavishly illustrated with paintings and etchings by Goya, Manet and Zuloaga.

The article's opening was in what had already become the characteristic Hemingway manner:

> Formal bullfighting is an art, a tragedy, and a business. To what extent it is an art depends on the bulls and the men who are hired to kill them, but it is always a tragedy and it is always a business.

But it was a flat account of business matters that occupied the rest of the article, Hemingway matter-of-factly explaining the economics of bull breeding and ring promotion and the enormous financial advantage held by the top matadors. In a letter he told Perkins the article was 'written in journalese full of statistics' and that he was 'keeping it as dull as possible'. But there was, he added, potential in the subject – if not in the method – for something better: 'Every aspect I touch on if I could go on and write about would make a long chapter in a book.'[6] Only at the end, with an appraisal of the American bullfighter Sidney Franklin, did the article turn back to something of the Hemingway manner with an elongated sentence on the potential for death in the bullring:

> He is very brave, very skillful, very artistic, and he kills very well, and he explained to me how bullfighting was really not dangerous, that there is always a way to avoid being gored, that, in the words of Ricardo Bombita, it is not the bull who gores the man, but the man who gores himself on the bull by some mistake in technique; and I, who have seen nearly every bullfighter in the first twenty seriously wounded at least once, wanted very much to believe him and hoped it was all true.[7]

The article finished, Hemingway turned at once to his big work of serious writing, ending a period of gestation that went back at least a half-dozen years. In his first letter to Perkins on 15 April 1925, while he was still under contract to the publishing house of Boni and Liveright, he had mentioned a book about bullfighting he hoped to do – 'a sort of Doughty's Arabia Deserta of the Bull Ring, a very big book with some wonderful pictures.' (The interest in photographs marked a change in attitude from his 'Pamplona Letter' in *the transatlantic review* the year before when he had declared that 'photographing kills anything, any good thing, just as it improves a bad thing.'[8]) But it took money to bum around Spain in the summer, he informed the editor, 'and writing classics, I've always heard, takes some time.'[9]

The model for Hemingway's future classic, if Perkins knew it, might well have given the editor pause – 'a book not like other books', T. E. Lawrence said of the massive personal account, part travel narrative, part ethnographic study, of desert wandering that ended, as would Hemingway's book, with a lengthy glossary.[10] Apparently hearing no more about the proposed work, Perkins, in a letter a year and a half after Hemingway first broached the subject, gently prodded his rising star, now free of Boni and Liveright and within the Scribner fold:

> Then you once spoke about a large book on bull fighting. This was to be, I gathered, something which would gradually accumulate, but it sounded like a most interesting and individual work. I thought that in thinking of the future, it might also be wise to

consider that, even though I am practically certain that you meant to make its preparation a matter of years.[11]

The editor was right; the bullfighting book was meant to accumulate gradually over the years. Hemingway had in effect been gathering material since his arrival in Europe as a correspondent for the Toronto papers. The *Star Weekly* in 1923 carried a lengthy article called 'Bull-Fighting Is Not a Sport – It Is a Tragedy' based on a trip to Spain in May of that year with Bill Bird and Robert McAlmon. The article began with a step-by-step account of a bullfight in Madrid, the first Hemingway had seen, then turned to a disquisition on the tragic nature of the three-act drama of the ring. A week later the *Star Weekly* carried 'World's Series of Bull Fighting a Mad, Whirling Carnival', an account of the best bullfight he had seen in Spain during Pamplona's annual fiesta of San Fermín. Gertrude Stein had suggested Pamplona, and his pregnant wife, Hadley, had accompanied him on the trip.

Both articles were miniatures of the book to come. They were written with an untutored Anglo audience in mind ('As far as I know,' Hemingway noted in the Pamplona article, he and Hadley 'were the only English-speaking people in Pamplona during the Feria of last year'), and consequently every aspect of bullfighting required detailed explanation by the knowledgeable narrator. Both pieces were lightened with moments of invented dialogue between the narrator and, in one case, the 'Gin Bottle King' and, in the other, 'Herself'; and both struck a dual tone of reverence for the beauty and danger of the spectacle of the bullring together with a sardonic awareness of the fraud and corruption of the business side. Near the end of the Pamplona article Hemingway suggested both in a brief exchange with his wife about a bullfighter:

> 'He is a very great kid,' said Herself. 'He is only twenty.'
> 'I wish we knew him,' I said.
> 'Maybe we will some day,' she said. Then considered a moment. 'He will probably be spoiled by then.'[12]

The two trips to Spain in 1923 and the *Star Weekly* articles that followed marked the beginning of Hemingway's enduring fascination with the bullring. In a letter in 1924 to Edward J. O'Brien he pointed to raw physical courage as the core of the attraction:

Do you remember me talking one night at the pub up on Mont-allegro about the necessity for finding some people that by their actual physical conduct gave you a real feeling of admiration like the sealers, and the men off the banks up in your country? Well I have got ahold of it in bull fighting. Jesus Christ yes.

I've got something that I really get fun out of again there. It looks as though it would last too. I wish we could go to some together sometimes, I know a lot about them now.[13]

Five of the prose miniatures of *in our time* that he published in 1924 were drawn from his bullfight experiences. In the fall of that year, following a third trip to Spain, he completed the long, detailed story about the heroic resistance of an aging bullfighter, 'The Undefeated'. The same year *the transatlantic review* carried his 'Pamplona Letter' with the concluding remark that 'if after about four more *San Firmins* [*sic*] I ever get so I can write anything worth a hoot about it you shall have it as you should naturally have it in any event.'[14] Two years later would come *The Sun Also Rises*. In the discarded closing section of 'Big Two-Hearted River' Hemingway had attributed to Nick Adams the passion for Spain and its tragic sport that so deeply marked the novel: 'His whole inner life had been bullfights all one year.'[15]

*   *   *

Composition of the book went slowly. This was due in part to the difficulty of working with factual material, with the need to update and verify, that led to considerable revision of the manuscript, but it was also caused by the pressure of events. Hemingway began writing in Key West early in 1930; before he was finished he would experience, as he laid them out for Perkins, a litany of physical problems:

. . . compound fracture of index finger – bad general smash up in that bear hunt – 14 stitches in face inside and out – hole in leg – then that right arm – muscular spiral paralysis – 3 fingers in right hand broken – 16 stitches in left wrist and hand. Eyes went haywire in Spain – with glasses now. Can't do more than about 4 hours before they go bad.[16]

The 'right arm' was a severe fracture suffered in a car accident in

Montana during his annual escape to the West from the summer heat of Key West, resulting in seven painful weeks in a hospital and a lengthy rehabilitation period. Additionally, there were work interruptions during the birth of a son when his second wife, Pauline, required a Caesarean section that was performed in Kansas City, and with the purchase of a new Key West home which required extensive renovation.

Seventy-four pages were finished by the end of June 1930, when he wrote to Archibald MacLeish that he couldn't sleep in the tropical heat and was looking forward to working in the mountains. By the end of the summer he reported to Perkins that it had gone as well as he had hoped in the new location: 'Have something over 40 000 words done. Have worked well 6 days of every week since got here.'[17] The auto accident in November stopped everything, and it wasn't until April that he was sufficiently recovered to resume work. From June to September he was back in Spain, following the bullfights (including the seventh fiesta of San Fermín he had attended in nine years) and working on the book. Apparently, much of what he did here was in the form of additions to the manuscript based on new eyewitness and historical material.[18] He wrote to Perkins in August that he had been 'working like hell last two weeks and am getting much done – work every day until my eyes poop out.' He was anxious to be finished but optimistic, telling the editor that 'this is really getting to be a hell of a good book I think.'[19] When he left Spain in September he had finished eighteen chapters and a glossary of bullfight terms. In November he told Perkins that everything was finished 'except this swell last chapter that I am still writing on,' and again he expressed confidence in the book: 'This is a hell of a fine book, Max. I've never gone better than lately.'[20] When Perkins tried to temper his enthusiasm by bringing up the hard times of the Depression and the likely effect on sales, Hemingway responded that 'they don't feel hard to me when I have been going as well as I have gone on the last three chapters of that book. Christ, when you can write well and get it as you want it nothing seems important . . .'[21]

Back in Key West at the end of the year after Pauline's delivery, he wrote to the editor that the manuscript would be sent on at any moment. But two weeks later he was complaining both to Perkins and his mother-in-law about the difficulty of working while house repairs were underway. He found sardonic consolation in the fact that Scott Fitzgerald 'had his wife go nutty which is much worse' while he was trying to work, and he recalled his own problems while writing his earlier books:

> During Sun Also plenty happened while during Farewell to Arrums – outside of Patrick being born only incident was my father shooting himself and me acquiring 4 new dependents and mortgages. Then some shitfaced critic writes Mr. Hemingway retires to his comfortable library to write about despair – Is that what I write about? I wonder.[22]

By the middle of January the manuscript was finished and forwarded to Scribner's. Perkins was soon sending back his usual hymns of unqualified approval:

> I read the book all yesterday – Sunday – and after it I felt good. . . . The book piles upon you wonderfully, and becomes to one reading it – who at first thinks bull fighting only a very small matter – immensely important.[23]

Two weeks later Perkins was even more more effusive, now professing to find virtue – slyly perhaps – even in the book's apparently random, free-flowing structure:

> In looking it over again, and reading it here and there, it seems immensely impressive, and it has a wonderful completeness too, although nobody could map out its organization. It gives the impression of having grown rather than of having been planned. And that is the characteristic of a great book.[24]

But there were still more difficulties ahead. When John Dos Passos came through Key West in February for some fishing with Hemingway, he read the entire manuscript at the author's request and offered enthusiastic praise ('the goddamnedest best piece of writing that's seen the light for many a day on this continent'). But he had reservations about Hemingway's lecturing tendencies and the book's considerable talk about writing. He repeated his views in a lengthy letter written after he had left Key West, deeply insightful in its sense of the work yet carefully shaped to Hemingway's thin critical skin:

> The Bull fight book is absolutely the best thing can be done on the subject. I mean all the description and the dope. It seems to me an

absolute model for how that sort of thing ought to be done. And all the accounts of individual fighters towns etc. are knockout. I'm only doubtful, like I said, about the parts where old Hem straps on the long white whiskers and gives the boys the lowdown. I can stand the old lady – but I'm pretty doubtful as to whether the stuff about Waldo Frank (except the line about shooting an owl) is as good as it ought to be. God knows he ought to be deflated – or at least Virgin Spain – (why not put it on the book basis instead of the entire lecturer?) and that is certainly the place to do it. And then later when you take off the makeup and assure the ladies and gents that it is really only old uncle Hem after all and give them the lowdown about writing and why you like to live Key West etc. I was pretty doubtful – don't you think that's all secrets of the profession – like plaster of Paris in a glove – and oughtn't to be spilt to the vulgar? I may be wrong, but the volume is so hellishly good (I'd say way ahead of anything of yours yet) and the language is so magnificently used . . . that it would be a shame to leave in any unnecessary tripe – damn it I think there's always enough tripe in anything even after you've cut out – and a book like that can stand losing some of the best passages. After all, a book ought to be judged by the author according to the excellence of the stuff cut out.[25]

Hemingway accepted the criticism, as he had earlier accepted Fitzgerald's acute reading of *The Sun Also Rises*, and began cutting. The idea of judging the book by the quality of the material left out no doubt appealed to his aesthetic sense of omission. He wrote to Dos Passos on April 12 that he had 'cut a ton of crap a day out of the proofs and spread it around the alligator pear trees which are growing to be enormous.'[26] On May 30 he told him the revisions were finished:

> Have gone over the book 7 times and cut out all you objected to (seemed like the best to me God damn you if it really was) cut 4½ galleys of philosophy and telling the boys – cut all of last chapter except the part about Spain – the part saying how it wasn't enough of a book or it would have had these things. That is OK.
>
> Left Old Lady in and the first crack early in the book about Waldo Frank's book – cut all other references to Frank. Believe Old Lady stuff O.K. – or at least necessary as seasoning.[27]

A few days later he conveyed to Perkins the same information about the revisions, adding that he had saved the excised material for possible future publication, in good man-of-letters style, in his notebooks:

Have cut a lot of text – with what is gone the book may be less fashionable (all this stating of creeds and principles which does not belong in literature at all by people who have failed in a lost belief in or abandoned writing the minute it got tough to save their bloody souls). But it will be permanent and solid and about what it is about. I will save what I cut and if it proves to be of permanent value you can publish it in my notebooks. . . .[28]

In the meantime he was struggling with the editor about some four-letter words in the manuscript and especially about pictures and their placement. From the beginning he had conceived of the book as lavishly illustrated with 'wonderful pictures', some at least in color, and he had spent considerable time and money – as he pointedly let Perkins know – gathering them. He insisted that the photographs were not illustrations (though finally they would be labeled as such in the book) but pictures that in their own right conveyed the feeling of bullfighting. Nonetheless, Perkins wanted to limit the number to keep down the cost in Depression times – only sixteen in all, according to Hemingway, whereas he himself had only been able to get the number down from over 200 to 112. He told Perkins the book had taken 'over two years in the actual writing and rewriting and plenty of years in getting the material and to hell with getting it out now in a preoccupied with business worries manner and selling it down the river to the Book of the Month Club to get some one a sure seven thousand dollars to cover margins with.' The 'irreducible minimum' number of pictures, he maintained, was sixty.[29] When it finally appeared, the book had a striking color frontispiece of *The Torero* by Juan Gris and sixty-four pages of black-and-white photographs.

There were also questions to settle with the editor about where the pictures should go in the text and about the placement of the captions (as it turned out, the pictures were grouped together at the end of the book before the appended matter, the captions on facing pages). Hemingway remained edgy about the constrained format. When he was finishing work on the galleys he reminded Perkins that 'limitations of space and costs have aborted any attempt to make the book exhaustive.' He didn't want the appended matter – the glossary, reactions of various anonymous figures to their first bullfight, a much inflated estimate of Sidney Franklin, and a listing of bullfight dates – called appendices since that would seem pretentious in such a reduced work. It was in the same letter of complaint to Perkins that he took issue with a typesetter's slug, 'Hemingway's Death', appearing at the top of each galley of the book. If he had in fact died, he informed the editor, it could be said that 'your goddamned lot put the curse on me.'[30]

A final problem was publication of excerpts from the book in *Scribner's Magazine*. Perkins had previously convinced him to allow a serialized version of *A Farewell to Arms* to appear in the magazine. 'It's mean business, picking articles out of a book like this,' the editor told him about *Death in the Afternoon*. 'But from the commerical standpoint, as we call it, it will help it.'[31] Hemingway was far from indifferent to that standpoint; he had earlier complained to Perkins about publicity coming from Scribner's that mentioned parts of the book he had cut from the galleys, thus possibly giving readers the impression of being shortchanged when they found the material missing. He told Perkins about the book: 'If you try to sell it as a great classic goddamned book on bull fighting rather than some fucking miscellany you may be able to sell a few.'[32] The mention of articles for the magazine got his back up in another way. He insisted that whatever the magazine published be called extracts from the book, with notes below the individual titles indicating the extracts came from 'Death in the Afternoon a book dealing with the Spanish bull fight.' Presumably, he was concerned that the material might be confused with his earlier journalistic articles. At any event, he went to great lengths to inform Alfred Dashiell, the magazine's new editor, that if he had wanted to write articles he would have since it was easy to do. His book, on the other hand, had a unity that wasn't to be found in articles. Apparently, Dashiell had suggested using Chapter Two of the book for one excerpt but without the chapter's closing paragraph, a colorful account of how a particularly durable bull met his end. Hemingway lectured him that the paragraph wasn't merely an afterthought. The seemingly casual way in which he introduced it was meant to 'avoid melodrama, local color and over-writing; these last two being the things which usually, by their presence, make "articles" as value-less as they are.' Another thing that 'distinguishes serious writing from the writing of "*articles*"', he informed Dashiell, was the amount of knowledge of a subject that the writer had behind him. He wanted it understood that the author of *Death in the Afternoon* had plenty of knowledge, certainly more than any ordinary journalist or writer of articles. [33]

Maybe because it became something of the mean business Perkins had predicted, the plan to carry excerpts from the book was scrapped. Instead the magazine accepted three new stories that were published during 1933 with much fanfare; and two years later Hemingway's non-fiction would make an appearance in the magazine with the serialization – Perkins urging it once again – of *Green Hills of Africa*.

Death in the Afternoon was finally published on 23 September 1932, with a large first printing of 10 300 copies. Sales were brisk at first, causing Hemingway to boast to his old newspaper friend Guy Hickok that he had tried to make the book 'completely unsaleable and offend everyone but you see – no bloody luck again.'[34] Then the book slumped. On 3 November Perkins wrote that 'things did look good for a while, but now they look bad again. Sales began to drop off about two weeks ago, which is much sooner than the seasonal drop in November.'[35] Hemingway's stature as a writer was enough at first, then the Depression, the unusual subject, and bad reviews took their toll. Hemingway would later complain to his son Gregory that *Ferdinand the Bull* made ten time more money than *Death in the Afternoon*.

In a review in the *New York Sun* on the day of publication, Laurence Stallings praised the book's originality but predicted, correctly, that it would be 'chopped to pieces in many a literary dissecting.'[36] There was generous, if not unqualified, praise from Malcolm Cowley and H. L. Mencken, and Robert M. Coates, who remarked that it was a thousand times better to see a bullfight than be told about one, nonetheless thought Hemingway had done some of his best writing since *In Our Time*. But it was Max Eastman's attack in an article in the *New Republic* nine months after the book was published, 'Bull in the Afternoon', that drew most attention, including Hemingway's. Eastman had two main points. One was that Hemingway simply had it wrong about bullfighting: it wasn't a tragic art but a blood spectacle in which a powerful but stupid animal is tormented, weakened and then killed by 'spryer and more flexible monkeys'. To take such bloodletting seriously, let alone claim it as art, was sophomoric at best, romantic nonsense at worst. Eastman's second, and more stinging, point was that Hemingway's romance of the bullring could only be explained as overcompensation for a lack of 'serene confidence that he *is* a full-sized man,' resulting in a 'literary style, you might say, of wearing false hair on the chest.'[37]

Archibald MacLeish interpreted the latter point as a sexual slur and sent a letter of protest to the magazine, providing a copy along with a copy of Eastman's article for Hemingway. Hemingway responded with a foggy open letter to the *New Republic*; to Max Perkins at Scribner's he vented his irritation directly. If Eastman ever published the article in a book he would sue for libel, he wrote the editor, and if he ever ran into Eastman in person he would handle matters himself. He was so angry he was tempted never to publish again. Everything he had written about Spanish bull-fighting was true and based on personal experience whereas Eastman knew nothing yet was paid for his views. Although he claimed to find the article too disgusting for further comment, he nonetheless plunged on in the letter with assertions of manhood and threats of retaliation.

An opportunity to even the score came four years later when Hemingway and Eastman accidently met in Perkins' New York office. The celebrated dust-up that followed spawned varying accounts; in Perkins' version, set out in a letter to Scott Fitzgerald, Hemingway bared a hairy chest, struck Eastman with a book containing a reprint of a revised version of 'Bull in the Afternoon', grappled with its author on the floor, then quickly regained his temper and ended up smiling. The story broke in the newspapers shortly thereafter with Eastman and Hemingway trading accounts. Fitzgerald found it a shameful incident yet cast a stone at critics for the hurt they inflicted on writers of Hemingway's caliber. 'After all,' he wrote Perkins, 'you would think a man who has arrived at the position of being practically his country's most eminent writer could be spared that yelping.'[38]

But confronted with *Death in the Afternoon*, critics were not inclined to spare the author, whatever his eminence. With the book of stories that followed, *Winner Take Nothing*, the critical hostility increased, and Hemingway's always acute sensitivity to any reservations about his work kept pace. Perkins had consoled him after Eastman's article that the quality of what he wrote couldn't be harmed by negative reviews, but such a sanguine position wasn't one he could adopt. Instead, he aggressively took on his detractors in letters and in print, insisting on the superiority of what he had written and threatening to bring them all to ruin.

*   *   *

'Just why did Ernest Hemingway write a book on bull-fighting?'[39] Malcolm Cowley began his measured review of *Death in the Afternoon* with the question, and over the years two answers have attached themselves to considerations of the work. One was provided by Hemingway himself: he wrote the book, he said in the biblio- graphical note at the work's end, because there was no introduction to the Spanish bullfight available in either Spanish or English. Hemingway is usually now given passing grades on this level; even critics who place the book among his lesser productions accept it as the classic literary account of bullfighting in, at least, English. A second answer to Cowley's question that has gained currency is that, more than an introductory handbook of tauromachy, *Death in the Afternoon* is a memorable evocation of Hemingway's long fascination with the Spanish landscape and spirit. The primary evidence here is the much admired final chapter where Hemingway abruptly switches from a lengthy account of the manner of killing in the bullring in the previous chapter to a collage of Spanish places and images and personal memories cast in the form of things that would have appeared in the book if it were 'enough of a book' (270). When Arnold Gingrich, the editor of *Esquire*, praised the chapter, Hemingway told him 'it is what the book is about but nobody seems to notice that.'[40] Earlier, he had informed Perkins that the last chapter contained the best writing he had done in the book.

Originally, the final section opened with a lengthy generalized introduction to the country, the nine initial paragraphs removed only after the manuscript was in galley proofs. 'It is a strange country, Spain, and few people have ever gone to it to find it as they expected,' Hemingway began. He then went on in the same broad vein to link Spain with northern Michigan and Italy, two other peninsulas he had loved and written about.[41] He had come to Spain, he said, only after they were ruined for him, and in Spain he had discovered a land and a people that reminded him of the American West. Spain had become for him the last good country, and in the final chapter, despite the limitations of knowledge and language he brought to the task, he meant to offer a lyric catalogue of some of its virtues. But the burden of the chapter was that even Spain was changing. It, too, would follow the downward path of his other beloved peninsulas. In the book as a whole he lamented the decline of modern bullfighting to a tourist spectacle, and in the final paragraph of the final chapter he turned again to the theme of destructive change:

> I know things change now and I do not care. It's all been changed for me. Let it all change.
>
> (278)

So the book about bullfighting, viewed from the perspective of the concluding chapter, was really about Spain. Even more, it was an elegy for the country, the last and best of the peninsulas he had known.

The two responses to why Hemingway wrote *Death in the Afternoon* – 'a Baedeker of the bullfight', as Carlos Baker calls it, as well as a 'summing up of ten years of intermittent experience with the Spanish earth and the people who lived on it' – have, once again, come to occupy most contemporary accounts of the book, softening some of the original criticism directed to it.[42] But one central critical approach, directed not only to the bullfight book but to Hemingway's non-fiction in general, has persisted, with the result that the non-fiction, praised here and there for interesting and even admirable qualities, is invariably relegated to a distant supporting role in relation to the fiction. Edmund Wilson, whose early praise helped launch Hemingway's career, established the overriding way of thinking about the non-fiction when he observed that when Hemingway wrote in his own voice, as against the voice of his fiction, 'the results are unexpected and disconcerting.' The admirable control and restraint of the fiction was replaced with floundering excess; everything became overdone and overblown, fatuous and maudlin. Wilson allowed that *Death in the Afternoon* had some value as a treatise on bullfighting, but it was nonetheless 'partly infected by a queer kind of maudlin emotion, which sounds at once neurotic and drunken.' The whole thing struck him as 'a little hysterical', including the much admired final chapter which was 'all too rich' and seemed, in its 'irrelevant reminiscences', an echo of Molly Bloom's soliloquy in *Ulysses*. The heart of the problem – though Wilson didn't put it such terms – was that what Hemingway said was essential for a good writer, a built-in shockproof shit detector, invariably seemed to fail him when he wrote in his own voice. Wilson's particular version of this was that 'as soon as Hemingway begins speaking in the first person, he seems to lose his bearings, not merely as a critic of life, but even as a craftsman.'

Wilson was obviously right in noting the change in voice from the fiction to the non-fiction. In *Death in the Afternoon* Hemingway writes in his own person, making explicit – often noisily so – what is ordinarily implicit in non-fiction, the writer presenting the material to the reader. And the effects of the changed voice are indeed different. The 'admirable miniaturist in prose', as Wilson called Hemingway the fictionist, is replaced by the dominating personality, prickly and ironic, occasionally hectoring and long winded.[43] The taut, rhythmic prose and implied meaning of the early fiction give way to an often aggressively loose language and a touchy, protective attitude toward the world of bullfighting. The calculated omissions of the fiction are replaced with a rush of detail that seems meant to overwhelm the reader with the entire iceberg rather than outline its dazzling tip. But the wholly different manner of the non-fiction is cause for regret only if measured against exclusive admiration for the fiction; taken by itself, it delights, giving the non-fiction its particular texture and flavor, forming the essential qualities of its lasting appeal. In the fiction Hemingway is guarded, secretive, suppressing more than he reveals, alert to Jake Barnes' remark that 'you'll lose it if you talk about it', but in the non-fiction the distinctive presence that has intrigued us so long leaps out of the mediating shadows of the fiction, offering itself – usually insisting upon itself – to the reader directly. Rather than the centrally destructive element, Hemingway's voice as Hemingway is a central source of pleasure in the non-fiction.

In a lengthy letter in 1926, Hemingway gave Perkins a foretaste of the bullfight book – and at the same time provided a revealing account of the complex aims of the work:

It will have illustrations – drawings and photographs – and I think should have some colored reproductions. It is a long one to write because it is not to be just a history and text book or apologia for bull fighting – but instead, if possible, bull fighting its-self. As it's a thing that nobody knows about in English I'd like to take it first from altogether outside – how I happened to be interested in it, how it seemed before I saw it – how it was when I didn't understand it – my own experience with it, how it reacts on others – the gradual finding out about it and try and build it up from the outside and then go all the way inside with chapters on everything. It might be interesting to people because nobody knows anything about it – and it really is terribly interesting – being a matter of life and death – and anything that a young peasant or bootblack can make 80 000 dollars a year in before he is twenty three does something to people. I think a really true book if it were fairly well written about the one thing that has, with the exception of the ritual of the church, come down to us intact from the old days would have a certain permanent value. But it has to be solid and true and have all the dope and be interesting – and it won't be ready for a long time.[44]

The book wasn't simply to be *about* bullfighting but something more intimate and immediate. Somehow it was to be bullfighting itself – a noble, if impossible, intention that recalls Agee's grand desire in *Let Us Now Praise Famous Men* to do no writing but provide actual elements of his sharecroppers' lives: lumps of earth, fragments of cloth, plates of food and of excrement. At one and the same time the book Hemingway envisioned had to be sufficient on the level of technical information and also interesting to readers who knew nothing about the subject. Even more, it had to possess permanent value. It had to be a factual work in the manner of a handbook yet possessed of literary quality.

As Hemingway apparently understood, the way to these vastly ambitious ends was to construct an expository account that would work on two levels – as he described it, an account with 'outside' and 'inside' elements. The approach from outside would come first and would establish his personal history as an *aficionado*; beyond that, it would establish his active presence in the book. From this point, the reader drawn into the subject through identification with the writer's developing interest, he could go inside the material in the sense of providing detailed, erudite chapters on each of bullfighting's elements. The dual approach roughly describes the structure of the book Hemingway finally produced. He began with the directly personal in the opening sentence ('At the first bullfight I ever went to I expected to be horrified and perhaps sickened by what I had been told would happen to the horses'), then moved on to a succession of instructional chapters. More importantly, the emphasis on outer and inner elements describes a dual perspective within the work that lifts it beyond the pedestrian tones of a mere guide to bullfighting.

F. O. Matthiessen argued that what separated *Walden* from the simple records of experience produced by Dana and Parkman was a quality of doubleness in Thoreau 'that made him both participant and spectator in any event.' Despite his submersion in a life in the woods, he was not, as Thoreau himself observed, 'wholly involved in Nature'. He was able to stand apart from the experience and his own place in it, capable of a detachment that allowed him – in Matthiessen's phrase – 'to possess the universe at home'. Hemingway professed not to be an admirer of Thoreau, claiming that he preferred his natural history free of literary trimmings; yet his method in *Death in the Afternoon* bears resemblance to *Walden*, though not in Thoreau's separation into participant and observer and with a consequent urge to universal meaning. In one of the dialogues with the Old Lady, however, Hemingway reacts to the charge that he is a prejudiced observer of bullfighting with a similar suggestion of division of mind:

> 'Madame, rarely will you meet a more prejudiced man nor one who tells himself he keeps his mind more open. But cannot that be because one part of our mind . . . becomes prejudiced through experience and still we keep another part completely open to observe and judge with?'
>
> (95)

Hemingway's typical doubleness is apparent in his capacity to give himself to the flow of fact about bullfighting while remaining apart from fact through insistence on his own commenting, reacting, feeling presence in the account. Throughout the book he maintains an outer as well as inner perspective that prevents him from being one with his material, wholly given over to a factual account. Fact is always colored with personality, charged with personal reaction. This is exactly the approach Thoreau admired, that of a writer who 'was satisfied with giving an exact description of things as they appeared to him, and their effect upon him.'[45] And it is precisely the two-level approach that Hemingway defined in the bibliographical note at the end of *Death in the Afternoon* when he said that the book explains Spanish bullfighting 'both emotionally and practically' (487).

The outer perspective of personal experience and feeling is, once again, firmly established at the beginning of the book when Hemingway raises the issue of the ethics of the bullring – especially the grim effect on horses in the days before protective padding – from what he calls 'a modern moral point of view'(1). Clearly, this is not to be an even-handed discussion since his own standard of morality, he informs us at once, is simply whether you feel good or bad afterward. He himself feels perfectly all right while a bullfight is going on, the feeling composed of the sense 'of life and death and mortality and immortality', and after the spectacle is over he feels sad yet 'very fine'(4). Once underway on the subject, he abruptly pauses to say he is not being personal because of any particular pleasure in doing so; he only wants to establish his emotional response to bullfighting on seeing it for the first time to make the point that he didn't become oblivious to the physical abuse of horses through long exposure. It wasn't a matter 'of the emotions becoming insulated through familiarity' (8). He then adds that the ordered ritual tragedy of the bullring actually prevents a separate emotional response to the fate of the horse. Only if one has 'no feeling of the whole tragedy' will he respond emotionally to such separate incidents (3). The *aficionado* naturally possesses such a sense of the bullfight in its entirety, attuned to it in the manner of the collective production of a symphony orchestra rather than the experience of individual instruments. But this sense of the whole is, once again, a matter of personal feeling, and Hemingway urges novices at a bullfight to 'only feel those things they actually feel and not the things they think they should feel' (10).

Another analogy occurs to him, with wine drinking, and he launches into one of those lengthy digressions ('This seems to have gotten away from bullfighting') that give *Death in the Afternoon* its agreeably unconfined, associative texture (11). Wine must be liked instantly and as a 'thing' before going on to the refinements of taste that come with time. The same is true of bullfighting: although it must be appreciated at once, it is unlikely that the first experience will be fully satisfying in an artistic sense since this requires the rare combination of good bullfighters and good bulls. Hemingway contemplates other, more likely combinations – brave bull, undistinguished bullfighter – and then plunges into a soaring account of the arrogant grace of the gypsy bullfighter Cagancho confronting a proper bull. He stops himself to say that what he has just written is 'the worst sort of flowery writing, but it is necessary to try to give the feeling, and to some one who has never seen it a simple statement of the method does not convey the feeling.' After noting that those familiar with bullfighting can 'skip such flowerishness and read the facts,' he continues with the account of Cagancho's style and the effort to try to convey the feeling aroused since facts alone are foreign to his dual consideration of his material (14).[46] The passage – and the book's opening chapter – ends with a less flowery though no less emotion-seeking statement of the critical importance of sunshine at one's first bullfight:

> The sun is very important. The theory, practice and spectacle of bullfighting have all been built on the assumption of the presence of the sun and when it does not shine over a third of the bullfight is missing. The Spanish say, 'El sol es el mejor torero.' The sun is the best bullfighter, and without the sun the best bullfighter is not there. He is like a man without a shadow. (15)

Personal feeling coming from, in Hemingway's terminology, outside the material remains a crucial element throughout the book. He frequently shifts from it to straightforward inner accounts of factual matters, as in the beginning of the second chapter with its definition of bullfighting as a tragedy involving certain death for the bull and danger for the man rather than the equal contest of a sport; yet the emotional response is always close at hand, interrupting the treatise, giving it life. So matters of definition quickly merge into the emotional memory of what he had 'really seen' and 'that which was important' in the goring of a novice bullfighter who had made a technical mistake:

> When he stood up, his face white and dirty and the silk of his breeches opened from waist to knee, it was the dirtiness of the rented breeches, the dirtiness of his slit underwear and the clean, clean, unbearably clean whiteness of the thigh bone that I had seen, and it was that which was important. (20)

Similarly, Chapter Four begins with practical information on where and when to see bullfights and the location of the best seats in the ring, then gives way to a vivid account of what Hemingway considers the best towns for initiation into bullfighting. Aranjuez, forty-seven kilometres from Madrid 'on a billiard smooth road', is 'an oasis of tall trees, rich gardens and a swift river set in brown plain and hills' (39). Valencia can be hot with the wind coming from Africa but at night on the beach you can lie 'in the barely cool water and watch the lights and the dark of the boats and the rows of eating shacks and swimming cabins' (44). The best season for bullfighting is the subject of the following chapter, but this quickly leads into a depiction of the bracing weather of Madrid and, finally, Hemingway's delight in his favorite Spanish city, the place that 'makes you feel very badly, all question of immortality aside, to know that you will have to die and never see it again' (51).

The chapter is also the occasion for a lecture on the tendency toward 'erectile writing' in books about Spain (53). In such work the effort to portray feeling loses touch with fact and becomes free-floating lyricism; it is 'journalism made literature' through the 'injection of a false epic quality' (54). The point, of course – in addition to the dismantling of a particular false Spanish epic in Hemingway's view, Waldo Frank's *Virgin Spain* – is to describe through contrast Hemingway's own aim in *Death in the Afternoon*. His bullfight book will centrally concern itself with feeling, but it will be true feeling because it will remain tied to fact, moderated and contained by real knowledge. It will be journalism made literature not through applied lyricism but through depth and clarity of information and an exactness of accompanying feeling. It will be, in a comparison offered in the book, writing that resembles the chaste simplicity of the Prado in Madrid where great paintings are hung with no attempt to create theatrical effect, emotion coming from observation of the work itself. Later in the book Hemingway provides another comparison with the art world in the celebrated remark that 'prose is architecture, not interior decoration, and the Baroque is over,' again suggesting the functional rather than applied role of feeling in his own work (91). The most telling analogy, however, is with bullfighting itself. Hemingway repeatedly insists that true emotion in the ring, as against false crowd appeal, is the product of difficult athletic feats performed with knowledge, style, courage and without tricks. Similarly, if feeling is crucial in his book, it is also crucial that it derive from fact and be controlled by fact. There is, admittedly, 'flowerishness' at times, yet such heightened language is never far removed from practical matters.

Hemingway was on firm ground in ridiculing what he called the 'bedside mysticism' practiced by Frank. At Dos Passos' suggestion he limited his attack to *Virgin Spain*, published a half-dozen years earlier (and a work, he might have calculated, his would be compared with), but he could well have examined Frank's book more closely, especially the ten pages allotted to bullfighting, since they bear no resemblance to what he was trying to accomplish in *Death in the Afternoon*.[47] Frank dissects a bullfight to explain its structure, but a generalized bullfight in a generalized setting; there are no actual bulls to measure or bullfighters to rank, though Belmonte materializes for an impeccable killing in the third act of the imagined drama. Specifics of time and place are not Frank's interest, nor is exact detail of any sort (with the exception of a single long footnote where information suddenly, and surprisingly, becomes practical and pointed). What he offers instead is detached feeling and ecstatic phrasing that fades to unintelligibility, as in the closing summary paragraph of the section:

> Gross comedy of blood; sex, dionysian and sadistic; the ancient rites of the brute and of the Christ meet here in the final image of stability. Spain's warring elements reach their locked fusion – Spain's ultimate form. For although everything is in the bull ring, and although anything may happen, *nothing happens*. Circus, blood, dance, death equate to nullity. Like life in Spain, this spectacle is self-sufficient, issueless . . .[48]

As *Death in the Afternoon* develops, an inner-outer approach to the material becomes an almost formalized rhythm. His presence in the work firmly established in the opening section, Hemingway now begins his chapters with practical matters about bullfighting practically described, then turns back at the chapter ends to matters of feeling or personal reaction. Chapter Two has a particularly satisfying conclusion. The wounding of a novice bullfighter leads to a discussion of provincial fights where amateurs of all sorts try their hand and a bull may appear many times in the ring, greatly increasing the danger faced by the matador. This leads in turn to the wonderful story of a brother and sister who pursue a bull which has killed many novices, their brother included. At length the bull is sent to a slaughterhouse where the brother and sister are given permission to conduct the kill. As a last act they remove the bull's testicles and roast and eat them alongside the street outside the slaughterhouse, enjoying a 'rare delicacy', as Hemingway pointed out to Alfred Dashiell of *Scribner's Magazine* when the story was removed from the excerpt set to appear in the magazine, while completing their sweet revenge.[49]

But with the ending of Chapter Thirteen – an account of the succession of physical and mental changes a bull undergoes in the ring, including an exact and detailed treatment of the *querencia*, the area of the ring where the bull is most comfortable and hence most dangerous – he is at his best. The placing of banderillas as part of the preparation of the bull for killing raises the question of the matador's physical prowess, and this brings to mind the exceptional case of the bullfighter El Gallo, who once quipped that what he did for exercise was smoke Havana cigars. El Gallo was crippled with horn wounds; he also notably lacked courage, openly admitting to fear and refusing to kill if the bull gazed at him in a certain way. ' "All of us artists have bad days," ' he offered as explanation (157). During one of his repeated retirement performances in the ring he solemnly and tearfully dedicated the bull to three different figures in the stands, then turned to his brother, Joselito, and said: ' "Kill him for me, José. Take him for me. I don't like the way he looks at me" ' (158). This leads Hemingway into a tongue-in-cheek reference to the implausibility of ever seeing El Gallo killed in the ring, then – ending the chapter – to a moving impression of the crippled and cowardly matador's skill, a skill as fragile as the structure of a spinet:

> El Gallo, in a panic, was still closer to the bull than most fighters when they were showing their tragic domination, and the grace and excellence of his work were as delicate as that lovely early Mexican feather work that is preserved at El Escorial. Do you know the sin it would be to ruffle the arrangement of the feathers on a hawk's neck if they could never be replaced as they were? Well, that would be the sin it would be to kill El Gallo.   (159)

*   *   *

With Chapter Seven Hemingway introduces the unfortunate device of imagined dialogue with the Old Lady, turning from feeling as a way of ending the book's sections in favor of satire. The exchanges with his interlocutor come through as arch and forced, Hemingway in his *The Torrents of Spring* manner. In only one instance, the Old Lady's appearance at the end of Chapter Eight, does an exchange serve to carry on the book's characteristic blending of fact and feeling. Here Hemingway provides a stirring account of the hard death of Manuel García, the bullfighter known as Maera. He and Hadley had seen Maera fight during their initial visit to Pamplona, never forgetting the unbreakable courage of the dark, thin-hipped, arrogant bullfighter, even then suffering from the tuberculosis that would kill him. Hemingway recalls Maera's stubborn struggle, while fighting with an injured wrist, to dispatch a bull that seemed made of cement, then tells of his eventual death

. . . that winter in Seville with a tube in each lung, drowned with pneumonia that came to finish off the tuberculosis. When he was delirious he rolled under the bed and fought with death under the bed dying as hard as a man can die. I thought that year he hoped for death in the ring but he would not cheat by looking for it. You would have liked him Madame. Era muy hombre.

(82)

The Old Lady calls attention to an earlier story about Maera in which, as a young banderillero, he had once been refused higher ˙ay by Juan Belmonte. Under questioning, Hemingway clears up the matter by noting the natural skinflint tendencies of bullfighters, themselves only recently escaped from the lowest rungs of society, when dealing with subordinates. Maera, however, altogether admirable, is an exception to the rule. When he became a full matador he lived with passion and a love for killing bulls and without meanness.

The appearances of the Old Lady seldom advance the book in such substantive fashion, though Carlos Baker suggests that the manufactured dialogue may at least have had the technical benefit of helping Hemingway carry on with the writing after a slow beginning. He had, at any event, employed dialogue before as a way of breaking the flow of fact ('necessary as seasoning', he had explained to Dos Passos) in his bullfight articles for the *Toronto Star Weekly*; the use now also serves the purpose of ridiculing bullfighting's detractors and settling old scores. One of the latter is the critical view of Hemingway the fiction writer as capable only of good dialogue, so in an instructional book lacking dialogue he arbitrarily provides it:

> Why isn't there more dialogue? What we want in a book by this citizen is people talking; that is all he knows how to do and now he doesn't do it. The fellow is no philosopher, no savant, an incompetent zoologist, he drinks too much and cannot punctuate readily and now he has stopped writing dialogue. Someone ought to put a stop to him. He is bull crazy. Citizen, perhaps you are right. Let us have a little dialogue.
>
> (20)

Yet whatever its intended function, without sufficient narrative context the book's dialogue seems only strained. Nowhere is this more evident than in 'A Natural History of the Dead', dropped into

Death in the Afternoon at the end of Chapter Twelve as a way of closing out a section on the breeding of fighting bulls, one of the least inspired in the book. Hemingway concludes the section with a list of the leading bull breeders in the land, then, sensing the need for a change of pace ('There is not a word of conversation in the chapter, Madame, yet we have reached the end'), turns to material he would later reprint as a story, repeatedly breaking into it for aimless exchanges with the Old Lady (32). When there is a fragment of narrative context, as in the account of Maera, the talk in the book works reasonably well, assuming some of the characteristics of the familiar fictional dialogue. Another example is the exchange between the horse contractor and the picador in Chapter Sixteen, or that between Hemingway and his son in Chapter Eighteen. Still, it is a relief, as Hemingway seems to have known himself, when the Old Lady vanishes two-thirds of the way through the book with the casual remark,

> What about the Old Lady? She's gone. We threw her out of the book, finally. A little late you say. Yes, perhaps a little late.
>
> (90)

The impulse to settle scores remains, however, as a way of balancing the instructional flow of the later chapters. In Chapter Sixteen the Old Lady gives way to self-initiated talk of 'higher things' that begins with a response to Aldous Huxley's portrayal of Hemingway as a self-conscious low brow (90). From this point Hemingway launches into a disjointed, though not uninteresting, statement of his literary creed that concludes with the celebrated iceberg image of the uses of omission. The following chapter ends the same way. 'Do you want conversation?' Hemingway asks. 'What about? Something to please Mr. Huxley?' (203). Higher things this time are a discussion of the merits of Goya, Velasquez and El Greco, with Hemingway pairing off El Greco's supposed homosexuality with Goya's manly – and Hemingwayesque – belief in

> . . . what he had seen, felt, touched, handled, smelled, enjoyed, drunk, mounted, suffered, spewed-up, lain-with, suspected, observed, loved, hated, lusted, feared, detested, admired, loathed, and destroyed.
>
> (205)

Chapters Eighteen and Nineteen depart from the pattern, perhaps because they deal with matters (the use of the muleta and killing) that Hemingway considers the heart of bullfighting, and so evoke throughout the sections some of the strongest moments of feeling in the book. About the muleta he says:

> It is impossible to believe the emotional and spiritual intensity and pure, classic beauty that can be produced by a man, an animal and a piece of scarlet serge draped over a stick.
>
> (207)

The opportunity of seeing skilled work with the muleta, always rare, then inspires one of the memorable flowery sentences in the work:

> If the spectators know the matador is capable of executing a complete, consecutive series of passes with the muleta in which there will be valor, art, understanding and, above all, beauty and great emotion, they will put up with mediocre work, cowardly work, disastrous work because they have the hope sooner or later of seeing the complete faena; the faena that takes a man out of himself and makes him feel immortal while it is proceeding, that gives him an ecstasy, that is, while momentary, as profound as any religious ecstasy; moving all the people in the ring together and increasing in emotional intensity as it proceeds, carrying the bullfighter with it, he playing on the crowd through the bull and being moved as it responds in a growing ecstasy of ordered, formal, passionate, increasing disregard for death that leaves you, when it is over, and the death administered to the animal that has made it possible, as empty, as changed and as sad as any major emotion will leave you.
>
> (206–7)

Some of Hemingway's best descriptive writing about bullfight action is also found in the two chapters on the faena and proper killing. The language here is clear and exact, yet there is always the close counterpoint of emotional reaction, especially when he considers the skills of such legendary figures as Belmonte and Joselito. He is thinking of Joselito when he says that the heart of bullfighting's emotional appeal is the feeling of immortality it provides both bullfighter and spectator:

He is performing a work of art and he is playing with death, bringing it closer, closer, closer, to himself, a death that you know is in the horns because you have the canvas-covered bodies of the horses on the sand to prove it. He gives the feeling of his immortality, and, as you watch it, it becomes yours. Then when it belongs to both of you, he proves it with the sword.

(213)

The subject of killing in the ring, especially killing in the classic *recibiendo* manner with the matador standing motionless and receiving the bull's charge, inspires a discussion of the physical and spiritual qualities of the good killer – and of the decline of modern bullfighting. It is rare now, Hemingway declares, to see killing done well and bravely, and he provides portraits of the manner of several matadors that has robbed killing of its emotion, that moment

. . . when man and bull form one figure as the sword goes all the way in, the man leaning after it, death uniting the two figures in the emotional, aesthetic and artistic climax of the fight.

(238)

Hemingway's account of the diminishment of the third and final part of the tragedy of the bullring, draining off much of its emotional appeal, leads him into a flat account of the future of Spanish bullfighting at the end of the section. He concludes that bullfighting will probably continue as an industry despite the present government's lack of sympathy for it, though any change in the breeding of fighting bulls would bring a quick end to it as a serious activity. Perhaps in reaction to the sober, matter-of-fact ending of the section, he turns in Chapter Twenty to the homage to Spain, 'a country you love very much,' as a way of returning to the counterpoint of personal response, of again interweaving fact with feeling, the emotional and the practical.   (277)

The device of writing about what he had failed to write about – all those evocative details of place and character that, if exactly captured, would 'make all that come true again' – was one Hemingway employed several times (272). It forms part of Harry's dying recollection in 'The Snows of Kilimanjaro', and in *The Garden of Eden* David Bourne carefully lists all the things he has not yet got right in the

African story he is writing. In *Death in the Afternoon* the device brings an emotional, sensuous response back to the center of interest and establishes Spain, the last good country, as the overriding subject despite the immediate focus on bullfighting. It concentrates attention on what is only intermittently, though powerfully, present before within the flow of practical matters – as, for example, in the description of the town of Aranjuez in the chapter on the best places to see a bullfight:

> The bull ring is at the end of a hot, wide, dusty street that runs into the heat from the cool forest shade of the town and the professional cripples and horror and pity inspirers that follow the fairs of Spain line this road, wagging stumps, exposing sores, waving monstrosities and holding out their caps, in their mouths when they have nothing left to hold them with, so that you walk a dusty gauntlet between two rows of horrors to the ring.

Hemingway adds that Aranjuez is 'Velasquez to the edge and then straight Goya to the bull ring' (40). In the same chapter he cautions against the use of field glasses at a bullfight because:

> . . .they will destroy for you some of the greatest and most startling beauties who will come in with cloudy white lace mantillas, high combs and complexions and wonderful shawls and who in the glasses will show the gold teeth and flour-covered swartness of some one you saw last night perhaps somewhere else and who is attending the fight to advertise the house.
>
> (41)

But the uninterrupted attention to Spain in the final chapter also recalls to mind, as does the section on proper killing in the bullring, the inevitable changes that have taken place in the country. In Pamplona new apartment buildings block the view of the mountains; in the forest of the Irati the trees have been cut down and the fishing ruined. The biggest change, of course, is that 'we are older.' Change itself occupies the final paragraph of the book, Hemingway maintaining without much conviction that he knows things change and doesn't care. Amid flux, all that endures is work and trying to do it well, which brings him around to the book at hand and a final movement of the counterpoint of fact and feeling. Although he may not have got all of his affection for Spain into the work, he decides that he has at least managed to say 'a few practical things' about the Spanish bullfight (278). From its outside opening, the book has come, in its final line, to an inside close.

What follows in the appended matter is in the practical vein as well, documentation now in the form of photographs, explanations, lists, and finally the bibliographical note. Yet even here Hemingway cannot confine himself to detached fact. The captions of the photographs are alive with personal reaction, the glossary even more so. Hemingway notes that the American equivalent for *mamarracho* – an insult directed at a poor bullfighter – would be 'awkward bum, stumble-bum, flat-footed tramp or yellow bastard'. The word *maricón* refers to a fairy or fag, causing him to remark that he only knows of two bullfighters who qualify, one of whom 'is almost pathologically miserly, is lacking in valor but is very skillful and delicate with the cape, a sort of exterior decorator of bullfighting.' The bibliographical note claims the use of 2077 works on bullfighting yet asks the indulgence of genuine *aficionados* for the book's inevitable narrowing to personal understanding. Of necessity, it is, finally, only 'one man's arbitrary explanation', a remark that reverses the ending of the main text, returning the book full circle to the personal, outer approach of its opening.

*   *   *

A discussion emphasizing matters of craft and design that elevate *Death in the Afternoon* from a dry handbook to a work suffused with passion and personality is brought up short by recalling Hemingway's advice to Perkins to promote the book simply as a 'great classic goddamned book on bull fighting', leaving it to the critics to 'claim it has something additional.' The book, he informed the editor, was simply 'a straight book on bull fighting'. As mentioned earlier, Hemingway was complaining about promotional matter that alluded to things he had already removed from the manuscript at Dos Passos' suggestion – 'all that story, dialogue, etc', as he characterized it, that was 'thrown in extra' – and also giving vent to his suspicion that the excised material was some of the best in the book.[50] So he insisted on the centrality of bullfighting even though, as an *Arabia Deserta* of the bullring, the book could hardly have avoided something additional. Critics have maintained as much ever since its appearance. In an early article in *Hound & Horn* Lincoln Kirstein announced that more than an introduction to bullfighting, *Death in the Afternoon* was a spiritual autobiography, a study of Spanish manners, and a study of the craft of fiction. Critics have subsequently gone to the book for evidence on a similar range of Hemingway topics, separating the ostensible text on bullfighting from a variety of more revealing subtexts. Nonetheless, a question to raise, taking Hemingway's remarks to Perkins at face value, is the importance of *Death in the Afternoon* simply as a treatise on bullfighting.

Allen Josephs, who has pursued the question at length, finds it complicated by the lack of other comparable works in English, yet concludes that *Death in the Afternoon* is a thorough account of the subject by any standard. He cites a Spanish critic, Shay Oag, a biographer of the bullfighter Antonio Ordóñez, who said that 'to say that his [Hemingway's] understanding of the bullfight was pro-found and fundamental is as impertinent a redundancy as to state that no one writing in English can as yet even begin to match him when he is writing about the bulls.'[51] Josephs tilts with the criticism in John McCormick's learned study *The Complete Aficionado* that Hemingway overemphasized the theme of death and consequently stressed the matador at the expense of the bull. McCormick quotes a matador who told him: 'We do not go into the plaza to die. We go there to live, to earn our bread. Why does this Hemingway not call his book *Life in the Afternoon?*'[52] Josephs' response is that it is the bull's death that takes place in the afternoon, and that Hemingway's fascination is with the bullfighter's performance – his life – con-ducted inches from the bull's horns. The tragedy of bullfighting, he points out, repeating Hemingway, is the bull, not the man.

Angel Capellán looks at Spanish reaction to the book as a bullfight treatise in *Hemingway and the Hispanic World*, noting that, despite some enthusiastic reviews at the time of publication, the book soon dropped from sight and wasn't translated into Spanish until the 1960s. When referred to at all, it was often misidentified as a novel. Hemingway's return to Spain in the 1950s on an assignment for *Life* magazine that resulted in *The Dangerous Summer* brought him con-siderable attention in the country, but Capellán says press coverage continued to reflect general ignorance of his bullfight book.

Capellán takes issue with the book's structure, arguing against digressions – particularly historical assessments of Joselito and Belmonte in the middle chapters – that break an orderly progression of sections on the elements of bullfighting. He also finds some facets of bullfighting missing in the book, yet believes it deals fully with the three things that monopolize Hemingway's interest, bull, bullfighter and the bullfight itself. With bullfighters, the period Hemingway knew best was the 1920s and early 30s, and here his judgements of individual figures were vividly subjective, often bearing little resemblance to what have come to be conventional assessments; his errors, seen in retrospect, stemmed from an over-emphasis on courage in a bullfighter as against technical proficiency. Still, Capellán has no quarrel with Hemingway's standing as a knowledgeable critic who knew the skills of the bullring and generally understood genius when he saw it. He concludes that Hemingway was 'the greatest of foreign aficionados of the Spanish bullfight', with an understanding of that world which 'was deeper, more knowledgeable, and comprehensive than that of other non-Spanish critics who have written about it, and equaling in technical accuracy that of Spanish bullfight critics, surpassing them in comprehensiveness.'[53]

Brief but similar evaluations have been offered by James Michener, like Hemingway a well-grounded literary commentator on Spain and the bullring. He has considered the book in the light of others in English (among them, Kenneth Tynan's *Bull Fever*, Angus Macnab's *The Bulls of Iberia* and John Marks' *To the Bullfight* – the last, Hemingway thought, the best book on bullfighting save his own) and concluded that 'the best thing so far written on bullfighting is Ernest Hemingway's *Death in the Afternoon*.' In an introduction to the book version of *The Dangerous Summer* Michener added about the earlier book that 'the remarkable illustrated essay' was 'loving, faithful, opinionated . . . It was one hell of a book.' [54]

Although Capellán concentrates on *Death in the Afternoon* as a bullfight manual, he slides off the subject to appraise it as literary criticism, following here a familiar track laid down by those who pursue something additional in the book beyond its formal subject. And with reason. Given Hemingway's personal approach to the material as well as his conception of bullfighting as an art form, finally rendered minor only because of its impermanence, it is natural enough that writing matters find a place in the book. Although he removed some of the 'lowdown about writing' at Dos Passos' suggestion, much was left in, with the result that the book contains some of Hemingway's most intriguing remarks on writing. With the second page he recalls his early efforts to learn to write and offers the distinction between journalism and the 'real thing' in writing. Thereafter, literary and artistic matters surface regularly, concluding in the final paragraph with the self-admonishment that 'the thing to do is work and learn to make it' (278).

Death in the Afternoon clearly has its uses as literary criticism, but Hemingway's views here have long since been worked into our understanding of his art, as have his views of Spain and the matador as an emblematic figure of grace under pressure and various other subtexts drawn from the work. What remains, with curious power to engage and delight, is simply the book itself as Hemingway described it, one man's arbitrary explanation of bullfighting seen both practically and emotionally. His accomplishment is that the book is still a lively reading experience, and for just the reason he hoped would give it lasting quality: the combination of a 'really true' subject that fascinated him in all its particulars with an unbuttoned personal manner. One without the other would have left the book a flat handbook or sheer exhibitionism. Together, they form an account that is always *about* something yet enlivened by the immediate presence of a powerful, reacting personality. It is always *someone's* account.

As Lincoln Kirstein remarked when the book appeared, 'Death in the Afternoon is, of all personal books, the most personal. The quality of its author's character is imprinted in the ink of the type on every page.'[55] It is the dominating presence of the first person, as Edmund Wilson saw, that separates the fact book so markedly from the detached mode of the fiction – and that leads to contemporary dismissals of the work in which critics, following in Wilson's wake, find Hemingway in his own voice only 'an overbearing know-it-all' and a posturing 'embarrassment'.[56] Yet it is exactly the personal element – excessive, insistent, always *there* – together with an accompanying preoccupation with subject, the effort to provide all the dope about bullfighting, that gives the book its distinction and durability as non-fiction.

Geoffrey Brereton, commenting on a British reissue of *Death in the Afternoon* in 1950, found the book 'a period piece – and something more'. It remained interesting long after its names and details had grown remote; indeed, the fading of topical interest was hardly a loss to the reader. 'On the contrary,' Brereton remarked, 'Hemingway's splashy reporting has set into a stalactite-show of freaks and oddities which may prove timeless enough to turn the book into a minor classic.'[57] More than half a century now since its appearance, the book's transcendence of the barriers of time and place seems all the more striking. Prior interest in Spain or bullfighting hardly matters, though the book still possesses its lingering authority as a

Baedeker of bullfighting. Around this central focus Hemingway erects a world complete unto itself, the names faded and the activity dulled, but Spanish bullfighting rendered as much a part of the literary landscape as Thoreau's pond or Agee's sharecropper South. He accomplishes this, as he did in the self-enclosed worlds of his stories and novels, partly through the means of the fiction – by dedicated attention, as he described his aim in fiction, 'to the sequence of motion and fact which made the emotion' (2). The addition in his true book is that the facts are a former journalist's observations together with a researcher's reading, the emotion personal and directly pursued, the two bound together in a richly textured back-and-forth movement. He said about fiction in *Death in the Afternoon* that, done right, it would be 'as valid in a year or in ten years or . . . always' (2). He might just as well have been accounting for the staying power of his rather technical book.

3

One Central Necessity

True narrative that is exciting and still is literature is very rare.

Bad reviews and poor sales didn't finish off Hemingway's interest in a factual approach to Spanish material. The film director Lewis Milestone wanted to make a documentary as a sequel to *Death in the Afternoon*, a Spanish collage following from the book's last chapter, shot on location and using non-professional actors; eager to sign on as advisor, Hemingway made a trip to New York to meet with the director. Later, he tried to recruit John Dos Passos for the project, painting a picture of the two of them roaming Spain in the summer of 1933 for the necessary spadework, breezily bypassing any role for Milestone:

> We will hire a car and work this movie out writing down what we work out, places and shots in a couple of five-cent notebooks. We will . . . go around and find out what we want to do exactly. Then we will have dope and will get some money (no milestoning or big shots) and make the picture the following summer. You would do better on your damned perpetual education of Henry J. Passos to go to Spain this summer than anywhere I believe. Really, and I won't bother you or anything. We can have a damned good time doing the movie thing, i.e. getting it all set in our heads and much enjoyment withall. Then with it all clear I will sell some bastard on the idea of making it even if I have to be polite.[1]

Nothing finally came of the scheme but Hemingway was soon involved in another, one that also had its roots in *Death in the Afternoon*.

Arnold Gingrich, then editor of a trade journal in Chicago called *Apparel Arts* and a collector of Hemingway first editions, had written to him in December 1932 asking him to autograph a copy of the work. Gingrich praised the last chapter, stimulating Hemingway's remark that it was what the book was about – and the boast that, bad reviews aside, 'Papa still feels pretty good and hasn't started to write the good ones yet.'[2] Shortly thereafter, Gingrich wrote to him about *Esquire*, the new men's magazine the editor was starting in the fall of 1933; he wanted Hemingway as a contributor, and was willing to pay $250 apiece for articles on hunting and fishing. He added that it would be a magazine of quality and, in the mode of *Death in the Afternoon*, have 'adequate cojones'.[3] It was the start of a long and fruitful relationship on both sides. Over the next half dozen years Hemingway would publish twenty-five articles and six short stories in *Esquire*, becoming a major factor in the magazine's rapid success.

Gingrich had definite ideas about the kind of articles he wanted from his prize contributor. They would focus on Hemingway's outdoor exploits, forming 'a sort of sportsman's notebook', and in the feeling they evoked they would resemble the last chapter of the bullfight book. Gingrich advised Hemingway to reread the chapter, hoping the approach employed in the book would 'spill over' into the first article about Cuba and fishing, conveying 'the sights and sounds and sweats and odors – the whole rhythmic pattern – of this separate life that revolves about the central fact of the fight with the swordfish as that other does about the fight with the bull.'[4] Gingrich kept insisting on the chapter as the emotional model for Hemingway to keep in mind: 'A law making it compulsory to read Chapter XX of Death in the Afternoon twice a year for the next five years couldn't hurt anybody – and that includes you.'[5]

The model for the form of the *Esquire* articles was the loosely written 'Pamplona Letter' Hemingway had published in *the transatlantic review* in 1924. Gingrich said he didn't expect a 'formal composition – a major effort involving gestation and labor pains', a bow in the direction of Hemingway's suspicion that *Esquire* was getting his work at a bargain-basement rate, though one Gingrich promised him was twice that paid other contributors. Typographically, however, the 'Pamplona Letter' wouldn't work for *Esquire's* layout since the disparate sections had been separated by thick dividing rules in the Paris journal. Gingrich once again advised following the example of the final chapter of *Death in the Afternoon* because 'it roams all over Spain, has no such divisions but manages, without the use of them, to string a lot of not very closely related subjects very closely together.'[6]

The link with the 'Pamplona Letter' precipitated a flap over titles for the *Esquire* articles. Hemingway assumed they would simply be labeled letters; when Gingrich added a more descriptive title he charged him with trying to deceive readers into thinking they were stories. The editor found the accusation 'pretty damn lousy', but he patiently explained that the magazine's style called for titles plus explanatory subheads on all pieces.[7] The first article in the fall of 1933, Hemingway's return to popular journalism after a decade's absence, carried the title 'Marlin off the Morro: A Cuban Letter', the form the magazine would use for most of his contributions. For his second article he turned back for material to Spain and bullfighting, bringing readers up to date on, among other things, the current crop of matadors in a meandering, unfocused piece.

Hemingway had no illusions about the importance of the articles he turned out for *Esquire*, as he frequently let both Gingrich and his readers know, thereby establishing his superiority to the hasty and lucrative work. Nonetheless, he once considered putting the articles in book form, suggesting to Max Perkins a collection, with the work that eventually would be called *Green Hills of Africa* as its centerpiece, under the title *The Highlands of Africa and Other Pieces*. The usual position he took about the articles was that he was writing them only for the money – in fact, paying back $3000 Gingrich had advanced against future articles, the money used by Hemingway as a down-payment on his new fishing cruiser, the *Pilar*. When he sent in an article that 'seems to be about fish' and had some technical information in it, he told Gingrich he would 'try to ease off on the science and let a good gust of shit blow over it in the re-writing.'[8] In 'Monologue to the Maestro: A High Seas Letter' he underscored for readers the distinction between his serious business of letters and the casual letters he turned out for the magazine. Gingrich, eager for Hemingway's presence in the magazine, raised no editorial objections. He told him to 'go ahead and write anything that comes into your head. No holds barred. If it's good journalism I'll be well satisfied. If it isn't I'll know it, as a person, but accept it and like it, as an "editor" '[9]

For subjects, Hemingway usually drew on what was immediately at hand, himself, dramatizing his exploits as a knowledgeable and widely traveled sporting figure, occasionally offering himself as a literary arbiter or political sage. What was at hand in 1934 was Africa. In December of the preceding year he had arrived in the country with his second wife, Pauline, and a Key West friend, Charles Thompson, beginning a well-financed three-month safari that had been planned while he was still working on *Death in the Afternoon*. Out of the experience came three *Esquire* letters published immediately after his return, with another, 'Sailfish Off Mombasa', appearing the following year.

In 'A.D. in Africa: A Tanganyika Letter' he recounted his bout with a serious case of amoebic dysentery during the safari, necessitating a flight back to Nairobi and treatment with emetine and bed rest. He made a stab at describing the African landscape, some of which reminded him of the brown uplands of Montana and Wyoming, other parts looking like an abandoned New England orchard 'until you top a hill and see the orchard runs on for fifty miles'; but it was the ailment and his reduced state as a writer that preoccupied him. Consequently, the letter was 'more dysenteric than the usual flow' of his articles and 'pretty well emetined', the doctor – conveniently, given the quality of the article – explaining to him that after such treatment 'you can't think coherently.'[10]

The second African letter, 'Shootism versus Sport', was a straightforward lecture on the proper way of shooting a lion – on foot rather than from a car or at night from a blind. 'Notes on Dangerous Game' began the same way, concentrating on the qualities of his white hunter, Philip Percival; but another theme quickly developed, Hemingway's insistence that the reader understand how little value he placed on his magazine work. He tossed off italicized parenthetical challenges to competitors (*'There are too many supers in these last two sentences. Re-write them yourselves lads and see how easy it is to do better than Papa. Thank you. Exhilarating feeling, isn't it?'*) and asides that established his awareness that writing for money required him to make, among other things, embarrassing comments about Percival's skill and bravery (*'Excuse me, Mr. P. You see I do this for a living. We all have to do a lot of things for a living. But we're still drinking their whiskey, aren't we?'*). Another aside promised an end to such asides, but the article concluded with a lengthy parenthetical reference to the ease of 'writing these letters' in which Percival, after his first deep-sea fishing experience (while waiting on the coast with the Hemingways for their ship home) is said to decide '"to write an article on it for Esquire. Call it Dolphin Fishing by One Who Knows."'[11] The point, it seemed, was that anyone could do one.

The *Esquire* articles aren't so lacking in interest or craft as Edmund Wilson had it when he dismissed them as 'rubbishy', but Hemingway clearly considered them hack work and churned them out with minimum effort.[12] A repeated question in his correspondence with Gingrich is how many he has to write before his debt is paid. In a letter written to the editor from Key West a few months after his return from the safari, he brought up the question again, then

turned to his desire to earn more money so he could get out to Africa
once more:

> As far as I know I have only one life to live and I have worked hard
> and written good stories, pieces etc. and by Jesus I want to live it
> where it interests me; and I have no romantic feeling about the
> American scene. Also pretty soon I will be long time dead and
> outside of writing I have two well developed talents; for sea
> fishing where there is a current and migratory fish and shooting
> with a rifle on targets at unknown ranges where the vital spots are
> not marked but have to be understood to be hit and for Christ sake
> why not go where I can use them instead of go out here and play
> around with chicken shit sailfish that I feel sorry for interrupting
> when I catch and never put my hand to a rifle from one year's end
> to the other . . . If I don't give a godamn about America I can't
> help it.[13]

The outburst was brought on by the tedium of Key West after East
Africa, a contrast all the more immediate since he was now writing
about the safari and was drawn back into the experience, causing all
else to pale. Unlike the *Esquire* journalism, the new work was
serious and demanding – 'a very long story', as he described it in a
letter to Scott Fitzgerald, and a 'hard one to write'.[14] When it was
finished he announced in another letter that the work was the best
he could write.

*   *   *

Unlike the lengthy composition of the Spanish book, *Green Hills of
Africa* was turned out with dispatch. It began as a short story 'about
while we were hunting in Africa' that Hemingway intended to
include with either his collected articles or stories, then quickly
evolved into a factual account in which he changed some names yet
remained close to the actual events of the safari while reconstructing
them in a fictional manner. Although he insisted that *Green Hills of
Africa* was the 'straight story, the actual things that happened,' it
was far from such a simple report.[15] Recreating experience even
from very recent memory inevitably altered the experience, and
there was as well the fiction-like shaping of characters and scenes
and the use of at least partially invented dialogue to develop
narrative movement and variety. Still, the book was an effort on

Hemingway's part to stay generally within the facts as he recalled them while the events and emotions of the safari were still fresh in his mind.

In New York on the return trip from Africa he had told reporters he would begin a season of intensive writing to earn money to return to the continent. At home in Key West in April 1934, just over a month after the safari ended, he started. By the end of April he had fifty pages, a false start as it turned out since he threw away thirty, saving only an account of a chance encounter with an Austrian with a broken-down truck. Work on the manuscript, with the title *The Highlands of Africa* and subtitle 'Hunters are Brothers', alternated with fishing expeditions for marlin off the Cuban coast in the *Pilar*. Hemingway's pride in the boat and pleasure in fishing carried over into the account of the safari, intensifying his memories of another outdoor activity performed with manly skill. In one instance the sea came directly into the book with mention of activities, hunting and fishing, 'which people do not consider a serious occupation and yet you know, truly, that it is as important and has always been as important as all the things that are in fashion', in a 400-word burst of a sentence on the wonders of the Gulf Stream.[16] By June, he informed Perkins that he had 20 000 words of 'triply re-written shit-removed mss', and in October he was up to 50 000 words.[17] His usual rate of progress was five or six pages a day, but there was one spurt of twenty-two pages, another of thirty. On 16 November he wrote Perkins that he had finished the book that morning – 492 handwritten pages, 73 650 words. In January, the editor got a look at a fresh typescript, the book now called *Green Hills of Africa*, during a vacation in Key West. The following month, less than a year after starting work, the manuscript was sent to Scribner's.

Perkins was as uncritically enthusiastic as ever. He told Hemingway it was 'extraordinary how wonderfully a factual account has been formed into a work of art'; he hadn't seen 'anything even approaching it in that respect'.[18] But there were, as usual, editorial questions about handling the book. He had already convinced Hemingway to publish it by itself rather than as part of a collection. Hemingway wanted to give readers an obvious value for their money as the best way to sell a lot of copies in hard times, but Perkins thought a collection would distract critics from the main work. The problem now was the exact nature of the book. As the editor saw it, the book transcended the ordinary narrative of an expedition, possessing the quality of an imaginative work, and so it was directed to Hemingway's usual literary audience. But it also had value as a factual record for the non-literary tribe of hunters and African enthusiasts. Perkins thought the book as a record would be enhanced by photographs, but 'the other and greater value, is injured by photographs.' He suggested a compromise – a picture as frontispiece and then sixteen pictures grouped at the end with long captions 'aimed at the people who would value the book as a record, and as telling about animals and hunting.'[19] The book would then resemble *Death in the Afternoon* in size and could be offered at the same price.

Hemingway's response was that he preferred to publish the book, as he put it, straight, with just a picture for the frontispiece and possibly another for the dust jacket. The photographs he had taken in Africa were inadequate; beyond that, he didn't think pictures would add to the book since he had already made pictures with his prose. A last point was that he had established a certain standard of quality in *Death in the Afternoon* and needed to beat that if the new book contained pictures. As it turned out, photographs were avoided entirely in favor of decorations by Edward Shenton, handsome drawings of animals and the hunt in an Art Deco manner that had been used in the serialization of the book in *Scribner's Magazine*, where Shenton's work routinely appeared.

Serialization had one troublesome moment. Perkins favored pre-publication, as he had with *Death in the Afternoon*, and the work easily fell into sections for the magazine. Hemingway wrote titles for the sections, then removed them for book publication, using titles only for the four major divisions, a change that he thought made the book appear less like a novel. He also provided a lightly humorous listing of characters for the magazine that he later chose to remove from the book, Perkins agreeing with some reluctance though retaining the listing for the dust cover:

POP – Mr. Jackson Phillips, called Mr. J or Mr. J. P. – a white hunter or professional guide. Not to be called Pop to his face
KANDISKY – An Austrian
DAN – A second white hunter
KARL – A lucky hunter
Mr. Hemingway – A braggart
Mrs. Hemingway – Wife of the above known as P.O.M. or poor old mama. Known to the natives as Mama
M'COLA – a gunbearer

CHARO – A gunbearer
KAMAU – A Kikuyu driver
DROOPY – A good native guide
ABDULLAH and GARRICK – Bad native guides
THE OLD MAN, and THE WANDEROBO-MASAI – Mysterious
    native guides
THE ROMAN, HIS BROTHER, HIS FAMILY – Excellent people
MASAI – Various Masai
There are also famine sufferers, various Hindus, porters, skinners,
personal boys, and a very good cook. There are many animals.

The problem was money. Perkins had mentioned $5000 for serialization rights when he read the manuscript in Key West; later he wired an offer of $4500. He said he knew that Hemingway could get considerably more from popular magazines such as *Cosmopolitan* and *Red Book*, but he maintained that it was all the money the unsound economic condition of the magazine allowed. Hemingway fired off a response outlining all he had done for the publishing house since 1926 and pointing out that, if its magazine had never run on a sound economic basis, neither had he. In the end, Perkins got *Scribner's Magazine* to offer another five-hundred dollars, Hemingway accepting with notable lack of enthusiasm.

As with *Death in the Afternoon*, there was a minor flap about language. In the proofs Hemingway had added an indirect reference to Gertrude Stein, and Perkins thought it 'better not to call the old girl a bitch.'[20] Hemingway claimed he didn't see what the fuss was about unless the editor thought it would give the critics something to jump on. He toyed with alternatives – fat bitch, lousy bitch, old bitch, lesbian bitch – settling finally on just female, a term he assured Perkins would make her far angrier than bitch in any of its varieties.

Serialization ran from May to October 1935, with the book appearing on 25 October. Despite the promotion value of magazine publication, sales were disappointing. After reading proofs of the first magazine installment, Perkins had predicted about the book that 'people are bound to like it immensely,' and Hemingway himself had happily anticipated sales in the fifteen or twenty-thousand range.[21] The book, he reasoned, had all the elements needed for success in that

> . . . it is a long and good story. It is straight and absolutely true
> autobiography, with no pulling of punches or lack of frankness.

With plenty of story interest, suspense and lots of conversation and it takes people bodily to a place they have never been and most of them can never go. Also it's the best writing I've ever done and the more often I read it the more I think it gets that extra dimensional quality I was working for.[22]

But less than two months after publication the optimism was gone and he unhappily concluded that the book had been ruined by three things: an inflated price; offense handed out to the critics; and too little advertising by Scribner's.

Perkins shrugged off the point about price, and he said that advertising was something that nobody could talk about positively. Hemingway's attack on the critics was another matter. The editor said he could have warned him about the effect of his 'plain truths' on the book's critical reception, but he knew Hemingway would have paid no attention; beyond that, he advised taking a long view since the truth-telling would only work against the book in the short run. Privately, he indicated that he had expected a critical attack on the book for another reason. Writers' careers had a natural ebb and flow; there was always a period when the critical tide ran against them whatever the merits of their work. In Hemingway's case there was some consolation in the fact that he had experienced such a reaction when he 'was writing books that are in a general sense minor ones.' To Hemingway himself, of course, Perkins couched his view of the minor nature of the two non-fiction books in heavily veiled fashion, suggesting it was merely the reading public's natural inclination for superficial impressions. With *Green Hills of Africa* the impression 'was that it was an account of a hunting expedition to Africa, covering a short space of time, and was therefore a distinctly minor piece of work.'[23] He should have foreseen the response, the editor added, since the public regarded Hemingway as a novelist and viewed the non-fiction merely as an interlude in his career.

As with the earlier fact book, the reviews of *Green Hills of Africa* were inconclusive. Few writers made much of Hemingway's swipes at the critics or lordly judgements on other writers; comparisons with *Death in the Afternoon* drew more attention. John Chamberlain thought the African book simply an account by a 'bullfight *aficionado* looking for variations on death in the afternoon'. Granville Hicks, in a *New Masses* review with the title 'Small Game Hunting', cared for neither work but thought them likely to be the best books written on bullfighting and hunting. Still, he found the subjects inherently limited and consequently dull, *Green Hills* comparing in tedium only to *Anthony Adverse*. Bernard DeVoto emphasized boredom as well, finding it a new experience in reading Hemingway, and T. S. Matthews suggested the month's shooting would have been better cast in a letter to a hunting pal. But Charles G. Poore found that as 'the Belmonte of his own hunting cuadrilla Ernest Hemingway has produced a fine book on death in the African afternoon,' the best on big-game hunting he had read. Carl Van Doren thought the various characterizations in the book skillfully handled and that the hunting country 'not only looks real, but sounds, feels, smells, and tastes real.'[24]

A particularly enduring view – an enduring view, once again, of the non-fiction generally – was laid down by Edmund Wilson in a *New Republic* article when he declared *Green Hills of Africa* Hemingway's most personal book and therefore his weakest. Hemingway had also fallen into the vein of what Wilson termed the 'Old Master of Key West' in *Death in the Afternoon*, but the predominance of practical information in that book had kept him from spoiling it. The African book had no such saving grace; it was all 'Hemingway maudlin'. Wilson thought the initial mistake was Hemingway's technical decision to use fictional methods yet limit himself to actual events, the effect being to illustrate the far richer experience of imaginative writing. He had simply chosen to treat his material in the wrong manner. But a deeper problem was his psychological approach to the material in which he put his literary personality at the center of the book, all else pushed to the side and seen in the dim light that remained. So about animals, Wilson said, the reader learns only that Hemingway wants to kill them, that the natives are simple figures who admire him, that his hunting companion inspires his envy, that his wife is fond of him. Even Hemingway himself in the book's self-portrait seemed an oddly reduced figure, a character apparently conceived in the image of the public writer-hero of the trashy *Esquire* articles. Removed from the detached mode of the fiction and talking in his own person, Hemingway the non-fiction writer seemed to Wilson invariably to lose all capacity for critical understanding. His sense of life, directly expounded, sounded only silly. *Green Hills of Africa*, Wilson concluded with a last turn of the knife, was the 'only book I have ever read which makes Africa and its animals seem dull.'[25]

James Joyce, for one, thought otherwise, though his enthusiasm may have been more for the idea of Hemingway's Africa than for the

African book. He recalled for an interviewer that he had met Hemingway in Paris before the safari and that Hemingway had promised him a 'living lion'. 'Fortunately we escaped that,' Joyce added. 'But we would like to have the book he has written. He's a good writer, Hemingway. He writes as he is.' (In the book Hemingway repaid the compliment, remembering Joyce in Paris and declaring that 'it was nice to see a great writer in our time' (p.71). Richard Ellmann has it that Joyce even discussed with Hemingway the possibility of going to Africa to add some raw experience to his life, an unlikely expedition yet one urged upon him by his wife. When Joyce mentioned an obstacle, that poor eyesight might prevent him from actually seeing a lion, Nora Joyce said: 'Hemingway'd describe him to you and afterwards you could go up to him and touch him and smell him. That's all you'd need.'[26]

Despite such occasional expressions on Hemingway's behalf, Wilson's perverse characterization of *Green Hills of Africa* has echoed through commentary on the book ever since, appearing to find added and conclusive support in the two famous stories drawn from the same safari material. While the non-fiction account is commonly dismissed as a failure, or at most a work of passing interest, 'The Snows of Kilimanjaro' and 'The Short Happy Life of Francis Macomber' are considered among Hemingway's certain masterpieces. Yet taken by itself – or taken in the context of Hemingway's other fact books – it is surely a major achievement and, together with *Death in the Afternoon*, one of the central works of American non-fiction. It is not as richly vigorous, as oddly curious and surprising, as the Spanish book, but much more studied and carefully executed. It isn't another compendium of Hemingway's expert knowledge but an attempt to recapture a fresh experience in a newly discovered place. The fact book competes with imaginative works – the issue Hemingway brought up in the foreword as a way of pointing to the experimental nature of the work, unfortunately so since it provided, then as now, a convenient means of dismissal – not in its measure with fiction but in the narrative methods and especially the fiction-like concentration brought to bear on a personal account. In Hemingway's non-fiction, *Green Hills of Africa* is his most formally ambitious work.

*   *   *

Hemingway said he wrote *Death in the Afternoon* because of a lack of books in English on Spanish bullfighting. *Green Hills of Africa* has similar roots in literary experience. In *The Sun Also Rises*, immediately after his remark that ' "nobody ever lives their life all the way up except bull-fighters," ' Jake Barnes turns the subject to Africa, asking Robert Cohn:

> 'Did you ever think about going to British East Africa to shoot?'
> 'No; I wouldn't like that.'
> 'I'd go there with you.'
> 'No; that doesn't interest me.'
> 'That's because you never read a book about it . . .'[27]

Unlike Cohn, Hemingway had done his reading. His interest in Africa went back to his early years in Oak Park where he had followed the progress of Theodore Roosevelt's safari in the magazines, devoured books about the continent in the public library, and joined in the community's passion for things African. For Oak Park, missionary zeal directed to Africa was the major concern; for the young Hemingway, it was the strenuous life in one of the last frontier places, hunting the great animals he had viewed with his father in Chicago's Field Museum of Natural History. Hemingway's first book review, written in Paris and published in the *Toronto Star Weekly* in 1922, was of a novel about the life and death of an African chieftain. Back in Key West in 1934, his dream of an African safari satisfied (and in the company of the same white hunter Roosevelt had used thirty years earlier), he began reading about Africa again – guides, memoirs, encyclopedias, travel books, all factual works and all in preparation for his own fact book. His research effort didn't appear as directly in the book as had his reading about Spanish bullfighting in *Death in the Afternoon*; it was a book that concentrated on a narrative of recent experience, but the reading was there as a foundation – and as a challenge, a body of work to be surpassed.

In his first *Esquire* article about Africa he had said that nothing he had read had given him any idea of the beauty of the country and the quantity of the game. The book manuscript completed, he repeated to Perkins that one of the sources of inspiration behind it was that he had 'never read anything that could make me see and feel Africa. It was not at all as I had imagined it or like anything I'd ever read. When I started the story, that was what I wanted to make.'[28] In the book, the white hunter, Pop, remarks that most safari books are ' "awful bloody bores" ', and Hemingway agrees. The only one he had ever liked, Pop goes on, is Daniel Streeter's *Denatured Africa*:

'"He made you feel what it was like. That's the best."' Hemingway mentions Charles Curtis' *Hunting in Africa East and West*, but Pop returns to Streeter's book: '"That man Streeter was damned funny though. Do you remember when he shot the kongoni?"' '"It was very funny,"' Hemingway agrees (pp.193–4).

Streeter's popular 1926 book takes a decidedly lighthearted approach to Africa and big-game hunting. The kongoni incident refers to twenty shots needed to finally fell a wounded and tracked animal, yet even then, the author out of ammunition and waiting alone for porters, the kongoni lifts its head and gazes at him with fixed eyes. A white hunter later explains that a last shot supposedly into the brain had only stunned the animal – and explains further that '"an animal is never dead in this part of the world until his pelt is nailed up on the barn door."'[29] Thereafter, the difficulties of genuinely killing African game become a humorous theme in a book in which everything about the land, the natives and the hunting is treated with a whimsical touch. No doubt the book's lack of solemnity – or any hint of the false epic quality of Waldo Frank's *Virgin Spain* – appealed to Hemingway and Percival together with some of its evocative descriptions of landscape and of hunting incidents. For the most part the book steers clear of the qualities that Pop says ruined most African accounts: '"They all have this damned Nairobi fast life or else bloody rot about shooting beasts with horns half an inch longer than some one else shot. Or muck about danger"' (94).

In addition to sharing Percival's enthusiasm for *Denatured Africa*, Hemingway may have been modestly influenced by the book. It has the same four-part structure as *Green Hills of Africa*, begins with a prefatory note that speaks (with heavy humor rather than with Hemingway's solemn declaration of intent) of the book's aim, and concludes, the author back in civilization, with a brief postscript. There is a similar preoccupation with the self (Streeter explains: 'Africa has been seen through thousands of eyes. Why do people go? How do they go? What do they see? How do they react to it all? I haven't the remotest idea, except as applied to myself'), and a similar – though more central and sustained – playful portrayal of the foibles of the self.[30] There is the same knowledgeable white hunter, the same hazy background of native figures, the same repeated pursuit scenes.

But admiration for Streeter's book aside, Pop and Hemingway agree that they haven't read anything about Africa that captures the way they feel about it. Their Africa is still virgin literary territory. So

Hemingway declares that he would ' "like to try to write something about the country and the animals and what it's like to some one who knows nothing about it." ' And Pop replies: ' "Have a try at it. Can't do any harm" ' (194). As with the bullfight book, *Green Hills of Africa* was in some sense meant to fill a literary void, though it was a book largely lacking the practical dimension, the instructional purpose, of the earlier work. Its ambitions were more wholly on the plane of feeling – to recreate the sights of Africa and the emotions it evoked through concentration on a narrative of the hunt. It was a book for the reader to live inside of rather than consult for information, and so it was more nearly the 'enough of a book' Hemingway had limned in the final chapter of *Death in the Afternoon*, a book to make experience come true again. In the African book he tells of reading a story of Tolstoy's during an interlude in the hunt that makes him feel he is 'living in that Russia again.' *Green Hills of Africa* has a similar aim. It attempts to draw the reader inside the work through description and narration, experiencing place and action that Hemingway had experienced. It is intended to enchant in exactly the manner of the Tolstoy story, allowing the reader to see

> . . . the river that the Tartars came across when raiding, and the drunken old hunter and the girl and how it was then in the different seasons.
>
> (108–9)

The discussion between Hemingway and Pop about safari books is preceded by talk about revolutions. Hemingway says he is going to write a study of them, but the problem is material – the need for the accumulation of many past performances and reliable information. You can only get the latter in revolutionary places where you speak the language, where you can talk with people and overhear conversations; without that ' "you don't get anything that's of anything but journalistic value". ' This was why he had never gone to Russia, a place in which the traveling journalist was restricted to handouts and sightseeing trips. Pop turns the subject back to Africa, telling Hemingway to ' "knuckle down on your Swahili then", ' but also pointing out that you still can't overhear because the natives talk their tribal languages. To which Hemingway responds with an encapsulated description of an African book, given the limitations he and Pop have just outlined, he might write:

'But if I ever write anything about this it will just be landscape painting until I know something about it. Your first seeing of a country is a very valuable one. Probably more valuable to yourself than to any one else, is the hell of it. But you ought to always write it to try to get it stated. No matter what you do with it.'

(193)

The book finished, Hemingway wrote to Perkins that when he began writing that indeed was all he wanted to do – make the country come alive as a landscape painting, capturing what he had seen and felt in Africa, filling the literary void of books that hadn't adequately prepared him for what it was like. It was all he could do given the brevity of his stay and his lack of languages. Although he didn't mention the contrast to Perkins, the African material lacked the depth of texture of the Spanish material for just these reasons. It was far closer to what he characterized as material possessed only of 'journalistic value' – or to the value of *Denatured Africa*, a funny book.

As landscape painting that made you 'think you will have been there,' the manuscript bore resemblance to 'Big Two-Hearted River'. But there were additional matters, Hemingway informed the editor, that he had discovered during the writing that made it more exciting. The completed work had structure and dialogue and action – it had a story, in other words, though not an invented one but just the actual things that had happened. It was no longer simply an account of his first seeing the country, something to get stated and of likely value only to himself; it was also 'that wonderful goddamned Kudu hunt – the relations between the people – and the way it all worked up to a climax.' It now seemed to him 'a very fine story', maybe the best thing he had ever written, since it was all true yet far removed from something of mere journalistic value. 'True narrative', he instructed Perkins, 'that is exciting and still is literature is very rare. Because first it has to happen, then the person that it happens to has to be equipped to make it come true, ie to realize it, so that it has all the dimensions.'[31]

In his emphasis on the story element in the book, Hemingway may in part have been responding to an earlier implied criticism from the editor. While he was nearing the end of the writing, Perkins had questioned him about the working title, 'The Highlands of Africa'. Wouldn't it be better, he wondered, to change it to 'In the Highlands of Africa', thereby implying 'something that happened, or things that happened there'? Otherwise the book might be mistaken for 'what they call a "travel" book.' Perkins was quick to add that the present title suggested a good deal to him; he only wanted 'to get in something that makes it seem as if it were a *story*'.[32] Hemingway replied only to the effect that he thought he could beat the working title. What he finally settled on didn't include the 'In' Perkins had wanted, but it hardly mattered; as Hemingway now saw it, there was plenty of story in the work to separate it from any confusion with a travel book.

*   *   *

During the talk about African books, Pop mentions that he once kept a diary about a trip to Alaska, an account of ' "what we did each day and how Alaska looked to an Englishman from Africa." ' When P.O.M. asks to read it, he tells her: ' "It'd bore you" ' (194). (Pauline's interest in the diary might have been stimulated by the diary account she was keeping while on the safari, an activity left unmentioned in Hemingway's book along with nearly everything else his wife did with her days.[33]) Hemingway's account of how Africa looked to an American from Key West is meant to be quite different, a true account that yields not a diary-like recital of events nor a journalistic travel book but an exciting story that resembles a work of the imagination. It is non-fiction with the dimensions of fiction, and in that sense it was something he hadn't tried before. In the foreword he named the two main areas of the experiment: the attempt to capture both the 'shape of a country' and the 'pattern of a month's action'.

With the portrayal of the country the book was more nearly the landscape painting he had mentioned to Perkins, but a literary landscape in which he insisted he was trying to capture Africa in the manner of an artist, not merely describe it as a diarist or journalist. In a letter written from Nairobi during the safari, he had told Perkins of his boundless enthusiasm for the new setting: 'This is the finest country I've ever been in. Believe we will settle out here. Wonderful people and splendid climate.'[34] The feeling for Africa found its way into the book through direct comment ('I loved this country and I felt at home and where a man feels at home, outside of where he's born, is where he's meant to go') and indirectly through exacting recreations of place (283–4). It was always one of his great strengths, the ability to convey a sense of place, and in the African book he was never better at it. At the same time, he wrote into the book revealing statements about his sense of the importance of landscape that have become among his more memorable passages. In any discussion of place in Hemingway's work, *Green Hills of Africa* is a central document.

His concern with country in the book is rarely panoramic. Landscape description tends to be tied to the narrative action of the final month of hunting and especially the last days before the rains bring an end to the season. Hemingway recalls Pop picturing the land to the south as 'a million miles of bloody Africa'; his own gaze is kept close to the scene at hand (159). Appropriately, the climactic action of the book takes place among green hills that are portrayed as 'an un-hunted pocket in the million miles of bloody Africa' (218). There are, however, some effective distant shots, such as when the hunting party comes into a country suggested by Droopy, one of the native trackers:

> It was green, pleasant country, with hills below the forest that grew thick on the side of a mountain, and it was cut by the valleys of several watercourses that came down out of the thick timber on the mountain. Fingers of the forest came down onto the heads of some of the slopes and it was there, at the forest edge, that we watched for rhino to come out. If you looked away from the forest and the mountain side you could follow the watercourses and the hilly slope of the land down until the land flattened and the grass was brown and burned and, away, across a long sweep of country, was the brown Rift Valley and the shine of Lake Manyara.
> (49)

Or when from a high vantage point with a view into the Rift Valley the hunting party see

> . . . the plain, the heavy forest below the wall, and the long, dried-up edged shine of Lake Manyara rose-colored at one end with a half million tiny dots that were flamingoes.
> (124)

And there is use of the familiar Hemingway contrast between plains and mountains that stimulates opposed emotional responses: hunting in cars on the vast and dusty Serengeti Plain brings flattened feelings, tramping through green hills and broken upland terrain lifts the spirit. While the killing of a lion on the plain is confusing and

unsatisfactory and recounted in a brief flashback, the extended hunt
for kudu in the hills, the book's centerpiece, ends in triumph. But
broad landscape portraits and a symbolic use of setting are minor
notes in the work, as are occasional parallels between the African
landscape and others Hemingway has known. Coming into a new
hunting territory, he tells Pop that they have

> . . . been through three provinces of Spain today . . . There's no
> bloody difference. Only the buildings . . . The limestone out-
> cropping in the same way, the way the land lies, the trees along
> the watercourses and the springs.'
>
> (151)

The African sky is compared to Italy, Spain and Michigan – the three
beloved peninsulas of *Death in the Afternoon* – and found wanting
even though the country remains matchless. 'You could beat the
sky,' Hemingway notes, 'but not the country' (72). For the most
part, the portrayal of country remains limited and practical, closely
tuned to hunting and the directly associated matters that Hemingway
says he hungered for in Africa:

> . . . the discomforts that you paid to make it real, the names of the
> trees, of the small animals, and all the birds, to know the language
> and have time to be in it and to move slowly.
>
> (73)

Given the concentrated focus, the rendering of country only
fleetingly embraces its native inhabitants. The Austrian, Kandisky,
has an academic interest in the natives and the languages; he has
accumulated books of notes. Of practical interest is the royal manner
of his life in the bush, a boy putting socks on him in the morning and
holding out his drawers. '"Don't you think that is very marvellous?"'
he asks Hemingway, and gets the bored response: '"It's marvellous."'
When he suggests that '"when you come back another time we
must take a safari to study the natives,"' there is no response at all
(31). Only as they merge with the action of the hunt do the natives
take on importance for Hemingway, and then they are lightly
sketched. Droopy, named on account of his eye lids, is a handsome
and stylish savage. Charo, a devout Muslim, nervously watches the
sun set during Ramadan, fingering a bottle of tea. The driver,
Kamau, wears tattered clothing discarded by hunters yet manages

to give an impression of elegance. M'Cola, assigned by Pop as Hemingway's gun bearer, has slim legs with Babe Ruth ankles but an upper body of shrunken muscles. Hemingway relates M'Cola's growing feeling for him after his early favorite, P.O.M., drops out of the shooting competition, but notes that the sense of comradeship was only temporary since the native's 'working estimations were only from day to day and required an unbroken series of events to have any meaning' (44). With M'Cola, Hemingway comes to share safari jokes about bird shooting, drinking, religion, and especially about hyenas shot at close range devouring their own intestines, the latter a 'dirty joke' that prompts one of the book's strongest paragraphs:

> 'Fisi,' M'Cola would say and shake his head in delighted sorrow at there being such an awful beast. Fisi, the hyena, hermaphroditic, self-eating devourer of the dead, trailer of calving cows, hamstringer, potential biter-off of your face at night while you slept, sad yowler, camp-follower, stinking, foul, with jaws that crack the bones the lion leaves, belly dragging, loping away on the brown plain, looking back, mongrel dog-smart in the face; whack from the little Mannlicher and then the horrid circle starting. 'Fisi,' M'Cola laughed, ashamed of him, shaking his bald black head. 'Fisi. Eats himself. Fisi.'
>
> (38)

Although he asks Pop about M'Cola's age (over fifty) and his children (worthless), Hemingway has no interest in the natives' lives beyond the hunt. His companions on the safari are given the same spare treatment, important only for the place they occupy in the business at hand. Karl (the name of Charles Thompson's brother and the nickname Hemingway finally pinned on his close Key West friend after first calling him Charles in the early parts of the holograph manuscript) and he live in the 'same small town', but it is only Karl's temperament as a hunter that matters, his need to be left by himself and to his own pace (86). Pop, past his prime when he 'galloped lion on the plain below Wami', is cheerful and wise, the gray eminence of the safari (73). P.O.M. is an indomitable terrier who remains in camp during the kudu hunting, wishing her husband well ('"*Oh*, good luck. *Please*, good luck."' (202)). Again, interest is reduced to what takes place for the hunter within the narrowly enclosed, time-bound world of camping, tracking, killing. Here

Hemingway constructs exact miniatures of setting. Trees along a stream possess

> . . . great smooth trunks, circled at their base with the line of roots that showed in rounded ridges up the trunks like arteries; the trunks the yellow green of a French forest on a day in winter after rain.
>
> (96)

The grass in the virgin pocket on the final kudu hunt appears

> . . . green and smooth, short as a meadow that has been mown and is newly grown, and the trees were big, high-trunked, and old with no undergrowth but only the smooth green of the turf like a deer park.
>
> (217)

Returning from a hunt, the car at night picks 'out the eyes of night birds that squatted close on the sand until the bulk of the car was on them and they rose in soft panic' (5). In the tiny eyes of a dead rhino 'a fresh drop of blood stood in the corner of one like a tear' (83). A felled kudu, suddenly come upon after hard tracking, is described in three tightly-packed, virtuoso sentences:

> It was a huge, beautiful kudu bull, stone-dead, on his side, his horns in great dark spirals, wide-spread and unbelievable as he lay dead five yards from where we stood when I had just that instant shot. I looked at him, big, long-legged, a smooth gray with the white stripes and the great, curling, sweeping horns, brown as walnut meats, and ivory pointed, at the big ears and the great, lovely heavy-maned neck the white chevron between his eyes and the white of his muzzle and I stooped over and touched him to try to believe it. He was lying on the side where the bullet had gone in and there was not a mark on him and he smelled sweet and lovely like the breath of cattle and the odor of thyme after rain.
>
> (231)

Minutes later the kudu is reduced to a bloody skin under M'Cola's 'fast, clean, delicate scalpeling with the knife', the cape finally freed from the neck and 'hanging heavy and wet in the light of the electric torch that shone on his red hands and on the dirty khaki of his tunic' (236).

With the emotional release of the kudu kill that draws the safari to a close, Hemingway turns reflective and expansive, the landscape painting of the book suddenly inflated to generalities that echo the grand literary declarations in the discussion with Kandisky in the opening pages. The subject now, prefiguring the concerns of a later ecological age, is the damage to the land wrought by man. 'A continent ages quickly once we come,' Hemingway intones. We cut trees, drain water, turn the soil, beginning the cycle that renders new countries old. Using machines, we take from the land and return nothing; in time, though the land remains, it is effectively ruined. A country was made to be left as it was found, but under man's restless hand 'they all end up like Mongolia.' The prophecy is grim, lightened only by the fact that there are 'still good places to go' – not in America anymore ('It had been a good country and we had made a bloody mess of it') but in Africa. He wouldn't be put off by his serious case of dysentery, the sort of ailment new continents tried to frighten you with, or by the possibility that the virgin country he had found might be shot over; there had to be other undiscovered pockets just like it. So he would make some money and come back to Africa and live his life in a place that interested him:

> Here there was game, plenty of birds, and I liked the natives. Here I could shoot and fish. That, and writing, and reading, and seeing pictures was all I cared about doing.

As for the interest in pictures while living in the African bush, Hemingway added that he didn't need to be near museums since he could remember all of the pictures (284, 285).

*   *   *

When Hemingway tells Pop that he liked Charlie Curtis' book about Africa, he specifies two of its qualities: 'It was very honest and it made a fine picture' (194). The 1925 account of a three-month safari in Kenya and Tanganyika, with Philip Percival as guide, is certainly that: direct, detailed, devoid of literary ambition. Curtis tells the story in flat, step-by-step fashion, providing portraits of place, camp life, natives and hunts for lion, rhino and buffalo, the whole illustrated with hand-drawn maps and snapshot photographs (the down-home captions reading, for example, 'Taken from where Richard shot his lion with the single shot').[35] It is the kind of factual record for hunters and African enthusiasts that Perkins had detected elements of in Hemingway's book, but beyond this passing resemblance it is wholly unlike the work Perkins also understood as 'something utterly different from a mere narrative of an expedition', something that was 'more that of a novel.'[36] The difference is the difference between travelogue and art.

Hemingway's ambition in *Green Hills of Africa* is evident enough in the painter's intensity he brought to the effort to capture the shape of a country. But it was the recreation of the pattern of a month's activity in that country ('that wonderful goddamned Kudu hunt – the relations between the people – and the way it all worked up to a climax') that lifted the account well beyond something of journalistic value or the fine picture of Curtis' book. Perkins had told Hemingway that nobody could map out the organization of *Death in the Afternoon*, a book that gave an impression of growth more than plan; *Green Hills of Africa* was the opposite. It had a carefully worked out, complex structure directed to a narrative center, the down-to-the-wire hunt for the elusive kudu. In Curtis' book, hunt follows hunt, events of equal import strung together like beads on a necklace; Hemingway constructs no such plodding account. His African book is elaborately orchestrated to arrive at the emotional climax and then release of a single central experience, shaping – as he put it – the actual things that happened during one segment of the safari into a damned fine story.

He chose to concentrate on the period from his return to the safari after medical treatment in Nairobi, with the shooting now in the upland country he favored and on foot rather than from cars on the plains, to the coming of the rainy season: a month's action. The book begins just before the end of that period – on the tenth day of failed hunting for a bull kudu antelope and with three days left for escape to the coast from the rain moving north from Rhodesia. Time pressing, Hemingway is feeling nervous. It isn't the way the hunt should be conducted, up against a time limit; 'the way to hunt is for as long as you live against as long as there is such and such an animal,' just as it is the way to paint or write (12). The connection, hunting and writing as all-demanding activities, opens the way for the literary conversation that dominates Part I and provides its title, 'Pursuit as Conversation'. The night before, the sound of a truck had ruined the pursuit of a kudu at a promising hunting blind on a salt-lick; returning to camp, Hemingway passed the now stalled vehicle with a bandy-legged Austrian in Tyroler hat and leather shorts beside it, Kandisky. When Hemingway gave his name, Kandisky recalled his poems published in the German periodical *Der Querschnitt*, so unlikely a meeting in so unlikely a place that Hemingway finds it 'too fantastic to deal with'(10).

After the next morning's hunt, the tenth for kudu, Kandisky is waiting in camp with Pop and P.O.M. and the talk turns literary. A time of 'verbal dysentery', Hemingway calls it, but in addition to offering a survey course on American writers he establishes his total absorption in the hunt. Kandisky asks: "'You really like to do this, what you do now, this silliness of kudu?'"

> 'Just as much as I like to be in the Prado.'
> 'One is not better than the other?'
> 'One is as necessary as the other. There are other things, too'
> 'Naturally. There must be. But this sort of thing means something to you, really?'
> 'Truly.'   (25)

Thereafter, with the exception of brief excursions back to literary matters, the pursuit of game is what matters, all else inconsequential in the engrossing necessity of the hunt. The literary talk ends with Hemingway off to hunt through the night at the salt-lick ruined by the truck the evening before.

At this stage of the safari he is hunting without Pop, a sign of the guide's approval, accompanied only by M'Cola, two trackers and a driver. Just as Pop's confidence in him has been won through experience, so has M'Cola's. The gunbearer had originally preferred Pauline, and during the drive out to the salt-lick Hemingway recreates the killing of the first lion near the Serengeti Plain, an unsatisfactory experience in that Pauline, given the opening shot, missed and he had to dispatch the lion with a second shot. M'Cola insists on Pauline's triumph ("'Mama *piga Simba*'"), and at the gunbearer's signal the porters ceremoniously carry her to her tent; thereafter, M'Cola looks with suspicion on Hemingway, change coming only when Pauline's license expires and Pop stays in camp and the two hunt alone together. Yet before that, Hemingway remembers, 'something had happened between us' (42, 44).

The recollection leads into Part II, 'Pursuit Remembered', a lengthy flashback section and the longest of the book's four parts. The time now is after the return from treatment in Nairobi during a foot safari for rhino in broken forest country. It is the kind of hunting Hemingway likes and the mood, in contrast to the opening section, is complete happiness. There is contrast with Karl as well, rejoining the safari after fruitless days of kudu hunting, Hemingway capturing his friend's ragged feelings with quick internal stokes:

> His mind was bitterly revolving eight blank days of hill climbing in the heat, out before daylight, back at dark, hunting an animal whose Swahili name he could not then remember, with trackers in whom he had no confidence, coming back to eat alone, no one to whom he could talk, his wife nine thousand miles and three months away, and how was his dog and how was his job, and god-damn it where were they and what if he missed one when he got a shot . . .
>
> (62)

Temperamental differences between Karl and Hemingway had been suggested in the opening section of the book (' "He gets so very excited," Pop said. "But he's a good lad" '), now they are developed and the shooting competition between the two outlined (15). Karl has killed the best buffalo and waterbuck and a good lion and leopard; he has, Hemingway insists, nothing to worry about. But he remains on edge, so Pop sends him off to shoot for meat while the rest of the hunting party moves to new country.

At first the new area is a loss, then Hemingway kills a rhino with a single shot at 300 yards, gaining Pop's approval and M'Cola's. But back in camp Karl also has a rhino, the severed head twice the size of Hemingway's; the response, foreshadowing the end of the climactic kudu hunt, is gloom. Hemingway, Pop and P.O.M. act 'like people who were about to become seasick on a boat, or people who had suffered some heavy financial loss.' Hemingway insists on his fondness for Karl and his pleasure in his own rhino, yet he can't shake the sting of defeat: 'But why couldn't he just get a good one, two or three inches longer? Why did he have to get one that makes mine ridiculous?' (84–5). The fact is that 'old Karl had put it on us all right with that rhino' (87). Pop now decides to send Karl for oryx while Hemingway and the rest of the party go to a new area Droopy knows about, three hours away, to try for a better rhino; then both Karl and Hemingway will join for the kudu hunt. ' "I'd rather get one, a good one, than all the rest,"' Hemingway says about that hunt, setting the terms of the final competiton with Karl (88).

Droopy's country has steep slopes difficult to hunt but the game is abundant. Hemingway shoots a buffalo, using a big gun with a rough trigger pull that feels 'like that last turn of the key opening a sardine can,' and also a rhino at a distance Pop estimates as 400 yards (102). Then they move on, deciding to rejoin Karl and return to the camp that had been their first in Africa, the trees there 'as big, as spreading, and as green, the stream as clear and fast flowing, and the camp as fine as when we had first been there.' The only difference now is warmer weather and the intervening time in which 'we had seen a lot of country' (123). In the dry and dusty Rift Valley they kill oryx for the black horns and zebra for hides for friends back home, but hunting on the plain is dull after the hills, broken only by an interlude of duck shooting on the edge of Lake Manyara where with the shots clouds of flamingoes rise into the sun, turning the horizon pink. From the old camp the safari moves on to yet another new location, this one near Babati.

Both Hemingway and Karl are gloomy after the Rift Valley hunting and on each other's nerves. The new camp improves nothing; the Prince of Wales had killed a kudu from it, but the country is infested with the tsetse fly and there is hard climbing in the hills. They hunt for five days, Hemingway sharply compressing the time ('Another time'; 'Another day'), before moving to a camp to the south toward Handeni, a reputedly miraculous country where kudu feed in the open and are easily taken (138–9). Here Hemingway acquires two native guides, Abdullah and Garrick, and after drawing straws with Karl he hunts a salt-lick while Karl goes into the hills. Hemingway is wildly encouraged by the first evening of hunting ('"It's airtight. It's foolproof. It's even a shame"'), then Pauline, overtaken with sympathy for Karl, blurts out that he is the one to hunt the lick in the morning (165). Hemingway and Pop cover up her mistake, agreeing that this is the plan, and the next morning Karl takes a kudu. (Pauline's diary kept during the safari gives a different view of the mix-up. She reported hearing an argument from her tent between Hemingway and Charles Thompson about who would hunt the salt-lick, who the hills. 'Distinctly heard 4-letter word,' she wrote, 'and Charles went to the lick.'[37]) Hemingway's consolation is that the head is ugly and heavy, 'a very strange and unfortunate kudu', and that Karl now moves down to sable country, leaving the field open for a better specimen (173).

With that – and the beginning of Part III, 'Pursuit and Failure' – the story shifts back to Part I, Hemingway riding out to the distant salt-lick. A few quick strokes pick up the threads of the action, returning the reader to the initial scenes. The remembered events of part two seem to have taken place 'a year ago'; the repeated failures of the kudu hunt are listed, including 'losing a shot the night before on this lick because of the Austrian's truck.' The events of the past have cemented Hemingway's friendship with M'Cola ('we were hunting together now, with no feeling of superiority on either side any more'), but time is still pressing (176). Only two days remain.

Rain and the presence of a native bowman cause another failure on the lick. Back in camp, Kandisky is gone but his recent presence turns the talk back to the literary matters of the opening. '"Give us that spiel on modern writers again,"' Pop says (191). The disappointing African books come up, and Hemingway mentions the work of landscape painting he could do – 'something about the country and the animals and what it's like to some one who knows nothing about it' (194). Then after another failure on the salt-lick only the unpromising evening is left. The kudu hunt '"looks washed up"', Hemingway tells Pop, the safari about to end on a dismal note (206).

At this late point an old farmer and a dirty Wanderobo arrive in camp with news of still another new country, this one abounding in kudu and sable but three or four hours away by car. A plan is hastily formulated: Hemingway will hunt the new country with a light camp while Pop and P.O.M. break the main camp; the three will join later with Karl to flee the country ahead of the rain. Hemingway is excited: '"It's just like when we were kids and we heard about a river no one had ever fished out on the huckleberry plains beyond the Sturgeon and the Pigeon."' Pop adds to the anticipation: '" I think this is the turning point. You'll get a kudu"' (210)

The stage setting complete – principal actors established, background experience and emotional setting laid out – Hemingway turns now to the dramatic center of the book, the final action in which success is snatched from failure. With Part IV, 'Pursuit as Happiness', he and his native entourage enter 'the loveliest country of Africa', that unhunted pocket in the great sweep of the continent (217). Here he encounters a village of handsome, laughing Masai, the most attractive people he has seen in Africa, who in their exuberance run alongside the car. Camp is made near a native building resembling a chicken coop and the hunt is abruptly begun with an hour left of daylight. Minutes later Hemingway has two bull kudu, one considerably more noble than Karl's. The skins and heads back in the temporary camp, there is a scene of joyful release around the campfire, Hemingway drinking beer and roasting meat with the natives, stumbling through conversation without a common language ('I spoke Spanish and he spoke whatever it was he spoke and I believe we planned the entire campaign for the next day') (244).

The following day there is a return to failure but of a new and momentary sort. A cow sable is shot by mistake and a wounded bull sable, doggedly trailed through the day, cannot be found, Hemingway feeling 'rotten sick' over the loss (272). Back in camp, the sight of the two kudu heads lifts his spirits, but on the drive out of the new country, joining up with Pop and P.O.M., he returns to a theme of the book's opening – the need to hunt without the pressure of time ('Why did I have to make a one night stand? Was that any way to hunt? Hell, no') (282). This leads to thoughts about returning to Africa, finding another unhunted pocket of good country despite the inevitable ruin of civilization, and hunting in the proper way – finally, not hunting at all but simply looking at the animals 'long enough so they belonged to me forever.' The passage is the proper conclusion of the confined portrait of a month's action, the account now widened out to an imagined and ideal safari, timeless and free of swings of emotion, killing for trophies subsumed into seeing for memory:

I'd make some money some way and when we came back we would come to the old man's village in trucks, then pack in with porters so there wouldn't be any damned car to worry about, send the porters back, and make a camp in the timber up the stream above the Roman's and hunt that country slowly, living there and hunting out each day, sometimes laying off and writing for a week, or writing half the day, or every other day, and get to know it as I knew the country around the lake where we were brought up. I'd see the buffalo feeding where they lived, and when the elephants came through the hills we would see them and watch them breaking branches and not have to shoot, and I would lie in the fallen leaves and watch the kudu feed out and never fire a shot unless I saw a better head than this one on back, and instead of trailing that sable bull, gut-shot to hell, all day, I'd lie behind a

rock and watch them on the hillside and see them long enough so
they belonged to me forever.

(282)

The loss of the bull sable is a let down after the two kudu, but the
true anticlimax comes with the return to camp. Karl has taken
another kudu, this one with 'the biggest, widest, darkest, longest-
curling, heaviest, most unbelievable pair of kudu horns in the
world,' repeating his earlier triumph with the rhino. Hemingway is
suddenly 'poisoned with envy', and Pop's suggestion that 'you can
always remember how you shot them' does no good (pp.291, 293).
But in the morning, dark feelings have vanished; his two kudu look
good beside the big one and he is at ease with Karl. He asks Pop
about the ritual of pulling thumbs he had gone through with the
natives after killing the kudu, learning it is a sign of brotherhood.
Pop explains: '"You're getting to be a hell of a fellow. You must be
an old timer out there"' (294). The final triumph is not simply the
two kudu but Hemingway's admission to a deeper level of African
experience (suggested in the book's early subtitle, 'Hunters are
Brothers'), a victory beyond the reach of Karl's streak of luck. On the
final hunt he has partially conquered the barrier of language that
limits accounts of new countries to journalistic value ('. . . it was as
freely discussed and clearly understood as though we were a cavalry
patrol all speaking the same language'); he has passed beyond the
fleeting experience of the hunter on safari into deeper union with
the land and its inhabitants (251). When Pop learns that M'Cola has
pulled his thumb as well, a last seal of acceptance, he says approv-
ingly, '"Well, well"' (294). The book Hemingway will write –
casually mentioned in the postscript, with a foreshadowing of post-
modernist self-referential fiction, as something to keep alive Pauline's
memory of Pop ('"I'll write you a piece some time and put him in"')
– will be more substantial than he first anticipated: '". . . something
about the country and the animals and what it's like to some one
who knows nothing about it."' The pursuit of the kudu, wresting
happiness from failure, had deepened the safari and the book to
follow from it, suggesting the possibility of a true narrative that is
exciting and still is literature.

*   *   *

For Edmund Wilson, as noted earlier, Hemingway's fundamental
mistake was chosing to treat the African safari as a series of real

happenings, reconstructed with a fiction writer's methods, rather than as material for imaginative work. A psychological flaw followed from a technical error: the concentration on the self which left Hemingway expounding his sense of life in his own voice rather than through the purifying indirections of fiction. The figure that emerged from the non-fiction, Wilson declared, was Hemingway's worst-drawn and least interesting creation.

A preference for imaginative use of the safari material is beyond debate. But if we grant Hemingway his decision to write a fact book, Wilson's strictures about the role of the self seem beside the point, fixed to exclusive admiration of the fiction and obscuring the essential art of the non-fiction. As Wilson saw, it is Hemingway's presence in his own person that sharply separates the non-fiction from the fiction, but it is exactly this direct presence – the forceful, mercurial presence of Hemingway himself, self-deprecating at times (aware of envy, righteousness, and sudden black anger as well as the inclination for 'evening braggies' around the campfire) yet immensely well satisfied with himself – that gives the non-fiction its vital character (240). It is *Hemingway* speaking, strengths and weaknesses in full light, life seen – in Walter Pater's definition of art – through a temperament.

In *Death in the Afternoon*, the self is strongly experienced yet counterbalanced by an externalized subject. In Hemingway's terms, there is in the book always a dual approach to the material, inner and outer, practical and emotional. In *Green Hills of Africa*, a work he chose to cast as a personal narrative, Hemingway himself is inevitably an even more direct and dominating presence, everything known and felt wholly in his terms, the subject deeply internalized. Nonetheless, the book is an effort to convey through personal experience the shape of a country and the pattern of a month's action; it is about something, not merely an exercise in extended self-indulgence (194). Wilson thought the 'personal interludes' of *Death in the Afternoon* had been rescued by the predominance of objective writing and solid information about Spain and bullfighting, while the African book was *'all'* such an interlude and consequently beyond redemption.[38] But this is hardly so. In his review of the book Carl Van Doren pointed out that most readers would probably take it as fiction since the narrative treatment has all the qualities of a novel, especially one in the Hemingway mold. The only thing that gives the work its non-fiction stamp, Van Doren added, is Hemingway's position as hero in his own person. Everything exists in the work as it existed for him – the country, the animals, the natives, the others on safari: 'He is the center of the action, the sensorium on which the action is recorded. His book about Africa is a book about Ernest Hemingway in Africa.'[39] This is just the case. Hemingway is the book's focal point, everything in the story filtered through him; yet through him place and action are conveyed. The book is what Pop says an African book should be, one ' "that could make you feel about the country the way we feel about it" ' (194). The country's importance is located in Hemingway's capacity to make it *his* country, just as big-game hunting is important because it is *his* hunting. It is all, as Van Doren saw, Hemingway in Africa – just as *Death in the Afternoon*, in its different manner, is Hemingway in Spain – yet the point finally is to provide the reader with a subject, though never one detached from the energizing presence of self. 'Where we go,' Hemingway says in the African book, merging self and subject, 'if we are any good, there you can go as we have been' (109).

Although *Green Hills of Africa* struck him as all insubstantial personal interlude, what appears to have disturbed Wilson most were passages where Hemingway stepped forward as the 'Old Master of Key West', no longer absorbed in his adventures but offering pronouncements on life and letters. At such moments he seemed to Wilson only 'fatuous or maudlin', giving his public what it had come to expect of him.[40] Here Wilson had a point. The major instance of the Old Master at work is the discussion with Kandisky at the beginning of the book, Hemingway arranging to interview himself on American writing. Although he makes a faint stab at undercutting the confident assertions of the scene (his tongue, he says, is loosened by beer; it is a moment of verbal dysentery), Hemingway here is the Hemingway frequently encountered in his *Esquire* articles or his personal letters, pontifical and reductionist. It is a part of the book (mirrored later in the jab at Gertrude Stein at the end of Chapter Three, the reflections stimulated by Tolstoy's story in Part IV, and the play with literary anecdotes in Chapter Ten) that a less enthralled editor than Perkins – or a reader with Dos Passos' dislike of Hemingway's tendency to strap on the white whiskers and give the boys the lowdown – might have suggested he remove. Yet in the book as a whole the intrusion is minor. Kandisky, hungry for conversation, says: ' "This is what I enjoy. This is the best part of life. The life of the mind. This is not killing kudu" ' (19). But literary talk – or mental activity of any sort, including the remarks near the end on the destructive march of civilization – doesn't form an essential part of the book, a book precisely about killing kudu. Presumably, the material was included to alter the book's pace, pursuit of literary game breaking up exclusive concentration on the pursuit of animals. The remarks bear some interest for the light thrown on Hemingway's literary tastes, his attraction to the literature of experience and disdain for the abstract and rhetorical, his bookishness yet ambition to write a non-literary literature in the manner of Twain. And they help define his goal in the African book by setting up the senuous recreation of experience as his principal aesthetic standard. But literary discourse, whatever its limitation or use, remains only a slight variation on the book's main business of recapturing place and action.

A more telling criticism than Wilson's aversion to Hemingway's direct and dominating presence in the book – to the presence of Hemingway the 'man', to use terms offered by Lionel Trilling, following Wilson, rather than Hemingway the 'artist' – is that he overvalued the material of a month's hunting action, the work finally lacking sufficient claim on the reader's interest.[41] Leo Gurko, while admiring the book, found that in the central kudu section 'the hunter's response to the situation is stronger than the reader's,' his emotion 'too large for the experience that arouses it.'[42] The novelist William Kennedy was more blunt, maintaining that 'the book perished in the bush from overkill: too much hunting detail, too much bang-bang banality, insufficient story.'[43] Such complaints aren't easily dismissed. The story Hemingway tells is confined to the enclosed world of the safari, the repetitious daily round of hunting with the dawn, rest in the afternoon heat, hunting again until dark, talk around the campfire; change comes only with the movement to new country and new pursuit. There isn't, finally, much to it. But from Hemingway's perspective the days are highly charged and of absorbing interest; he wants only to lengthen them out, then repeat them in the future. The attempt is to draw the reader into sharing such exhilarating preoccupation with sharply narrowed place and action, all else blotted out for the moment, non-existent. The story line that does emerge from the experience – 'the way it all worked up to a climax' – seemed to Hemingway a compelling element, assuring the reader's interest; but the real meat of the book is in the reconstruction of riveting physical and emotional involvement with the hunt.

In a passage deleted from the holograph manuscript, Hemingway constructed a dialogue with Pauline about the pleasure he derived from brave exploits. She would better understand his feeling, he says, if she had 'known any yellow bastards'. They agree that Karl is a genuinely brave fellow, then Pauline returns to the question of Hemingway's enjoyment of daring deeds. '"It's nice,"' she says about them, '"but it's sort of silly."' To which he responds with a comment that replaces the pleasure found in bravery with the exhilaration he found in all engrossing physical activities:

> 'Listen. The things that please me are very simple things. Most of them seem to have to do with natural reflexes and co-ordination. Like things that happen so quickly in trout fishing, correcting from a cast already started in the hundredth part of a second in the air. When I was a kid every time I would do that I would be pleased. Now shooting and all the things that are made up of so many things to do and think at once all surrounding one central necessity please me.'[44]

The essential experiment of the book was in the attempt to capture one of the simple things that pleased him so much – the minute play of action and feeling that had seemed, during a month's hunting in Africa, an absolute necessity. In a letter to the Russian critic Ivan Kashkin just after the publication of *Green Hills of Africa*, Hemingway referred to the book's subject while distinguishing (as he had in the book in dialogue with Kandisky) between the joys of writing and those of action. 'The minute I stop writing for a month or two months,' he said about the latter, 'and am on a trip I feel absolutely animally happy.'[45] On this level – the true account of an action that had stimulated an animal happiness – the book is as compelling as Hemingway thought it was. His landscape painting and the intricate structure he worked out and the drama of the kudu hunt add to the pleasure, but it is the portrayal of total, mesmerizing absorption in physical activity that gives the book its special flavor.

4

A First Class Life

*Africa was where he had been happiest in the good time of his life, so he
had come out here to start again.*

Six months after *Green Hills of Africa* appeared, Max Perkins suggested
a book of stories that would also include some of Hemingway's
better journalistic efforts, especially two recent articles with strong
political overtones, 'Wings Always Over Africa' from *Esquire* and
'Who Murdered the Vets?' from *New Masses*. It would make an
unconventional book, the editor reasoned, and one that might
increase Hemingway's stock with what he termed certain radical
elements. But when Hemingway replied that he didn't want to mix
fiction and non-fiction – something he had earlier brought up
himself with the idea of including the African book with stories – the
editor backed off. Hemingway's view, he said, was sound policy.

There may have been something else behind Hemingway's
response other than policy: Perkins' explanation in the wake of the
weak sales of *Green Hills of Africa* was that his public wanted fiction,
not non-fiction. If that was the case, he was ready to oblige. After a
concentrated period of fact writing that had produced two major
books but little enthusiasm, he plunged back to fiction, drawing on
Havana and Key West material for *To Have and Have Not* and the
African safari for two stories. Nearly twenty years would pass
before he ventured on another sustained period of fact writing.

With *Death in the Afternoon* and *Green Hills of Africa* he had been at
the peak of his powers, still young and vibrant, dazzlingly successful.
When he returned to extended non-fiction in the final decade of his
life his health, physical and mental, was in precipitous decline,
there had been long dry periods of writing, and though his commercial stock had soared his critical reputation had been severely
battered. He liked to describe himself now as a crafty old lion in the
African veldt who knew his limits yet could still transcend them
when he wanted. In the field in which he chose to spend most of his
energy at the end, non-fiction, he managed to write three book-
length works, each drawn from returns to the locales of past

exploits: Africa, Spain, Paris. But effort was more evident in the final decade than cunning. Two of the accounts – one left unfinished and both left unpublished – were swollen and often flat performances, clearly lacking the overall quality of his earlier Spanish and African books. Although the Paris sketches that came to be called *A Moveable Feast* inspired a warm wave of critical applause after the book's posthumous publication, the work as a whole provided only occasional echoes of his best undertakings in non-fiction. In the end, the old lion turned once again to the fact writing with which he had begun his career, and with dogged effort, but he could rise above the burden of his last years only fitfully and with no real sense of satisfaction.

*   *   *

Although he concentrated on fiction after *Green Hills of Africa*, Hemingway kept his hand in as a fact writer with occasional magazine and newspaper work. He produced more letters for *Esquire*, his agreement with Arnold Gingrich altered to six articles a year rather than twelve (yet for the same amount of money, he happily informed Perkins), and he began writing for *Ken*, a new left-leaning, though anti-Communist, opinion journal with an insider tone that was launched under Gingrich's direction in 1938. In promotional material Hemingway was listed as one of the magazine's editors, but the first issue took note of disagreements and announced that he was simply a contributor. Kenneth Lynn suggests the rift had to do with Hemingway's displeasure over the magazine's Red baiting; at any event, in less than a year's time – from April 1938 to January 1939 – he contributed thirteen fact pieces and the story 'Old Man at the Bridge'.

The year before, he had been in Spain as a foreign correspondent during the civil war, his first return to newspaper journalism since the abrupt departure from the *Toronto Star* in 1923. A comfortable contract with the North American Newspaper Alliance paid him $500 for cabled stories up to 400 words, $1000 for mailed pieces up to 1200 words, the work distributed to some sixty newspapers, among them the *Kansas City Star*. As in his Paris days as a roving corre-spondent, Hemingway was free to pick his subjects and write as he chose for what was essentially a feature service used to supplement regular news coverage of the war. In 1937 he was also involved in the making of a propaganda film for the Loyalist cause, *The Spanish*

Earth, following the filming across the country and eventually writing and delivering the narration.

Although it was a productive time for Hemingway the journalist – the articles for *Ken* plus thirty newspaper dispatches from Spain – there was nothing distinguished about the work he turned out. It was generally facile and undemanding, marked only by flashes of effective detail or bright character sketches. The best of the Spanish material gathered on his journalistic rounds was saved, as had always been his practice, for his fiction. Phillip Knightley, in a study of war correspondents, finds Hemingway's performance in Spain 'abysmally bad' both on a technical level and in his suppression of material harmful to the Loyalists. He eventually told all in *For Whom the Bell Tolls*, yet Knightley insists on the reader's 'right to expect all the news the correspondent knows at the time, not as interpolations in a work of romantic fiction published when the war is over.'[1] This may well be so, but the public's right to know was never a burning issue with Hemingway in his journalistic guise. In Spain he was a celebrity journalist, and his journalism was a means to a private end – a well-paid stay in the country, involvement with a political cause he believed in, and fresh war stories to transmute into fiction. Jeffrey Meyers suggests Hemingway viewed the experience as a 'great adventure – rather like a hunting expedition with political over-tones.'[2] By 1939, journalism was temporarily put aside and he was back in Key West, Havana and the mountain West, turning the adventure into the Spanish novel.

In 1940 he married Martha Gelhorn, novelist and journalist in her own right, and the following year both were in the Far East as correspondents, Martha with *Collier's* magazine and Hemingway with Ralph Ingersoll's newspaper *PM*. The newspaper carried a series of seven dispatches on the Sino-Japanese conflict and prospects of American involvement, Hemingway writing in an unusually im-personal, analytical manner – perhaps because the Far East, unlike Spain or Africa, seemed to exercise no hold on his imagination, leaving him in a journalistic mood of rare detachment – even though the series was treated with much fanfare, including an opening interview conducted by Ingersoll that underscored the renown of the special correspondent. It wasn't until 1944, his involvement with the Second War until then notable for its absence, that he again went back into action as a newsman.

Hemingway was in Europe as a correspondent for seven months between June and December. It was an exhilarating time in what

seemed a thoroughly good war, but it resulted in even less journalistic effort than his Spanish and Far Eastern adventures. He managed
six loosely written articles for *Collier's* – 'only enough', he acknowledged, 'to keep from being sent home' – that concentrated mainly
on personalities and his own exploits.[3] His typical approach was to
involve himself in combat and then write about the experience ('. . .
the day we took Fox Green beach . . .'; 'The day we advanced on
Paris . . .'), depending considerably more on his reputation as a
writer than on his diligence as a reporter.[4]

Back in Cuba after the war, he set his war experiences aside in
favor of very different material – recollections of his marriages to
Hadley and Pauline, fascination with reversed sexual roles, and the
sun-washed setting of the south of France that he stirred together in
a long novel he would call *The Garden of Eden*. He also made a
tentative beginning with his novel of the sea, *Islands in the Stream*.
Stimulated by a visit to northern Italy late in 1948 with his fourth
wife, Mary, he broke off work on these projects in favor of his
stored-up war material and *Across the River and Into the Trees*. After
the full blast of critical disapproval that greeted the Venetian story
came the overwhelming success of *The Old Man and the Sea* in 1952.
His occasional journalism during these active half-dozen years of
fiction writing was limited to an article for *Holiday* on the mechanics
of Gulf Stream fishing, another for *True* that he characterized as an
antelope story. But now, in his early fifties, fiction was essentially
behind him.

*   *   *

The return to fact writing was both a matter of private need and
financial gain – an attempt to recapture past pleasures by returning
to some places he loved together with plush magazine assignments
that underwrote the nostalgic travels. A return to Africa had long
been high on his list of things to do. In 'The Snows of Kilimanjaro' he
had attributed to Harry his own desire to return to the country in the
hope of recapturing a vital, energetic way of life:

> Africa was where he had been happiest in the good time of his life,
> so he had come out here to start again. They had made this safari
> with the minimum of comfort. There was no hardship; but there
> was no luxury and he had thought that he could get back into
> training that way. That in some way he could work the fat off his

soul the way a fighter went into the mountains to work and train in order to burn it out of his body.[5]

His youngest son, Patrick, was now living on a farm in East Africa and sending back enthusiastic hunting reports, further stimulating Hemingway's interest in a second safari. He wrote Bernard Berenson that, after putting in two and a half years of hard work in Cuba, the time had come to 'get up in the hills'. 'Out of Africa', he added, 'there is always something new.'[6]

Plans for the safari caught the attention of *Life* and *Look* magazines, both of whom wanted to send photographers along for a picture story. Hemingway resisted, writing to a *Life* editor that a photographer would turn the safari into work rather than a vacation. He also claimed to be worried that any magazine journalism he wrote would use up material he might employ in fiction. 'If I went out for you,' he told the editor, 'and wrote as good journalism as I could . . . I would use up what I might write in three stories. The last time I was in Africa I wrote only two short stories, The Snows of Kilimanjaro and The Short Happy Life of Francis Macomber. I cabled some very basic journalism to Esquire.'[7] In May of 1953, just after Hemingway learned that he had received the Pulitzer Prize for *The Old Man and the Sea*, a *Look* editor came to Cuba to make a personal pitch for the picture story. The plan was for a photographer to accompany the safari only for the first two or three weeks, disturbing the hunting as little as possible. Hemingway kept resisting, then bowed to what Mary remembered as the 'simple arithmetic' of the proposition: $15 000 for the picture story with captions written by Hemingway, another $10 000 for a story of 3500 words or more.[8]

Before leaving for Africa Hemingway urged his wife to take up Swahili and organized a crash reading course that included two works by Philip Percival's brother as well as Isak Dinesen's *Out of Africa*, a book he would recall in *A Moveable Feast* as the best he had ever read about the country. They arrived in Africa in late August of 1953 after stops in France and Spain. Percival, now sixty-eight years old, came out of retirement to join the hunting party that included Hemingway's Cuban friend Mayito Menocal, *Look* photographer Earl Theisen, and Mary. Charo was again part of the entourage, well past seventy and dimly aware of his literary role in *Green Hills of Africa*; although M'Cola was dead, Hemingway soon became attached to his new gunbearer, N'Gui, persuading himself that the native was M'Cola's son. The safari proceeded at a leisurely pace, the hunting going well at first despite the photographer's presence. (The picture story, 'Safari', would appear in *Look* in January 1954, Hemingway dramatically displayed on the cover and inside sixteen pages of photographs drawn from some 3000 taken by Theisen, with captions and a single opening page of hasty stage-setting turned out by Hemingway, ending with the remark, 'I hope the pictures are better than the words.'[9]) It soon became clear, however, that Hemingway's shooting skill had deteriorated; Menocal, as Charles Thompson before, consistently took the better trophies. Denis Zaphiro, a young game warden whom Percival asked to serve as the safari's white hunter, told Jeffrey Meyers that, except for lion, Hemingway was not much interested in shooting and after Theisen and others left the safari he preferred merely to drive around and watch the animals.

As Hemingway reported it in letters at the time, this was the best part of the second African adventure. He and Mary were alone, Zaphiro joining them only part of the time, and the competitive pressure of hunting with Menocal was off. Mary later remembered that 'we did an awful lot of walking in Africa and of course if we found something that looked remarkably good in the way of a head we might possibly . . . But we passed up a great many animals who were just too sweet to shoot. Both of us did'.[10] An appointment as an honorary game warden, gained with Zaphiro's help, gave added purpose to Hemingway's days. He handled the position with a mixture of seriousness and high spirits, touring shambas on patrols, fielding a steady stream of complaints, dispatching marauding animals. There were also curious experiments in going native by shaving his head, hunting with a spear on night-time prowls, and dallying with an unkempt Wamkaba girl he insisted on calling his fiance. Although the contrast with the hunting intensity of the first African safari was considerable, it was a time that pleased him deeply – a 'first class life', he confided to Harvey Breit.[11]

The safari's ending, however, turned into a nightmare of repeated bad luck. On a sightseeing flight to the Belgian Congo the plane carrying Hemingway and his wife crashed. Their injuries were minor, but a second crash the following day while on the way for medical treatment resulted in serious harm for Hemingway, including a fractured skull, dislocated shoulder, and severe internal injuries. While still in a dangerous condition he responded to numerous cabled requests for stories by dictating a 15 000-word article for *Look* – for a fee of $20 000 – on what he called the late unpleasantness that had prompted premature obituaries around the world. Later, waiting near Mombasa for a ship to Europe, he was seriously burned while helping put out a brush fire near a camping site.

Look published 'The Christmas Gift' in two installments in April and May 1954. Perhaps because the article was dictated (to a Mrs Figgis, Mary remembered), and under trying circumstances at best, it was loose, padded and oddly flat. Hemingway tried to treat the crashes and their aftermaths with disinterested humor, but the effect was mostly forced. He mentions, for example, a dialogue with a curious elephant at the first crash site that

> . . . was conducted, I am sure, on both sides in a rather unpleasant fashion. I can recall stating to the elephant, 'Debark, you un-speakable elephant, before you are called upon to take the consequences.' The elephant replied in her own language which by this time I was commencing to have a small knowledge of.[12]

He said he had decided to give a true and accurate account of the experience after reading absurd versions in the press, and the article offered a step-by-step recounting of the mishaps together with a report on what it was like to read one's own obituaries. It offered as well meandering excursions into such side issues as how Senator Joseph McCarthy would react in a crisis, a dream sequence recounted as a challenge to Freudian interpretation, and the adoption of a stray dog in Idaho.

Back in Cuba in the summer of 1954 after a return journey by way of Italy and Spain, Africa was still much on his mind. For a while there were plans for a documentary film on African wildlife, then he turned to a new writing project – a series of short stories drawn from his recent experience in the country. One quickly expanded to book length in the form of a discursive, untitled, mostly factual day-to-day journal of the safari. He told Bernard Berenson in September that he was working on it at only about half capacity, in part because of a depressing period of rainy, muggy weather that caused him to write in an air-conditioned room. He said he liked to put the weather outside into his books, but now he had the feeling of writing in the pressurized cabin of a plane. He was getting the work done 'but it's as false as though it were done in the reverse of a greenhouse.' Because of that he thought he might 'throw it all away, but maybe when the mornings are alive again I can use the skeleton of what I have written and fill it in with the smells and the early noises of the birds and all the lovely things of this finca which are in the cold months very much like Africa.'[13] In October came the announcement of his Nobel Prize, and in a letter shortly thereafter to his World War II comrade Buck Lanham he was considerably more optimistic about the book. Despite the domestic turmoil brought on by the prize, he was now in another 'belle epoque writing' and had 'gotten back into the country and I live in it every day.'[14] He thought the book had some stuff in it Lanham would like.

By late October of 1955 the book stood at 650 typed pages. On 30 November, working at a pace slowed to 300 to 400 words a day because of various new ailments that kept him in bed, he noted in a letter that he was up to page 703, and added: 'I love the book.'[15] He told his lawyer, Alfred Rice, on 24 January 1956 – the second anniversary of his second plane crash in Africa – that the manuscript stood at 810 pages. Work was abruptly halted on 27 February, on the eight hundred and fiftieth page, in the midst of a sentence:

> 'That's too bad,' I said and I remembered the old days and how you looked forward to the one beyond all price in . . .[16]

The manuscript was wrapped away in cellophane and Hemingway flew off to Peru for the filming of fishing sequences for *The Old Man and the Sea*. When he returned, he tossed off 'The Situation Report' for *Look* to accompany another series of photographs, Hemingway-at-home this time, taken by Earl Theisen during a visit to Cuba. In the article he told about interrupting writing on 'a book that you loved and believed in on the eight hundred and fiftieth manuscript page,' and promised never again to allow himself to be side-tracked from the work he was born and trained to do.[17] In the morning, he said, he was going back to it.

But the African book stayed in its cellophane wrap, apparently never worked on again. Hemingway spent the summer on minor stories drawn from his World War II experiences, and in the fall he was in Spain for the bullfights. From Spain he traveled with Mary to Paris where, in the Ritz Hotel, they discovered two trunks left behind and forgotten when the move was made to Key West in 1928 following the break-up of the marriage to Hadley. The contents, notebooks and clippings and sheaves of typed fiction, were delightful reminders of the past. According to Mary, Hemingway sat for hours on the floor beside the trunks reading his early work, pleased to discover writing had been as hard for him then as it was now. When he returned to Cuba, the Paris material went along with him together with the first stirrings of a new kind of fact book.

*   *   *

The African book remained hidden away until the winter of 1971–2 when *Sports Illustrated* magazine published three lengthy excerpts. The manuscript's existence had come to light in a 1969 inventory of Hemingway materials by Philip Young and Charles Mann, described as an 850–page typescript, unfinished, dated 1955, an 'autobiographical account of duties as volunteer ranger at the Masai game preserve at foot of Mt. Kilimanjaro in late 1953.'[18] Ray Cave, an editor of *Sports Illustrated*, contacted Mary Hemingway (who had published an article in the magazine on the bullfighter Antonio Ordóñez, 'Holiday for a Wounded Torero', some years before) and asked if the work had anything to do with hunting. He learned that it did, and that she was willing to let the magazine see it. Cave handled the editing, following two rules agreed to with Mary: all deletions would be indicated with ellipsis marks, asterisks and space breaks; and there would be no editorial changes or additions beyond spelling and punctuation corrections and the use of dashes to mark deletions of profanity. The published excerpts totaled some 55 000 words, just over a quarter of the manuscript, and were trumpeted by the magazine as a literary revelation and a major non-fiction addition to the body of Hemingway's outdoor writing.

The 'African Journal', the title chosen by the magazine for the untitled manuscript, exhibits Hemingway's usual blending of fact and fiction – a work of non-fiction only in the sense of his decision to stay more generally within the facts than he typically did in his fiction. In her remarks about the work Mary, who was in a position to judge, put stress on the fictional element in the mixture, identifying the work as 'semifictional' and 'fiction based on fact'. Yet she also paid tribute to the 'tape recorder in his head' that enabled Hemingway, who had made no notes in Africa, to capture the safari with considerable accuracy. 'I have checked my diary to verify things,' she told Ray Cave, 'and he was consistently correct. He might embellish a scene, but he did that with everything in life.'[19] 'No dates,' she noted about the work in her autobiography, *How It Was*, 'but places described and sharp characterizations of people, also dialogue.' She added, perhaps putting the best face possible on her critical estimate of the work, that she found it 'entertaining'.[20]

The *Sports Illustrated* excerpts obscured the diary structure of the manuscript, emphasizing instead two thin narrative lines, Mary shooting a lion and Hemingway a leopard. The period treated is in the third month of the safari (beginning, Hemingway wrote, 'on a windless morning of the last day of the month of the next to the last month of the year') and covers a span of three weeks.[21] In the first two excerpts, both called 'Miss Mary's Lion' by the magazine, Percival (named Wilson Harris this time) has left the safari and Hemingway and Mary are alone with the native hunting party, trying to fulfill Mary's three-month determination to kill a lion. The particular lion in question is a marauder who has destroyed cattle belonging to the Masai. In his position of quasi-official responsibility as an honorary game warden with the Kenya Game Department, Hemingway is charged with killing the animal but he has passed up two chances in favor of Mary, who because of her lack of height has difficulty hunting in high grass and at the moment is shooting poorly. Unlike Pauline's distant supporting role in *Green Hills of Africa*, Mary is a featured figure, with Hemingway presenting himself as her stalwart protector, eager to have her get her lion yet concerned that nothing go wrong. '"Take really good care of her,"' Percival instructs him before leaving the camp, adding that he should '"think properly."' There is a veiled reference to Hemingway's bad shooting early in the safari, but now it is all right. '"Better than all right, actually,"' Percival emphasizes.[22] Hemingway is fully in charge, wise in the ways of the bush yet cautious, taking his time to build up Mary's confidence and the overconfidence of the lion. He has announced to the natives that the lion will be killed before Christmas, yet the hunt goes ahead with none of the time pressure of *Green Hills of Africa*. The end of the safari is still a long way off, and the concentration on a lion for Mary, unlike the inner necessity of a prize kudu, is only a magnanimous gesture on Hemingway's part. While he was writing the 'African Journal' he told Buck Lanham, 'Buck you should have been around when I was being responsible for Miss Mary in Africa and her with the valour of ignorance.'[23] The remark catches exactly the selfless, solicitous image he projects in the work.

Hemingway explicitly contrasts the safari with the first African trip when he was eager for trophies and there was little time to learn the country. This time he has settled into a particular district, thanks to his temporary job as a stand-in for Denis Zaphiro, and he shoots for meat or to dispatch predators. His only 'fixed engagements' are Mary's lion and his leopard. The unhurried pace of this phase of the safari is reflected in the leisurely digressions of the magazine selections, Hemingway breaking the shaky narrative line with memories of past shooting exploits, portraits of native figures, and vignettes of camp routine, including the steady consumption of alcohol and books. A rainy day is a pleasure on both counts but especially for the reading:

> Everything had been taken out of my control for a moment and I welcomed the lack of responsibility and the splendid inactivity with no obligation to kill, pursue, protect, intrigue, defend or participate and I welcomed the chance to read.[24]

With the second installment Denis Zaphiro, known as G.C. (for Gin Crazed), rejoins the hunting party, setting up passages of bantering dialogue with Hemingway similar to those with Pop in *Green Hills of Africa*. When the talk turns to Mary's and G.C.'s memories of London, Hemingway meditates on Paris and the good cafes he has known there and the effort to keep them secret; later, Paris comes back into the account with his recollections of Ford Madox Ford and Ezra Pound. After a bout of dysentery that keeps Mary in camp, slowing the already slow pace of the lion hunt, Hemingway and G.C. at last spot the massive, black-maned lion stretched out over the mound of an anthill, 'molded to its top as though he were sculptured there,' surveying his domain.[25] By the time Mary is brought to the scene the lion has moved and a stalk begins. Hemingway guards a flank to keep the lion from escaping into a forest across an open plain; G.C. and Mary work directly toward the lion. Although G.C. takes her dangerously close, Mary's shots are off target and she hits the lion first in the foot and then in a haunch. When the lion breaks for cover Hemingway hits him, then G.C. brings him down with a final shot. The description of the scene, briefly treated in a series of quick strokes, Hemingway found unsatisfactory. In a note in the margin of the manuscript, reproduced in the magazine excerpt, he reminds himself to 'improve the shooting. Make lion clearer and sharper.'[26]

Though the long wait for the lion is over, Mary is displeased, accusing Hemingway of shooting before she did. G.C. confirms that she shot first and hit the lion and the natives noisily celebrate her triumph (as natives had celebrated Pauline's similar triumph in

Green Hills of Africa), but she remains unconvinced. The installment ends with Hemingway, awake in the night while Mary sleeps, recalling Fitzgerald's remark that in the dark night of the soul it is always three o'clock in the morning; later, he reads a guidebook about birds and realizes that, preoccupied with the hunt for Mary's lion, he hasn't paid enough attention to them. 'This looking and not seeing things' he professes to view as a great sin, and he decides that 'we did not deserve to live in the world if we did not see it.'[27]

The third installment, 'Imperiled Flanks', opens with Mary's continuing 'sorrow' over the way the shooting of the lion has turned out (an emotion that doesn't appear in her autobiography, where she says only that she was embarrassed during the natives' celebration, not knowing until later whether she had actually hit the lion), then switches to the story of the hunt for a leopard. After Mary leaves for Nairobi and Christmas shopping, Hemingway is lonely and indulges in stray thoughts about absent friends, the novelist John O'Hara ('fat as a boa constrictor that has swallowed an entire shipment of a magazine called *Collier's*'), a Christmas tree Mary wants ('an extra-potent type of marijuana-effect tree'), and the possession of white skin in Africa. The leopard in question has killed seventeen goats and must be dispatched, but the killing has additional 'conscience-clearing' value because of an earlier incident in which Hemingway had posed for the *Look* photographer with a leopard actually shot by Mayito Menocal, then promised Mary he would kill his own leopard before the magazine published the picture. At length, the leopard is found in a tree and dropped with a single shot, then has to be tracked into an island of heavy brush before he is killed. What remains of the installment is given over to disjointed memories of spear hunting under moonlight ('It was more than a little bit theatrical; but so is *Hamlet*') and tennis matches with Ezra Pound together with the tumbling night-thoughts of a habitual insomniac.[28]

*   *   *

Judging from the selections published in *Sports Illustrated*, Carlos Baker's assessment of the African book as a 'slightly fictionalized day-to-day diary of the safari, almost completely formless, filled with scenes that ranged from the fairly effective to the banal' seems essentially correct.[29] Charles Scribner, Jr, included the second of the magazine installments in his 1974 anthology, *The Enduring Hemingway*, yet he said he found the work rambling and informal, wholly different from the usual Hemingway manner. The personal voice, clearly Hemingway, is present again in the non-fiction, though it is not as dominating and authoritative, as insistently present, as before. And there is nothing of the taut, carefully managed structure of *Green Hills of Africa*, nothing of the earlier absorbed attention to African landscape painting. For readers who find the hunting tedious in the account of the first safari, this time there is a minimum of step-by-step shooting detail. The killing of Mary's lion, and especially the killing of Hemingway's leopard, are relatively un-eventful affairs, wholly lacking the intensity and extended drama of the hunts in the first book for rhino and kudu. There are some strong passages in the work – in one, dry cider and pillows stuffed with balsam needles suddenly remind Hemingway of the tastes and smells of Michigan when he was a boy. But for the most part the writing is as limp and uninspired as the opening sentence of the first magazine installment: 'Things were not too simple in this safari because things had changed very much in East Africa.'

Ray Cave found the manuscript as a whole unstructured and undisciplined. Although Hemingway edited as he went along and, judging from notes for changes and additions in the margins, apparently considered much of what he had written in final form, the editor concluded that the work was no more than a rough draft. He isolated, however, five themes apparent in the manuscript: the hunt; Hemingway's playing at going native by dying his clothes a Masai rust color, hunting with a spear, and conducting a romance of sorts with the Wakamba girl; ageing and the power that followed from it; the Mau Mau uprising of the time and the weakening of British rule in Kenya; and religion. Only the first was given promin-ence in the magazine excerpts, the theme that loosely tied the manuscript to *Green Hills of Africa*, to the public image of Hemingway the hunter, and to the magazine's focus on sport.

Cave speculated that the diversity of themes kept Hemingway from giving the work a cohesive focus. Nonetheless, the very variety of interests, if only as glimpsed in the published excerpts, gives some indication of the kind of work he may have had in mind. In *Green Hills of Africa* he told of his desire for a second and leisurely return safari, one in which there would be no time pressure and no need to accumulate trophies. This time he would *live* in the country, writing when he chose and observing the animals. He would 'lie behind a rock and watch them on the hillside and see them long enough so they belonged to me forever.'[30] The second safari, in other words, would be a much larger, ruminative experience of Africa, embracing the diverse thoughts inspired by the country together with the action and characters it provided, rather than the experience of Africa simply as a hunting ground. The honorary game warden's position gave Hemingway the altered relationship to Africa that he wanted, one in which he to some degree settled in; Denis Zaphiro is lauded for giving 'us this great privilege of getting to know and live in a wonderful part of the country and have some work to do that justified our presence there.'[31] The work might have provided a firm enough spine for the book, just as the kudu hunt had in the earlier African book and as the instructional, handbook mode had in *Death in the Afternoon*. And it might have lent to the book a greater depth of awareness about Africa, responding to the criticism of old African hands like Graham Greene that *Green Hills of Africa* had been a shallow affair in which Hemingway had skipped 'off on a month's safari arranged by a travel agency' and then written only 'about white hunters and shooting lions – the poor half-starved brutes reserved for tourists.'[32]

Hemingway toiled on the manuscript for some sixteen months, each writing day totaling his word count on the page as a talisman of his labors. But the hard work or insight or plain luck that had provided him with effective structures for the Spanish and African books eluded him this time. Before, there had been enthusiastic letters to Perkins outlining the plan of the bullfight manual and telling of discovering the 'story' of the kudu hunt. This time there was only the accumulation of 200 000 words. Consigning the manuscript to cellophane oblivion seems to have been a wise act – suggesting he had come through the shattered end of the second safari with his critical powers not wholly diminished – if an unfortunate one given the African sequel he might have produced.

5

This About the Bulls

It would have been simple if either Luis Miguel or Antonio had been killed. Luis Miguel was pretty well destroyed but is still functioning and that makes it no easier to make a story which has any permanent value.

After a summer of neglecting the African manuscript while he worked on stories, Hemingway left Cuba with Mary in late August of 1956 for Europe and the fall season of bullfights in Spain. The two leading matadors of the day, Antonio Ordóñez and his brother-in-law, Luis Miguel Dominguín, both of whom Hemingway had met during his return to Spain in 1953, had passed through Havana the previous winter on their way to engagements in Central and South America, rekindling his interest in bullfighting. He had written to Harvey Breit that needed a break from work on the African book and planned to see the two fight in Caracas, a trip eventually abandoned because of illness and lengthy bed rest.

In Spain that fall he followed Ordóñez's string of triumphs and was a triumph himself, cheered by crowds at the *corridas* and surrounded by swarms of autograph seekers. The attention was gratifying but Africa remained on his mind. He would later write in *The Dangerous Summer* that after the bullfights he and Mary planned to 'go on out to Africa where we had unfinished business.'[1] He had in fact booked passages for a return to Mombasa and a third safari, one on which he meant to introduce Ordóñez to the thrills of big-game hunting, with his son, Patrick, serving as white hunter. Continuing health problems stood in the way; although a Spanish doctor told him Africa was out of the question, Hemingway none-theless insisted he was good for one more trip. Nasser's closing of the Suez Canal, greatly lengthening the sea route to Mombasa, finally cut short the plan. In mid November, Spain was put behind for France, Hemingway glumly resigned to the abandoned safari. It was in Paris at the Ritz Hotel that the rediscovered trunks stimulated a new writing project, Africa replaced with a different effort to recapture the past.

Back in Cuba, he began leisurely but steady work on the series of sketches that would become *A Moveable Feast*. He continued working on the book as well as a revision of *The Garden of Eden*, his novel begun several years before, both in Cuba and Ketchum, Idaho, through the spring of 1959 when he and his wife again returned to Spain. Ordóñez and Dominguín were going head to head now in a series of *mano a mano corridas* – each bullfighter killing three bulls rather than the usual bullfight card of three matadors and two bulls each – that Hemingway was determined to see. His health had improved, leaving him in the best condition he had been in since the African fiasco. In his sixtieth year, drawn again to Spain and the bullring, he was looking ahead to what he enthusiastically called a 'wonderful summer'.[2] Mary, however, would remember the period differently – as one of tension and continued physical and mental decline, a thoroughly 'disturbing summer'.[3]

*   *   *

Just before he left Ketchum for Spain, Hemingway had informed L. H. Brague, Jr, an editor at Scribner's, that 'probably the next book to publish is the Paris stuff.'[4] The manuscript was typed, he added, and he planned to take it to Europe and possibly add more sketches. But he was in no hurry to get the book to his publisher, in part because he had hatched another writing task for himself, one that provided a professional excuse for the return to Spain. Scribner's was planning to reissue *Death in the Afternoon* and he wanted to update it by adding an appendix dealing with the current bullfight scene. The publisher had told him, he wrote to Patrick, that the fresh material would create the effect of a whole new book.

Some sort of revision of the bullfight book or a sequel to it had been on his mind since the moment of publication in 1932. In October of that year, less than a month after the book's appearance, he wrote to Max Perkins that when Scribner's had recovered from the Depression 'I will bring the book up to date and put in a few more dirty stories, and we can get it out with illustrations by Robert Domingo in colour – say 8 plates – that would be swell.'[5] Perkins was in hazy agreement, writing back to Hemingway to the effect that 'some day we will get out that new edition, and put in the colored pictures.' Of greater interest to the editor was a fresh non-fiction book Hemingway might write: 'By the way, couldn't you write a wonderful book about fishing sometime, full of incidents about people, and about weather, and the way things looked, and all that?'[6] In 1946, while he was working on *The Garden of Eden*, Hemingway complained to Perkins about *Death in the Afternoon* being out of print and reminded him of the old plan to update the work:

> It should be republished now and kept in print and later should be brought up to date in an entirely new edition. I could do that after I finish this long novel. Have kept up my research all the time and have a vast amount of stuff I can boil down . . . I have kept up all my contacts with the bull fighters and have some wonderful new stuff to go in a sequel to D. in A.[7]

The following year Perkins died, and with that nothing more was heard about the addendum to *Death in the Afternoon* until plans developed for the Spanish summer of 1959.

Life magazine got wind of what Hemingway had in mind for the book and sent correspondent Bill Lang from its Paris bureau to Spain with an offer of prior magazine publication. On the magazine's side, there was eagerness to have Hemingway again in its pages, where he hadn't appeared since the immense success of *The Old Man and the Sea* in 1952. For Hemingway, there was the temptation of another lucrative magazine deal (as it turned out, $90 000 for the English-language rights to the material, another $10 000 for the Spanish-language rights). The agreement with *Life* called for 5000-word news story, the piece to appear shortly after the bullfight season, with the focus on what it was like to return to Spain and on the summer's rivalry between Ordóñez and Dominguín.[8] It must have struck Hemingway as an undemanding task, and one that avoided the ephemeral nature of magazine work since the material eventually would be recycled in the reissue of *Death in the Afternoon*. Although he hadn't yet written a word on the book project, he readily accepted *Life's* proposal.

From his wife's point of view, an unhappy side of the arrangement with *Life* was that Hemingway was obliged now to follow the Ordóñez–Dominguín duel through the summer to its end. With an entourage that included Bill Davis, whose elegant home near Málaga provided a base for the Hemingways, and his friend and factotum A. E. Hotchner, he hurtled around Spain on an arduous schedule of bullfights and accompanying revels. His physical condition was only relatively better, he was drinking heavily again, and there were increasing signs of mental instability. In October, Mary left Spain to ready the houses in Cuba and Ketchum but also to escape humiliations heaped on her by her husband's erratic, self-absorbed behavior. He stayed on to work on the *Life* article, beginning it on 10 October with an account of his return to Spain in 1953, the first time he had been back to the country since Franco's victory in the civil war. By 15 October he had over 5000 words behind him, what *Life* wanted but not what it was going to get. As the Spanish journalist José Luis Castillo-Puche, who was close to Hemingway at the time, described it, the work lurched forward amid confusion and increasing anxiety:

> I had seen him . . . up there in his hotel room that was almost like a prison cell putting sheet after sheet of paper away in his files and then taking them all out again, pages only half finished, pages so full of corrections that they were scarcely legible. For the first time since I had known him, I saw him get all confused, tear up whole sections of his manuscript, rip up photographs or fling them across the room in a fit of temper, swear at those present in the room and others elsewhere, and swear at himself. For the first time in his life Ernesto had made a mess of what he was writing.[9]

Back in the less hectic settings of Cuba and Ketchum he kept adding to the bullfight manuscript. By April 1960 he was up to 60 000 words. He wrote to Charles Scribner, Jr, that he hadn't anticipated the manuscript running to such length but it wouldn't be a loss for the publishing house since the material was a 'property' and could go in the revised edition of *Death in the Afternoon* – or, a new idea, it could appear as a separate volume. Although the manuscript had ballooned, he gratuitously added that he was 'no Tom Wolfe' since 'all the words have to make sense.'[10] By the end of May he felt he finally had a first draft, some 120 000 words, of 'this about the bulls that comes after Death In The Afternoon.'[11] But the ending still wasn't right. Since Ordóñez and Dominguín were going to resume their competition, a return to Spain was necessary to gather new material he needed to complete the work.

Earlier, Hemingway had put off *Life's* editors by indicating the difficulties posed by the magazine assignment. At first, he pointed out, the assumption was that one of the bullfighters would be killed, creating a dramatic, news-story end to the season. His job in this case was to provide coverage for the magazine. But it had turned into a different kind of story, what he characterized as 'the gradual destruction of one person by another with all the things that led up to it and made it.' So he had had to establish the different personalities of the two matadors and their different approaches to the art of the bullring as well as provide an account of the events of the dangerous summer, and this had led to the swollen length of the manuscript. Another factor in the increased length was the need to make something of lasting quality after the Ordóñez–Dominguín duel was no longer newsworthy. In his explanation to *Life* Hemingway was laying the ground for boosting the price of his work from the $30 000 originally agreed by the magazine, yet the position seems genuine given the new idea of eventually using the material for book publication. What he was writing wasn't to be understood as a mere journalistic account but, as he had insisted before about *Death in the Afternoon* and *Green Hills of Africa* something of permanent value. It was to 'have some unity and be more than the simple account of the mano a manos which were no longer news and had been picked over by various vultures and large bellied crows.'[12] *Life*, for its part, seems to have done nothing to discourage the larger aim. Ed Thompson, the magazine's managing editor, wrote to Hemingway that he wasn't dismayed by the added wordage, and noted: 'If you are running that much longer than you expected you must have a hell of a story.'[13]

But with the work finished, there was the problem of how to cut it for the requirements of magazine publication, and here Hemingway was as helpless as he had been with finding an effective shape for the manuscript of the second African safari. After wrestling unsuccessfully with the task for a month, and after rejecting *Life's* offer to cut the work for him, he summoned Hotchner to Cuba to help. As Hotchner described their collaboration, it was a struggle to get Hemingway to eliminate anything. 'What I've written is Proustian in its cumulative effect,' he insisted, 'and if we eliminate detail we destroy that effect.'[14] But after three days of protest, he began grudgingly going along with Hotchner's suggestions; at the end of nine days, 54 916 words were excised from the manuscript. It was as far as he could go. His stuff didn't cut well, he complained to Charles Scribner, Jr, because 'everything depends on everything else and taking the country and the people out is like taking them out of The Sun Also Rises.'[15] It was agreed that Hotchner would take the work, now called *The Dangerous Summer*, to New York; there, he and *Life's* editors would finish the revisions. At the airport in Havana,

Hemingway passed Hotchner a sheath of notes for reading on the plane that countermanded some of the cuts already made and suggested others. Hotchner decided to interpret the new material not as instructions for more editorial work but as Hemingway's private notes to himself.

Another of Hotchner's tasks in New York was to negotiate with *Life* for a higher price for the expanded manuscript. In New York there were also frequent worried calls from Hemingway about what should be published first, a book edition of the bullfight manuscript or the Paris sketches. Hotchner suggested turning the question over to his publisher, and Charles Scribner, Jr, and Harry Brague were given copies of both manuscripts. They decided the bullfight manuscript should be published first, and soon, to capitalize on the publicity gained from publication in *Life*, then abruptly changed course in favor of the Paris book before settling once again on the bullfight book. Hemingway, who had previously indicated that he thought the Paris sketches should appear first, said he would consider the third change of plan.

While Hemingway returned to Spain to work on the ending of *The Dangerous Summer* and gather photos, Hotchner stayed on in New York to work with the *Life* editors on the bullfight manuscript. The first of three lengthy installments appeared in the magazine on 5 September 1960, the white-bearded writer featured on the cover and accompanied by photos that illustrated events and figures in the story – though with more photos devoted to Hemingway than either of the two bullfighters – and one section, reminiscent of the photos in *Death in the Afternoon*, showing Ordóñez and Dominguín performing basic bullfight maneuvers. An editorial note indicated that the complete version of *The Dangerous Summer*, running to 120 000 words, would be published the following year by Scribner's.

Although Mary reported to him that the first *Life* installment had been enthusiastically received in New York, Hemingway was anything but pleased. He wrote back that the magazine 'made me sick . . . the horrible face on the cover . . . the comparing journalism with "The Old Man". Just feel ashamed and sick to have done such a job.'[16] When Hotchner arrived in Spain in October he found Hemingway in a deeply paranoid state and obsessed with the pictures the magazine had used, certain that Ordóñez and Dominguín would interpret them as maliciously showing them in a bad light. He was troubled as well about Spanish reaction to a disparaging remark he had made about Manolete and about whether his treatment of Domínguín had been fair. He claimed to be mightily sick of the whole project now but was hoping he could work his way through, as he had during bad times in the past, to another happy period of good writing. He wrote to Mary that although he was faced with 'hells own amount of problems' and was afflicted by 'not sleeping, tricky memory, etc bad,' he now had an ending for the bullfight book and could return home even though the Ordóñez–Domínguín rivalry went on. 'Must get out of this and back to you,' he told her, 'and healthy life in Ketchum and get head in shape to write well. I can say that they went on and did this, whatever it turns out, but that I had to get back to Ketchum – can see how to do it – in the writing I mean.'[17]

When friends managed to get him on a plane back to the States it was the beginning of the end. The long ordeal of the bullfight manuscript was over; in the half a year left to him the only work he did was fitful retouching of the Paris sketches. After the desperate departure from Spain, Hotchner had gone back to Hemingway's hotel room to retrieve a bottle of Scotch whisky that Hemingway wanted him to have; near the bottle was a neatly written paragraph on a page of typing paper, apparently a final addition to the bullfight book – and a fitting conclusion to the entire ill-starred effort:

Nothing is as much fun any more as it was when we first drove up out of the grey mountains above Malaga onto the high country on the road to Madrid we drove so many times that year. Everything you read in the paper every morning makes you feel too bad to write. Probably the moral is you never should have got mixed up with bullfighters. I knew that once very well and I should not have had to learn it twice.[18]

* * *

For a full-length work by a writer of Hemingway's stature, *The Dangerous Summer* had a curious publishing history as a book. That it wasn't published immediately on the heels of the *Life* installments, as *The Old Man and the Sea* had been after its appearance in the magazine, may have been due to its poor reception. In his introduction to the book version, James Michener recalls that readers were impatient with digressions in the magazine pieces; rumor had it that *Life* considered the series a disaster, even that the magazine had considered canceling before the series was finished. But if *Life* was unhappy with its second venture in publishing Hemingway, it carefully kept the news from him. After reading the published installments, Bill Lang praised the work, telling Hemingway 'it had pace, it had interest, suspense, and a conclusion.'[19] Two months after the series appeared, Ed Thompson expressed interest in publishing the Paris sketches. He praised Hemingway for working 'hard and effectively' on the bullfight material and cautiously brought up his complaints about the photos used by the magazine – an academic question now that the series was out, Thompson noted, 'but your views would be valuable for the next time I hope there will be.'[20]

In her autobiography, published in 1976, Mary mentioned *The Dangerous Summer* (as well as the African manuscript) among the Hemingway works still awaiting editing and publication. She thought some of the observations about Spain removed by *Life* merited book publication but that many bullfight descriptions might, as she phrased it, be put to rest. Carlos Baker believed publication was delayed because Charles Scribner, Jr, 'thought it was not worth bringing out in book form as it was,' and added his own corresponding view that the writing was 'not always up to the Hemingway par, it tended to grow loquacious. But honed down sufficiently, the book should be pretty good.' Scribner took the same position. The work, he said, 'badly needed editing' for book publication. Although he had 'managed to whittle it down some over the years,' he was 'never really satisfied.'[21] It wasn't until 1984, when the manuscript was turned over to a young editor in the publishing house, Michael Pietsch, that Scribner was sufficiently pleased to go ahead. The book version of *The Dangerous Summer* finally appeared in 1985, a quarter of a century after Hemingway's death.

According to Hotchner, the manuscript Hemingway presented him with in Havana in 1960 had 688 typed pages and 108 746 words. The two of them got it down to 53 830 words, the manuscript subsequently submitted to *Life's* editors.[22] The book version, edited from that manuscript, has about 45 000 words and includes a lengthy introduction by Michener and a glossary of bullfight terms drawn from *Death in the Afternoon*. A question, of course, is how much of what Hemingway intended was left after the trimming and shaping of various editorial hands. Hotchner, who wasn't involved with the book version (though he is thanked on the copyright page for research assistance), found it substantially the same as the magazine version that he was involved in editing. Although he felt

Scribner's should have published the full manuscript because that was what Hemingway had intended, the book seemed to him faithful to the spirit of the original work.[23]

Hotchner's recollection is only partly borne out by an examination of the original manuscript (both the holograph and the typescript), deposited with the Hemingway papers at the John Fitzgerald Kennedy Library in Boston following publication of the book version. The book version has an orderly structure of chapters whereas the manuscript has no internal divisions, and the book eliminates detail on other bullfighters that caught Hemingway's attention, leaving a more narrow focus on Ordóñez and Dominguín than the manuscript reveals. Beyond this, the manuscript lacks the smoothness and concentration of the book; it is a rougher, meandering, generally less polished performance. Bill Davis, to take a minor example, is usually called 'Negro' in the manuscript, a joking reference to the title *El Negro*, the ghostwriter, bestowed on him by Ordóñez when he saw all the books in the Davis home, later used to reflect Davis' unflagging attendance on Hemingway. In the book the name becomes simply 'Bill'. More significant alterations are the removal of digressions that recall the uneven progress of *Death in the Afternoon*, detail about Spain, and a greater richness of characters. Nonetheless, the book generally follows the manuscript through the first 493 pages of the 688-page typescript, ending – as the *Life* series ended – with the dramatic goring of Dominguín at Bilbao. The considerable difference is that the typescript goes on for another 195 pages, broadening attention to an entire season of bullfighting rather than the book version's concentration on the Ordóñez–Dominguín contest, and altering the overall mood of the book version through the addition of a more personal and somber aspect.

Hemingway went on in the manuscript version to describe the rest of the bullfights that summer after Dominguín was shelved because of his wound, his attention now on the larger question of how the dangerous summer of *corridas* came to an end rather than simply the Ordóñez–Dominguín rivalry. A particular focus in the final third of the manuscript is on what Hemingway calls the picador business, an infraction of the complex rules governing the pic-ing of the bull by the picadors in Ordóñez's *cuadrilla*. A technical violation has taken place, if not an intentional one, and an investigation is begun. Eventually, Ordóñez, who continues to fight during the investigation in the belief the matter will be cleared up, is arrested, briefly jailed, and suspended from bullfighting for a month, bringing an end to his season in Spain. The manuscript recounts in detail one last fight at Nîmes in France, Ordóñez still performing with brilliance. As Hemingway puts it, the bulls finished Domínguín while only the Spanish authorities could stop Ordóñez. He adds that, with the two leading figures absent, the rest of the bullfight season turned into a financial disaster for the promoters.

In the manuscript, the Nîmes *corrida* is the final piece in the story, concluding the season that Hemingway had doggedly followed from early spring through the end of September. He says he has the story now that he had promised Ordóñez he would write, one from which he will try to create something of permanence to memorialize the year. But he doesn't end the manuscript here. He goes on to describe the visit of Ordóñez and his wife to Cuba, and after that a cross-country car trip with the matador out to Ketchum. He finally brings the manuscript to a close when he is back in Cuba, working on the book, his mood decidedly down. He includes here the paragraph that Hotchner had found in his hotel room ('Nothing is as much fun anymore . . .'), and remarks that a new bullfight season has begun in Spain, one he half–heartedly feels he ought to attend to check on new developments. Still, his work about the past season is finished, the monument to it made. If it hasn't been, he adds in a melancholy and wholly out of character remark, he hopes someone else can carry the task forward from where he ends.

*   *   *

Presumably, the decision to publish *The Dangerous Summer* (and, later, *The Garden of Eden*) in a reduced version was based on a desire for a more commercially appealing book in size and manner. From a scholarly standpoint, or simply the standpoint of a decent regard for the integrity of Hemingway's work, it seems only a misguided exercise in editorial tampering. If the book was to appear in a cut version, the publisher might well have imposed the scrupulous editing guidelines followed by Ray Cave in presenting excerpts from the second African manuscript in *Sports Illustrated*. Readers should have been alerted to where cuts had been made and generally reminded that they were reading only a portion of Hemingway's manuscript. Ideally, the work should have been published as Hemingway left it. Certainly he anticipated it would appear in its complete form, one that included the material about the country and the people that he had lamented removing, with Hotchner's assistance, from the manuscript handed over to *Life*. While the magazine was still considering the manuscript, he told Charles Scribner, Jr, referring to the *Life* manuscript, that 'there is so much that I don't use that it should, with the other material to come, and for the appendix, be a good book I think whenever we publish it.' He added that in case *Life* didn't want the work he would have 'wasted five months on the article but no time on the book.'[24]

Nonetheless, the Scribner's book is the book at hand for the time being. It generally follows the first two-thirds of Hemingway's manuscript, though, once again, edited into a far smoother and orderly version of that material; and there is at least some justification for the book ending where it does, with the goring of Dominguín in Bilbao. A note in the margin of the manuscript, initialed by Hemingway and placed after the description of Dominguín's wound and just before the concluding scene in the clinic, indicated that the work could be ended at this point. No doubt Hemingway was also referring to this ending when he wrote to Ed Thompson that 'the present end of the bull piece is OK if anything should happen to me as things sometimes do.' He told Thompson that for the additional material – presumably, some of the material that went into the final 195 pages of the full manuscript – he would 'have to go to Spain to get what I need for the end and to check certain things nobody will write or tell me on the telephone.'[25] Until *The Dangerous Summer* appears in Hemingway's full version, the only useful approach is to consider the Scribner's book in the light of the other published version available, the installments in *Life*.

Michael Pietsch's impression of the manuscript Hemingway and Hotchner submitted to the magazine was that it was weighted down with excessive detail, especially detail about bullfighters in addition to Ordóñez and Dominguín, and foggy with repetitive language used to describe bullfight action. The editor found, however, a clear story line buried in the detail, and the manuscript had an effective ending; as he saw it, the editing problem was to remove the encrusted detail and so highlight the story line. Scribner's gave consideration to publishing in book form the version that *Life's* editors had carved from the edited manuscript, but Pietsch found the magazine installments awkward and hard to read and still heavy with extraneous detail. He described his editorial approach to the *Life* manuscript this way:

> In editing the manuscript I pulled out passages that might have required a bit of patience on the reader's part, in order to highlight

the parts of the manuscript that were excellent. . . . Most of what I removed is large sections of an almost documentary nature (which I think Hemingway wrote out of something like journalistic habit) in which he describes the second and third bullfighters at corridas where Dominguín and Ordóñez fought. Taking out these easily exciseable sections left the strong, clearly connected stories of Hemingway's return to the pleasures of Spain and the rivalry between the two great bullfighters.

'The wonderfulness of *The Dangerous Summer*', Pietsch added, 'is all Hemingway's.'[26]

The book version is undoubtedly smoother than the magazine version, in part because of greater care given to the work's structure and the thinning out of detail. The magazine version jumps from Hemingway's first return to Spain in 1953 to the return for the summer of 1959 with a single paragraph of transition; the book version, separated into chapters as against the three-part structure of the magazine version, devotes the five-page second chapter to the intervening years. The loss of detail is apparent in the handling of the account of the Hemingways' passage to Spain aboard the *Constitution* and arrival in Algeciras – a matter of five paragraphs in the magazine, one in the book. Such changes are minor at most, and in these instances improvements. Elsewhere, however, the elimination of detail in the book version results in the loss of some rich, narrative-slowing asides. The following passage, for example, quintessentially Hemingway in his irascible, instructional mode, was left on the editing room floor:

I am trying to avoid using a Spanish word whenever I can explain in idiomatic English. This is not always possible but I think it is better than the peppering, larding and truffleing with bullfight terms and phrases that you get from the newly erudite writers that have disgusted me with trying to read anything about bullfighting in English. But this time, if I were not trying as far as possible to say it in English or whatever it is I write, you could be so snowed under with Manoletinas, Giraldillas, Pedresinas, Trincherillas and other varieties of ballroom bananas that you could not see the paper for the words. Just remember that any pass that ends in *ina* or *illa* is probably a phony and was invented to impress a gullible public.[27]

And this one, Hemingway in his comic vein playing with a supposed business relationship between himself and Ordóñez:

> The Spanish press was always very curious about our business projects which were usually on a great and imaginative scale. Someone would send me a clipping of an interview with Antonio from which I would be delighted to learn we were erecting a chain of motels along some stretch of coast that I had never visited. One time a newspaper man asked us what were our immediate projects in America. I told him that we were trying to buy Sun Valley in Idaho but that the Union Pacific was being difficult about the price.
>
> 'Then Papa there is only one move for us to make,' Antonio said. 'We must buy the Union Pacific.'
>
> By this type of rapid decision and our vast reserves of ready cash that we hold in all countries due to the translation of our books and Antonio's winter fights in Latin America we have been able to acquire for the benefit of the press a controlling interest in Outer Mongolian Opium Production, certain interests in Las Vegas, a few tin mines, Lucky Strike, a bull ring here and there, La Scala opera house in Milano, a number of good hotel chains (unpulled) and we are dickering with the Du Pont people for their General Motors stock.[28]

The effect of cuts such as these is to make the book version seem less in any sense a sequel to *Death in the Afternoon* and more an antiseptic and clean-flowing, though for lengthy stretches generally flat, documentary. Despite the editorial surgery, much of the work still seems written, in Pietsch's phrase, out of journalistic habit and with little freshness of insight or language, about Dominguín, for example: '. . . I was convinced he was a great bullfighter and Antonio was an all-time great fighter') (153). Still, some strain is apparent between the journalistic necessities of the work with its origin in a magazine assignment and Hemingway's desire to shape it, as he had the earlier bullfight book, into something of enduring value. Castillo-Puche thought he approached the *Life* articles (a mistaken venture to begin with since, as the Spanish journalist saw it, the Ordóñez–Dominguín duel was little more than a publicity stunt) as 'though they were up-to-the-minute news bulletins, an approach to the assignment that was bad both for his literary style and for his nerves.'[29] Clearly, there was a considerable amount of tedious fact gathering involved, which no doubt did Hemingway's physical and mental condition no good; but he had more in mind for *The Dangerous Summer* than news coverage for *Life*. In a passage that appears in the book version though not in *Life*'s installments, he says that before coming to Spain he wrote to Ordóñez that he

> . . . wanted to come over and write the truth, the absolute truth, about his work and his place in bullfighting so there would be a permanent record; something that would last when we were both gone.[30]

How to craft such a lasting record from the relatively thin journalistic material of a summer's spectacle was the hard task he had set himself.

*   *   *

Part of Hemingway's approach is simply the piling up of bullfight detail, an attempt to create permanence through density – an easy target, as it turned out, for the editorial pencil. In his introduction to the book version, Michener accommodates himself to the editing of *Life* and Scribner's yet wistfully laments the loss of such material ('purely bullfight passages') that would have charmed the devout *aficionado*.[31] A more important approach is found in the personal stamp Hemingway gives the account, linking it to the rest of his non-fiction even though his distinctive presence is far less dominant and intrusive than in either *Death in the Afternoon* or *Green Hills of Africa*. He once again locates himself at the center of things, the central observer if not, as in the African book, the principal actor. The two matadors seem finally to perform for him, awaiting the implacable judgement that will consign them to their places in bullfight history. On the deepest level, his personal domination of the material involves transforming it into a dramatic account of familiar Hemingwayesque dimension, one that may have had little to do with the reality of events. He found or created, as he had earlier with the hunt for kudu in *Green Hills of Africa*, the 'story' meant to give life to events.

From the beginning, the return to Spain in 1953, Hemingway is center stage. He had pledged never to return as long as friends from civil war days were still in jail; now they are free and he can honorably return. At the border an inspector studies his passport, discovering his identity as the writer just as Kandisky (' "You know

Hemingway the poet?"'') had done along an African road. The inspector asks if he is "any relation of Hemingway the writer?"

'Of the same family,' I answered . . .
'Are you Hemingway?'
I pulled myself up to modified attention and said, '*A sus ordenes*,' which means in Spanish not only at your orders but also at your disposal . . .
Anyway he stood up, put out his hand and said, 'I have read all your books and admire them very much . . .'

(44)

But just as Hemingway had come to Africa to hunt rather than talk about books, he is in Spain not to write but to renew his interest in bullfighting. Even when he returns for the dangerous summer of 1959, writing remains in the background; there is no indication of his journalistic task – and unlike his other ventures into non-fiction, no disquisitions on writing or writers dropped into the text. The sole mention of any work comes in a single line just after his 1959 arrival: 'I had to get the remaining material I needed to finish an appendix for *Death in the Afternoon*' (62). He has returned to Spain to acquaint himself with a new generation of bullfighters, and although experience has taught him not to have bullfighters for friends because of the emotional drain involved ('I suffered too much for them'), it is clear that this is precisely what will happen (49). He will not only see the new bullfighters but draw close to them, an insider as always, and his emotional reaction to the Spanish summer will be a central ingredient of the work.

Immediately thereafter he introduces the two bullfighters who will be the focus of his attention – and immediately he takes sides, scarcely pausing for even the pose of the detached journalist. 'I could tell he was great from the first long slow pass he made with the cape,' he says of his first sight of Ordóñez in action (49–50). When Ordóñez summons him to his hotel after that first fight, Hemingway reminds himself about friendships with bullfighters, especially one of Ordóñez's talent where there will be 'much you will have to lose if anything happens to him.' He dismisses the advice, of course, and with the meeting a friendship is cemented (51). There is friendship with Dominguín as well, though at once the older, long-successful matador is established as the less attractive figure. Hemingway, invited to lunch at Dominguín's ranch, describes him as 'a charmer, dark, tall, no hips, just a touch too long in the neck for a bullfighter, with a grave mocking face that went from professional disdain to easy laughter.' The telling detail is a life-size statue of the bullfighter at the ranch ('a rare thing for a man to have around his own finca in his own lifetime') that appears, to Hemingway's eye, more noble than Domínguin in the flesh (53).

Hemingway professes admiration for Domínguin as a cynical, worldly-wise companion and for his grace and skill in the ring. As a banderillero he is unsurpassed. But there is a crucial weakness: his style of handling the cape 'did not move me at all'; later, he will find that Domínguin also has a penchant for cheap, crowd-pleasing tricks in the ring (54). He maintains that the summer of 1959 was 'terrible' for him because of his friendship with the matador; he professes to be absolutely just in his appraisals, striving for a position of neutrality (55). Yet there is never a question about which side he is on. At one point he describes a lunch at Ordóñez's ranch where both men are present and 'we were all being friends,' but he adds that between the two 'the chips had been down for a long time' (108). They are for Hemingway as well from the moment the book opens.

When Hemingway arrives in Spain in 1953, Domínguin is in retirement, the pre-eminent matador in the land. When he returns in 1956, Domínguin has returned to the ring in France and North Africa; by 1959 the rivalry with Ordóñez is underway, Domínguin receiving more money because of his fame, and Ordóñez, at the peak of his artistry, out to prove he is actually the superior figure. At first, Domínguin and Ordóñez fight in separate locations, Hemingway following Ordóñez and reporting what he is told about Domínguin's fights, the narrative following a pattern of long auto trips, meals, hotels, *corridas*, the bulls frequently of poor quality. Other matadors draw brief attention – among them the diminutive Chicuelo II, 'braver than a badger' but inclined to the crowd-pleasing tricks of Manolete who, Hemingway remarks, 'had brought bullfighting to its second lowest ebb and then been killed and dying had become a demi-god and so escaped criticism forever' (90, 92). But the work of others only highlights the dominance of Ordóñez.

At Aranjuez, Ordóñez is gored in one buttock yet valiantly kills the bull while bleeding heavily. It is the twelfth serious horn wound of his career. In the hospital his wife, Carmen, asks how it happened and Hemingway explains that it was due to pointless rivalry with Chicuelo II. Carmen, wanting her husband to change his ways, says to Hemingway:

'You tell him.'
'He knows it. I don't have to tell him.'
'You tell him anyway, Ernesto.'

(97)

Throughout, Hemingway is the intimate friend who is wise in the ways of the bullring and everything else. When the bullfight surgeon, Dr Tamames, treats Ordóñez in the hospital – described in one of the book's most effective scenes – Hemingway is his assistant:

'Come here,'' he said to me. 'Distinguished colleague. Stand here. Roll him over. Roll over yourself, you, and lie on your face. You're in no danger from Ernesto or me.'

(99)

When Ordóñez is to be released from the hospital, it is into Hemingway's expert care, the surgeon asking him:

'Will he come to you at Málaga to get in shape?'
'Yes.'
'Good. I'll ship him down as soon as he can travel.'

(100)

After Ordóñez's wounding, Hemingway sees Dominguín fight for the first time that summer. His work is formidable but the horns of his bulls have been reduced, a small matter to even the 'knowledgeable people' taken up in the spectacle of the ring, yet for one with Hemingway's far greater knowledge a matter of grave significance since 'a diet of this type of bull with his defenses altered would unfit him, subtly but permanently, for the real bulls when he had to face them' (106, 107). Here, seventy pages into the book, Hemingway sets the stage for the appearance of the two bullfighters on the same card with an effective summary passage:

Luis Miguel had his place to maintain. He claimed to be the number one bullfighter and he was rich . . . He also wanted to be paid more money than Antonio per fight and that was where the deadliness came in. Antonio had the pride of the devil. He was convinced that he was a greater bullfighter than Luis Miguel and that he had been for a long time. He knew that he could be great no matter how the horns were. Luis Miguel was being paid more than Antonio was and I knew that if this occurred when they fought together Antonio would turn loose that strange molten quality he had inside himself until there would be no doubt in anyone's mind and especially Luis Miguel's who was the greater fighter. Antonio would do that or he would die and he was in no mood to die.

(111–12)

The meeting takes place in Zaragoza. It is the first time Ordóñez and Dominguín have been in the ring together in seven years. Although Ordóñez performs well, Hemingway gives the nod to Dominguín due to the luck of drawing better bulls. The journey now swings rapidly to Valencia and Barcelona and Burgos, Hemingway describing countryside that had once been the field of civil war engagements, places that 'could scare me still by their bare nakedness' (119). The festival at Pamplona follows, 'rough as always' with noise and overcrowding and non-stop drinking. Hemingway's entourage is swollen with young women taken as 'prisoners' ('not a wife but favored them with her approval,' he disingenuously notes) and there are benign interludes in the Irati forest that at the end of *Death in the Afternoon* he had expected to be destroyed but finds still the 'last great forest of the Middle Ages' (136, 138). At a Pamplona bar a young American journalist accuses Hemingway of wasting his time 'sitting in a bar seeking adulation, making wise cracks with your sycophants and signing autographs.' Hemingway reports the accusation but gives it no consideration, tossing it off instead in an exchange with Hotchner:

> 'Why do you waste time on that creep?' Hotch said.
> 'He's not a creep,' I said. 'He's a future editor of the *Reader's Digest*.'
>
> (139–40)

After Pamplona, it is on the road again to Valencia where Ordóñez and Dominguín once more appear on the same card. As usual, Dominguín is brilliant with the banderillas, and Hemingway's description is exact and moving:

> The bull waited for him close to the fence, his flanks heaving, blood streaming down one shoulder from the pic wounds, and his eyes watching Miguel who walked in to him slowly, his arms

spread wide, the harpoon pointed sticks held straight forward. Miguel walked past the point where he should cite the bull and make him charge, then past the point where this way of putting in the sticks was still safe, then past the point where it was possible with the bull still watching him to be sure of catching him. Then the bull charged at three paces and Miguel feinted with his body to the left and as the bull's head followed him brought the sticks down and pivoted on them to come out over the opposite horn.

(150)

But when it is time to kill, Dominguín has trouble. Five times his sword strikes bone. 'The crowd was strangely silent,' Hemingway notes. 'They were watching something happen to a man that they could not understand' (151).

As Hemingway adds it up, Dominguín is showing the signs of pressure. Ordóñez has wounded his confidence, winning every time save one when they have fought on the same card; now, at the festival in Valencia, they fight *mano a mano* for the first time that season, and without a third bullfighter on the card there is no escaping his rival. During the contest the wind catches Dominguín's muleta, exposing him to the bull, and he is badly gored. Meanwhile, Ordóñez excels with his remaining bull, 'doing consistently and continually what no one could do and doing it happily and lighthearted' (162). The first head-to-head meeting belongs to Ordóñez.

Then fate intervenes. Immediately after Valencia, in a fight in Palma de Mallorca, Ordóñez is gored and flown to Madrid for treatment. The two matadors find themselves in the same hospital, Dominguín relaxed now and with his confidence restored since, as Hemingway interprets it, his rival has been revealed as vulnerable. The second *mano a mano* between the two, fought in Málaga, turns out to be a classic of the bullring. Both men surpass themselves in brilliance, the statistics of approval finally totaling ten ears, four tails, and two hooves. Yet, Hemingway remarks,

. . . these meant nothing. What was important was that the two brothers-in-law had fought an almost perfect bullfight that had been unmarred by any tricks by the mean or shady maneuvers by the managers or promoters.

(176)

Michener calls Hemingway's account of the Málaga *corrida* one of the finest bullfight summaries ever written and suggests he might have ended his report at this point, the two matadors at the top of their form. But the story Hemingway is after is quite different, an enduring story of ultimate triumph and failure ('the gradual destruction of one person by another') rather than a journalistic account of what happened, and so he plunges on to recount other fights and the deepening personal involvement ('I suffered too much for them') announced at the book's beginning.

In the third *mano a mano*, in Ciudad Real, Dominguín is again outclassed, Hemingway putting into Hotchner's mouth his own sentiments. Ordóñez's brilliant movements in the ring, Hotchner says, are 'impossible to do'.

> 'He isn't leaving much of Luis Miguel.'
> 'Miguel will be all right when his leg is sound,' I said and hoped it was true.
> 'This is doing something to him though,' Hotch said. 'Watch his face.'
> 'It's an awfully good bull,' I said.
> 'It's something else,' Hotch said. 'Antonio isn't human. He does things all the time no human being can do. Look at Luis Miguel's face.'
> I looked and it was quiet, sad and profoundly troubled.
> 'He's seeing ghosts,' Hotch said.
>
> (185–6)

During the festival in Bilbao, before the most severe of bullfight audiences and with Franco's wife in attendance, the destruction is complete. Dominguín is seriously gored, a horn entering his groin and penetrating to the abdomen. Ordóñez, competition now removed and alone in the limelight, kills his last bull in *recibiendo* fashion, the classic, dangerous, and nearly forgotten way of killing Hemingway had celebrated so profusely in *Death in the Afternoon* as 'the most arrogant dealing of death and . . . one of the finest things you can see in bullfighting.'[32] He said in that book that he had seen it properly completed only four times in over 1500 kills. With Ordóñez he sees it once again.

Back in 1956, Ordóñez had killed bulls *recibiendo* as well, and in one instance he had dedicated a bull to Hemingway with the words, 'Ernesto, you and I know that this animal is worthless but let's see if

I can kill him the way you like it' (58). Now, at the end of the summer of contests with Dominguín, he repeats the dangerous act, turning the book at last into an approximation of an appendix to *Death in the Afternoon* that had provided the inspiration for Hemingway's renewed study of bullfighting. It is the high moment of the dangerous summer:

> So now Antonio drew himself up, sighted along the blade of the sword, and bent his left knee forward as he swung the muleta toward the bull. The big bull charged . . .
>
> (203)

When the sword hits bone and buckles, Ordóñez prepares to kill again in *recibiendo* fashion. 'No one in our time cites twice recibiendo,' Hemingway remarks (203). The method of killing links Ordóñez to the legendary eighteenth-century matador Pedro Romero, who regularly killed *recibiendo* and had provided the name for Hemingway's flawless young bullfighter in *The Sun Also Rises* (a figure in turn modeled on Ordóñez' father, the bullfighter Cayetano Ordóñez). Once more the sword hits bone, and to the astonishment of the crowd Ordóñez cites *recibiendo* yet again. In the hush of the bullring Hemingway can 'hear the click behind me as a woman's fan closed.' This time 'the blade slid in slowly high up between the very top of the shoulder blades' (204).

The rivalry is over. Dominguín's goring and Ordóñez's glittering triumph in Bilbao settles the issue of superiority beyond all question, at least as far as Hemingway is concerned. It could, he says, only be raised again 'technically' or to generate more money (205). The story ends, emotion dispelled, with a visit to Dominguín in the clinic, the bullfighter much in pain and his room crowded with visitors. A brief exchange reaffirms Hemingway's rightful place at the center of things. '"I missed you,"' Dominguín says to him, referring to Hemingway's capacity to take charge and remove people from the room.

> 'I'll see you in Madrid,' I said. 'Maybe if we go some of them will go.'
> 'We all look so nice together in the rotogravures,' he said.
> 'I'll see you at Ruber's.' Ruber's was the hospital.
> 'I've kept the apartment,' he said.
>
> (206)

*   *   *

The ending of the magazine version wasn't so cleanly handled. Before the closing exchange with Dominguín, Hemingway mentioned later fights of Ordóñez's and the matter treated at length in the original manuscript, the 'sordid disaster about the picadors'. An editor's insertion in the magazine explained that Ordóñez's picadors had been suspended for violating rules. Hemingway himself remained oblique: 'It was noble for a while, all the way, really, and then suddenly it was sordid and ugly because somebody lied.'[33] A coda for the installments was provided by a telegram from Hemingway, printed in cable form and vaguely accounting for the two matadors' careers in the year that had elapsed between the summer rivalry and *Life's* publication of the series. According to Hemingway, Ordóñez was still brilliant and Dominguín was getting his old confidence back, but another series of *mano a mano* contests seemed too dangerous unless, Hemingway cryptically noted, 'it were arranged to their complete mutual financial and artistic interest.'[34]

The coda, with its effort to bring the journalistic story up to date, only highlights the difficulties posed by *The Dangerous Summer* considered as a work of reporting. Spanish observers have pointed out that Dominguín and Ordóñez didn't have a true rivalry in the sense of matadors of equal standing in competition over a number of years and involving a great many *mano a mano* encounters. Hemingway's presence turned the attenuated duel into a media event, his eventual story thus – in one commentator's view – 'an excessive monument to a not-so-great event.'[35] Nor was Dominguín destroyed, as Hemingway had it, as a major *torero* as result of three head-to-head contests with his chief rival. The careers of both bullfighters went on; the ending Hemingway told Mary he had found, emphasized all the more in the reduced book and magazine versions, was more the creation of a storyteller than the observation of a journalist.

The work's troublesome quality as journalism is seen as well in the lordly judgement handed down on the two rivals. Michener takes Hemingway to task for his overwhelming bias in favor of Ordóñez, finding it an abuse of his role as an impartial reporter and constituting an 'unwarranted attack on Dominguín, who was not as outclassed in that long duel as Hemingway claims.'[36] Spanish *aficionados* have long agreed, with the slighting of the sainted Manolete only adding to their ire. Dominguín himself stoutly resisted

Hemingway's characterization, and maintained that the writer had threatened him with destruction ('I'm going to ruin you for life, Miguel . . . I'll have you kept out of the ring') and deliberately heightened his rivalry with Ordóñez into deadly competition.[37] Michener, who saw Ordóñez fight many times after 1959, found him invariably disgraceful – evasive, using the very tricks Hemingway despised, killing the bull from the side. In Hemingway's defense as a journalist, Eric Sevareid, who attended the famous Málaga bullfight and wrote about it in *Esquire* before the *Life* installments appeared, drew a similar portrait of the contest (though one, since he was in Hemingway's company at the time, that might have been influenced by him). Sevareid's enthusiasm for Ordóñez also compared with Hemingway's in his conclusion that 'no bullfighter will ever seriously challenge Ordóñez while he remains in his physical prime; and he will stay in his prime for years.'[38] Others, including Michener, have paid tribute to the technical accuracy of Hemingway's accounts of bullfight maneuvers.

Still, taken as journalism, *The Dangerous Summer* remains suspect. Castillo-Puche believed that Hemingway intended the work as a 'great piece of reporting', and as such 'something entirely new about bullfighting'.[39] As a work of reporting, the work would indeed have stood in marked contrast to *Death in the Afternoon*, and Hemingway may well have pondered it in this light. Certainly the assignment for *Life* – as against the way Hemingway may have conceived of the work when it existed in his mind only as a sequel to *Death in the Afternoon* – gave *The Dangerous Summer*, unlike his earlier efforts in extended fact writing, a news-story center and the broad form of a work of topical reporting. But a rigorous journalistic effort – the pursuit of the 'absolute truth' that he claimed as his overriding aim in the work – was something for which he had little experience and less inclination; his journalism was invariably a form of anti-journalism, emphasizing an imaginative story and his own dominant presence. Hemingway had made clear to *Life* what it was that most deeply engaged him about the summer rivalry of Ordóñez and Domínguín, informing Ed Thompson that it 'would have been simple if either Luis Miguel or Antonio had been killed. Luis Miguel was pretty well destroyed but is still functioning and that makes it no easier to make a story which has any permanent value.'[40] This was hardly a true story in a journalistic sense, but it was the one that caught his imagination and that he sought to form into an account of universal value, one that would hold up as the truth of art long after the truth of events had faded from memory.

The returns to Spain, culminating in the hectic summer of 1959 and its aftermath, were an effort to recover imaginatively a past when he was young and vital and bullfighting was a new, all-engrossing world. In 1924 he had told Edward J. O'Brien of his wonder in discovering people whose physical conduct he could admire totally: 'Well I have got ahold of it in bull fighting. Jesus Christ yes.'[41] In *The Sun Also Rises*, the wonder particularized itself in the golden youth Pedro Romero, in 'The Undefeated' and again in *Death in the Afternoon* in the indomitable Maera. With Antonio Ordóñez, Hemingway recreated his idealized matadors, blending, as he always did, recollection and observation with what he made up, coming around full circle to one of the great imaginative centers of his work, the man of physical conduct worthy of unqualified admiration.

Yet if he could join the past in imagination, he couldn't wholly summon the creative energy needed to escape the confines of documentary journalism. *The Dangerous Summer* is never as deliciously imprinted with the personal as *Death in the Afternoon* or *Green Hills of Africa*, nor does it delve deeply into the lives and personalities of the two matadors, making their rivalry seem more than a sporting event, giving it the tragic edge he sought. The story of the destruction of Domínguín by Ordóñez, as against the account of triumph and failure in the bullring, is argued more than revealed and never seems a matter of serious consequence. In addition, the ability to impose a fresh and engaging shape on his material remained as elusive as it had been during the long labor on the account of the second African safari. In an admiring review of the book version of *The Dangerous Summer*, William Kennedy offered the fanciful notion that Hemingway's 'spirit' had returned to Scribner's to 'tell the folks there how to prepare the text.'[42] The reality is indeed that others, Hotchner and *Life's* editors and Michael Pietsch, whether guided by Hemingway's spirit or not, had to take up where he left off, giving his manuscript its published form in the magazine and book versions.[43] The last line of the original manuscript, Hemingway holding open the possibility that someone else might carry the work forward, may have been a plea for just such assistance, his recognition that what he had made in 'this about the bulls' was neither precise reporting nor that rich admixture of fact and imagination that could transform reporting into a story possessed of permanent value.

Beyond the moving conception of Ordóñez as perfect matador and the saga of his triumphant summer, what endures best in *The Dangerous Summer* as enduring Hemingway are bits and pieces of the account, isolated passages nearly as good as any he ever wrote. The pleasures of food and drink, for example, now and then come to familiar sensuous life:

> We drank sangria, red wine with fresh orange and lemon juice in it, served in big pitchers and ate local sausages to start with, fresh tuna, fresh prawns, and crisp fried octopus tentacles that tasted like lobster. Then some ate steaks and others roasted or grilled chicken with saffron yellow rice with pimentos and clams in it.
>
> (125)

There are moments of the old sure touch with dialogue, as in a passage in which Dr Tamames lectures about Ordóñez's thigh wound in the brusque manner of Nick Adams' father in 'Indian Camp':

> 'Now your pain. Your famous pain,' he said. 'The dressing had to be fastened on securely. You understand? The wound swells. That is natural. You can't poke something bigger around than a hoe handle six inches up into you there and make all that destruction in the muscle without making a wound that will pain and swell. The dressing constricts it and that makes it worse. Now this dressing is comfortable. Isn't it?'
> 'Yes,' said Antonio.
> 'Then let's have no more about pain.'
> 'You didn't feel the big pain,' I said.
> 'Neither did you,' Tamames said. 'Fortunately.'
>
> (100)

And there are bright flashes of descriptive writing that bring to mind the exact landscape painting of *Green Hills of Africa*:

> The rest of us headed for Alicante, then through date palms and the rich, crowded, flat farming and fruit country of Murcia, past Lorca, to break out and up into the wild mountain country and along the lonely valleys with the white-washed houses of the villages and the herds of sheep and goats raising dust along the road until we came down out of the hills in the dark past the entry

to the ravine where they had shot Federico Garcia Lorca and saw the lights of Granada.

(163–4)

Ordóñez's final victory in Bilbao is a sustained piece of strong work, with the heart of the account the killing in classic *recibiendo* fashion. Hemingway here repossesses the 'real thing' in writing he had sought in his early fiction and announced in *Death in the Afternoon* – that recreation of 'the sequence of motion and fact which made the emotion and which would be as valid in a year or in ten years or, with luck and if you stated it purely enough, always . . .'[44] The description of the moment of death, strongly marked by Hemingway's reacting presence, could well have taken its place in a sequel to the first bullfight book:

. . . and the blade slid in slowly high up between the very top of the shoulder blades. Antonio's feet had not moved and the bull and he were one now and when his hand came flat onto the top of the black hide the horn had passed his chest and the bull was dead under his hand. The bull did not know it yet and he watched Antonio standing before him with his hand raised, not in triumph but as though to say good-bye. I knew what he was thinking but for a minute it was hard for me to see his face. The bull could not see his face either but it was a strange friendly face of the strangest boy I ever knew and for once it showed compassion in the ring where there is no place for it. Now the bull knew that he was dead and his legs failed him and his eyes were glazing as Antonio watched him fall.

(204–5)

6

How Things Truly Were

. . . the old things are nowhere except in our minds now.

Hemingway had broken off work on his Paris sketches to take up *The Dangerous Summer*, yet, according to his wife, after the manuscript was finished and the *Life* installments had appeared he was so repelled by the venality of the bullfight business that he put book publication aside and returned to the sketches for some final tinkering. After his death in July 1961, Mary found the typed manuscript in his workroom in Ketchum together with a draft preface for the book and a list of titles, including *A Moveable Feast*. Since picking a title was among the last things he did in preparing a work for publication, she concluded that he considered the book finished.

A detailed letter Hemingway sent to Harry Brague of Scribner's just six months before his death supports the notion that the book was at least close to final form. He told the editor he had eighteen chapters finished and arranged and that he was working on a nineteenth and last chapter as well as a title. The title of the moment, *The Paris Stories*, wasn't right since, as he put it, 'Paris has been used so often it blights anything.' He gave Brague a rundown of the page lengths of the chapters – and then a fussy accounting of page wordage (240 words per page, he calculated) that led to an estimate of a book of between 42 000 and 45 000 words:

Averaging words (5 pages):
3 pages all type no conversation   209
    266
    335
conversation   222
all conversation   171
$5\sqrt{1203}$
240

There were complaints as well about the hard circumstance of his work in Ketchum without access to his Cuban library, but he also offered his usual self-congratulatory tribute to a manuscript soon to be in his publisher's hands. 'All the truth and magic', he assurred Brague, was in it.[1]

Mary and Harry Brague saw the manuscript through publication. They settled on the title, and, as Mary later indicated, there was some minor editing that included adding and removing commas and some cutting of repetitious language. In addition, the order of a couple of the chapters was changed for what was described as the sake of continuity. Mary insisted, however, that nothing was added to the book. When *A Moveable Feast* appeared on 5 May 1964, the first of Hemingway's posthumous books, it bore no mention of the editorial work, a note by Mary saying only that the book was finished in Cuba in the spring of 1960 and some revisions made in Ketchum the following fall. One last editing chore before publication had been a trip to Paris to check Hemingway's recollection of the city's layout, Mary concerned that he might have placed a street where it didn't belong. She found only two errors in the spelling of street names; 'otherwise', she said, 'his memory had been perfect.'[2] It was a deceptively casual remark, for nothing about the Paris book, neither the circumstances of its development and publication nor the reliability of Hemingway's memory, was quite that clear-cut.

*   *   *

The appearance of Gertrude Stein's *The Autobiography of Alice B. Toklas* in 1933 got Hemingway, revenge in his eye over the charge that he was yellow, talking about another man-of-letters endeavor: memoirs. In the 'Pamplona Letter' in 1924 he had declared that 'it is only when you can no longer believe in your own exploits that you write your memoirs.'[3] Now he told Janet Flanner that 'By jeesus will write my own memoirs sometime when I can't write anything else. And they will be funny and accurate and not out to prove a bloody thing.' In case Flanner thought this just 'big promises by Hem', he insisted that 'By God I will.'[4] Max Perkins received the same promise. After mentioning reading an installment of Gertrude Stein's book in the *Atlantic Monthly*, Hemingway pledged: 'I'm going to write damned good memoirs when I write them because I'm jealous of no one, have a rat trap memory and the documents.'[5] His memoirs, however, were something for the far future when the well of fiction had run dry. In the meantime, Perkins was assured, there was plenty to write first, and over the years the memoirist largely confined himself to letters as the place for his occasional offerings of 'true gen' about the past.

The old days in Paris was a subject that especially needed straightening out. Hemingway had claimed for Malcolm Cowley's benefit that he instructed his children on how it had been then – and that, the perfect audience, 'they love to hear about Scott and Jim Joyce and how things truly were instead of the accepted version.' They even fed him just the right straight lines: 'Papa what is the *true* gen on so and so or such and such.'[6] In his writing, Paris in the famous past made only cameo appearances. In *Green Hills of Africa*, reading Tolstoy's *Sevastopol* suggests the Boulevard Sevastopol which in turn stimulates impressions of the city and his life there when he was starting out. In 'The Snows of Kilimanjaro', Harry evokes the Paris quarter in which 'he had written the start of all he was to do' but that he had never captured in his work: 'No, he had never written about Paris. Not the Paris that he cared about?[7] In the part of the unfinished African manuscript that appeared in *Sports Illustrated*, Paris makes a passing appearance as a city known and loved so well that 'I never liked to talk about it except with people from the old days.'[8]

In the most extended comment on Paris, 'A Paris Letter', published in *Esquire* in 1934, Gertrude Stein's book cast a considerable pall over Hemingway's observations. Paris in the fall compares unfavorably with a previous fall in Wyoming, the city gloomy and filled with death and dying – a preview of a dark strain that would run through *A Moveable Feast*:

> This old friend shot himself. That old friend took an overdose of something. That old friend went back to New York and jumped out, or rather fell from, a high window.

At the root of the somber mood is the fact that another 'old friend wrote her memoirs', later in the article revised to read that 'legendary people usually end by writing their memoirs.' After a review of the French boxing scene, Hemingway ended the magazine article with a passage that suggested another strain that would appear in *A Moveable Feast*, Paris now viewed as the lovely, wistful place of youth:

> Paris is very beautiful this fall. It was a fine place to be quite young in and it is a necessary part of a man's education. We all loved it

once and we lie if we say we didn't. But she is like a mistress who does not grow old and she has other lovers now. She was old to start with but we did not know it then. We thought she was just older than we were, and that was attractive then. So when we did not love her any more we held it against her. But that was wrong because she is always the same age and she always has new lovers.[9]

Despite the early references to writing his memoirs and, in his work, the scattered recollections about the old days in Paris, it was apparently the discovery in 1956 of the trunks in the Ritz Hotel that actually launched him on *A Moveable Feast*.[10] Friends had also noticed that, following the ordeal of the African plane crashes, he was more given to spinning stories about the past. Perhaps, an added stimulus, there was the feeling that he was near the end of the line as a fiction writer, the time having come to turn memoirist in earnest. He began in Cuba in the spring of 1957 with an account of Scott Fitzgerald ('how I first met him and how he was') that he was thinking of sending to the *Atlantic Monthly*, where he had once read some of Gertrude Stein's autobiography and which had asked him for a contribution to its centenary number.[11] He found the remembering easy but the writing hard, and he finally put the piece aside, telling Harvey Breit that 'when I read it over I remembered that character writing about his friend Mr. Dylan Thomas and thought people would think I was doing that to Scott and him dead.'[12] But the reluctance to do in Scott in the manner of John Malcolm Brinnin's *Dylan Thomas in America: An Intimate Journal* was only a temporary affair of conscience; in the meantime he kept working on other remembrances that he called sketches, a sardonic reference to the early characterization of his short stories by uninterested editors. In *Green Hills of Africa* he had remembered

> . . . *all of the stories back in the mail that came in through a slit in the sawmill door, with notes of rejection that would never call them stories, but always anecdotes, sketches, contes, etc. They did not want them, and we lived on poireaux and drank cahors and water.*[13]

Mary recalled that by December he had completed sketches about writing a story in a Paris café and about Gertrude Stein and Ford Madox Ford, the latter a revision of an account of Ford deleted from the original opening material of *The Sun Also Rises*. She was typing the sketches as he gave them to her ('correcting spelling and punctuation and consulting him about phrases which I thought needed reorganization') and didn't hide her disappointment. '"It's not much about you,"' she objected. '"I thought it was going to be autobiography."' Hemingway's response was that he was writing 'biography by *remate*' – a jai alai term that Mary interpreted as meaning that he was trying to create a portrait of himself by 'reflection', his life revealed only in the light of the lives of others.[14]

As a memoirist, Hemingway was indeed working with considerable indirection, moving freely across the time frame of the years 1921–6, establishing only a tenuous continuity among the sketches, leaving more out than he put in, and relying on well-worn anecdotes. The story of how his relationship with Gertrude Stein ended had, for example, been retailed in a letter to Edmund Wilson in 1951, and no doubt many times before that. Nonetheless, the discrete, usually brief sketches, ordinarily opening with a generalized page or two about a place or activity and coming around to an anecdotal ending, were an inspired form at this point. Although Hemingway was working on *The Garden of Eden* at the same time, the Paris book grew rapidly, and by the summer of 1958 he thought he was virtually done. He had eighteen sketches behind him and one or two more in mind. In September he declared to Buck Lanham that he had written 'a book, very good, about early earliest days in Paris, Austria, etc. – the true gen on what everyone has written about and no one knows but me.'[15] Early the following year he was telling Harry Brague that he thought the next book to publish was the 'Paris stuff', though he added that he was taking the manuscript with him to Paris on a locale-checking trip to 'go over it all and maybe do a couple more of the pieces. It is a hell of a good book – really.'[16] In November of 1959 during a stop-over in New York he dropped off the manuscript with Charles Scribner, Jr, but he still wasn't ready to commit himself to publication. He left instructions that it be returned to him in Ketchum for final work.

According to A. E. Hotchner's account of the final year and a half of Hemingway's life, little was ever done to the manuscript again. After *The Dangerous Summer* was behind him and he had returned to the sketches, he spent long hours poring over the pages but did no real writing. Hotchner remembered him complaining bitterly about his inability to finish 'the bloody book':

'I've got it all and I know what I want it to be but I can't get it down . . . I *can't*. I've been at this goddamn worktable all day, standing here all day, all I've got to get is this one thing, maybe only a sentence, maybe more, I don't know, and I can't get it. Not any of it. You understand, I *can't*. I've written Scribner's to scratch the book. It was all set for the fall but I had to scratch it.'

When Hotchner suggested that Scribner's could delay publication until spring, Hemingway repeated his anguished certainty that he would never finish the book:

'No, no they won't. Because I can't finish it. Not this fall or next spring or ten years from now. I *can't*. This wonderful damn book and I can't finish it. You understand?'[17]

*   *   *

If the typescript his wife found after Hemingway's death wasn't finished to his full satisfaction it was as near to finished, as Carlos Baker remarked, as it would ever be. But the published book produced by Mary and Harry Brague departed significantly from that final manuscript. Baker cautiously skirted the issue in his discussion of the book in *Hemingway: The Writer as Artist*, noting simply that the chronology of composition given by his wife in the note to *A Moveable Feast* differs from that which appears in one of Hemingway's letters and also one of Mary's, both written while the book was in progress. He also pointed out that an eight-page sketch of his son, Bumby, that Hemingway meant to use as chapter eighteen of the book was omitted, inadvertently it seems, because it was found in longhand rather than typescript. Other critics have been less circumspect, maintaining that changes made in the published work were so substantial that a revised text is necessary if we are to read the book Hemingway actually left behind.[18]

Alterations at the beginning and end of the work seem especially damaging. The preface, with its accounting of omissions in the story and thus echoing the closing chapter of *Death in the Afternoon*, appears to have been collated from various draft prefaces. Baker noted that he hadn't seen the original of the published version, and noted further that errors in spelling and usage suggested that Hemingway didn't regard that version as final. More problematic is the opening sentence of the third and final paragraph of the preface: 'If the reader prefers, this book may be regarded as fiction.' The sentence doesn't appear in any drafts of the preface in Hemingway's handwriting; what does appear in several instances is a direct assertion that 'this book is fiction.' One of the draft prefaces, however, indicates that Hemingway was more concerned with fending off potential libel actions with the remark than with accurately labeling the book:

> This book is fiction. I have left out much and changed and eliminated and I hope Hadley understands. A book of fiction may eliminate and distort but it tries to give a fictional picture of a time and the people in it. No one can write true facts in reminiscences. Evan would back you up but he is dead. Scott would disagree. Miss Moorhead would sue if you published anything against Walsh and she has many letters and much basis to sue on. The story about Walsh will have to come out.[19]

Analysis of the several editorial alterations worked on the heavily revised concluding chapter of *A Moveable Feast* suggests that one thing Hemingway apparently intended was a return at the end of the book to the thought that much about Paris had been omitted, material that he planned to treat in another book. In the preface he had left the door open for a second work ('It would be fine if all these were in this book but we will have to do without them for now'), and Mary underscored the possibility in her remarks about the published book: 'He had planned, I guess, to do a second book about Paris . . .'[20] In draft material for the concluding chapter, Pauline was portrayed in a wholly different light – not as the rich interloper who destroyed the marriage to Hadley but as a good wife who had loved truly. She was to receive her due, Hemingway maintained, in the book to come:

> There is no mention in this book of Pauline on purpose. That would be a good way to end a book on these days except that it was a beginning not an ending . . . That part, the part with Pauline, I have not eliminated, but have saved for the start of another book . . . It could be a good book because it tells many things that no one knows or can ever know and it has love, remorse, contrition and unbelievable happiness and the story of truly good work and final sorrow.[21]

More damaging than the loss of references to Pauline and a second book in the last chapter are insertions of material from earlier drafts about the 'pilot fish' and the 'rich' that Hemingway apparently meant to remove from the final version of what took place in Schruns. Left in, they cause the book to conclude with a portrait of the innocent, unsuspecting author – elsewhere in the sketches revealed as hard-headed and all-knowing – as a victim of circumstance. In the ending Hemingway seems to have preferred, he excuses the rich, shoulders some measure of blame for the failure of the marriage, and offers apologies to Hadley.[22]

Yet whatever its inadequacies as the book Hemingway intended, the published version of *A Moveable Feast*, like that of *The Dangerous Summer*, is the one at hand for the time being. It is the most widely read and admired of Hemingway's non-fiction books – the book that has been seen as the fitting capstone of his career. A commercial and critical success when it was published following the fanfare of excerpts in *Life* illustrated with lavish color photographs of Paris, it has continued to draw attention from critics who ordinarily attend only to the fiction and to hold special appeal for the legion of Hemingway admirers. In part, the attraction has to do with the bottomless charm of the subject matter, Paris in the Twenties; in other part, it stems from the story-like manner of the book's form and suggestive parallels with the early short fiction. Frank Kermode expressed a widespread view when he declared *A Moveable Feast* 'Hemingway's best book since the 1920s and that makes it altogether exceptional.' In similar fashion, Jeffrey Meyers has praised the book as 'infinitely superior' to Hemingway's books after World War II and his 'greatest work of nonfiction'.[23]

*   *   *

'Hemingway's tragedy as an artist', Cyril Connolly once said, 'is that he has not had the versatility to run away fast enough from his imitators . . . A Picasso would have done something different; Hemingway could only indulge in invective against his critics – and do it again.'[24] The charge, if it has merit at all, applies far more to the fiction than the non-fiction, for the latter, while always in a personal mode, shifts notably each time: Hemingway at the center of an instructional handbook, a travel narrative, a discursive journal, a work of reporting. With *A Moveable Feast* the genre is again different, a memoir approached through a loose mosaic of twenty self-enclosed sketches – the personal voice, far from the often aggressive and lurching manner of *Death in the Afternoon*, generally muted and wistfully reflective now, resembling more the detached authorial voice of the fiction than the aggressively personal Hemingway of the earlier non-fiction that Edmund Wilson had found so offensive. The mixture of fact and fiction in the book resembles the fiction as well in that it contains an even higher proportion of invention than usual, Hemingway reshaping his life to the end.

But for all that, *A Moveable Feast* isn't fiction. Hemingway clearly approached the book as a work of non-fiction drawn from recollection, though with the libel-inspired disclaimer in the preface that the book could be regarded as fiction and with his usual awareness, as he had said in *Death in the Afternoon*, that 'memory, of course, is never true.'[25] One large aim – perhaps primary, as suggested by the Fitzgerald sketch with which he began – was to set the historical record straight about old days and old acquaintances. Arthur Mizener's biography of Fitzgerald had long been on his mind ('supposed to be history'), and after he had read Harold Loeb's *The Way It Was* that appeared in 1959 he remarked that Loeb was searching 'for how he wished things to have been.'[26] In his correspondence with Charles Fenton, trying to deter scholarly use of autobiographical material he might work up himself, he had mentioned his interest in getting things right about Paris days: 'It is important that I should write about the Paris part as no-one knows the truth about it as I do and it is an interesting time in writing.'[27] The record-straightening aim was highlighted in the preface with the remark that the book might 'throw some light on what has been written as fact.' It was to be a factual book, then, to revise what others had claimed as fact, but a book free of illusions about recovering historical truth in any exact sense. Early in the book the process of remembering rises to the surface in a dialogue with Hadley ('"Do you remember . . ."'), and in the account of Schruns in the final sketch the reliance on memory is again directly acknowledged:

I remember the snow on the road to the village . . .
I remember the trails up through the orchards . . .
The worst thing I remember of that avalanche winter . . .
I remember the smell of the pines . . .
I remember all the kinds of snow . . .[28]

Yet it was exactly such slippery slopes of memory that he had warned Fenton against, instructing the Yale scholar that 'the basic mis-conception in your approach is that most people can't remember anything accurately.'[29] The remark applied equally to his own exercise in memory. Contrary to his boast to Perkins, he had neither a rat-trap memory at this stage of his life nor the necessary documents; if he was finally getting it right about Paris in *A Moveable Feast*, it was only in the sense of setting out some of a survivor's 'true gen'. Moreover, it was true gen in the service of present concerns, the past remade to fit the fictions of the moment. His work of memory, just as each of his earlier efforts in non-fiction, was inevitably colored by the demands of his life now. In *A Moveable Feast* he didn't recreate the past as it had been but, in the pose of a memoirist this time, fashioned it through selection and invention into the way he now wished to remember it.

In the preface, he offered a cursory list of the book's omissions:

> There is no mention of the Stade Anastasie where the boxers served as waiters at the tables set out under the trees and the ring was in the garden. Nor of training with Larry Gains, nor the great twenty-round fights at the Cirque d'Hiver. Nor of such good friends as Charlie Sweeney, Bill Bird and Mike Strater, nor of André Masson and Miro.

He might have gone on, for approached as a thoroughgoing account of the Paris he had known, and especially that 'interesting time in writing' he had dangled before Fenton, *A Moveable Feast* is far from satisfying. Hemingway's interest is limited to a set of highly eclectic memories, and memories always in the service of the self, everything aimed inward. So he recalls old friends and enemies, settles old scores, retells old tales, takes pains to have the last word in his uneasy relationships with Gertrude Stein and Scott Fitzgerald – all arranged to place himself in attractive light, the 'egotism and mental laziness' of his chosen cast of flawed figures set off against, as he remarks at one point, his own sterling 'discipline' (30). When Stein informs him that the young people of the lost generation are drinking themselves to death, Hemingway says, '"Have you ever seen me drunk?"' '"No,"' Stein is made to admit, and then pointedly add: '"But your friends are drunk"' (29).

This side of the book is, of course, not without interest. The three sketches devoted to Stein are directed with skilled vituperation to a passage of overheard conversation, Hemingway delivering in print the low blow he had long been saving up. Ford Madox Ford is dismissed with a barrage of comic overkill as physically distasteful ('I had always avoided looking at Ford when I could and I always held my breath when I was near him in a closed room'), a snob and a liar (83). The early friendship with Ezra Pound is saluted, though not without careful shading: 'His own writing, when he would hit it right, was so perfect, and he was so sincere in his mistakes and so enamored of his errors, and so kind to people that I always thought of him as a sort of saint' (108). The 'Jim Joyce' that Hemingway had regaled his children with makes only passing appearances while the forgotten poets Ernest Walsh, Evan Shipman and Ralph Cheever Dunning are featured figures. There is, though, a fetching still-life of Joyce and his family glimpsed through the window of Michaud's restaurant:

> . . . he and his wife against the wall, Joyce peering at the menu through his thick glasses holding the menu up in one hand; Nora by him, a hearty but delicate eater; Giorgio thin, foppish, sleek-headed from the back; Lucia with heavy curly hair, a girl not quite yet grown; all of them talking Italian.
>
> (56)

Fitzgerald, Hemingway's chief rival from the Paris days, is on the receiving end of the most extended recollection, one ordered with a ponderous hand to show Hemingway's contrasting superiority. As Hemingway establishes it, the heart of the difference is the matter of masculinity: he abounds in it, Fitzgerald is comically lacking. The result, or so Hemingway seems to have hoped, is that Fitzgerald, diminished as a man, would be equally diminished in literary reputation. At their first meeting in the Dingo bar, Fitzgerald's face is said to resemble a boy's and to possess a mouth that, 'on a girl, would have been the mouth of beauty' – a telling contrast with the manly Hemingway whose dark beard and uncut hair caused him to be called 'the Black Christ' by peasants in Schruns (149, 206). Fitzgerald dresses smartly but his ever-knowing companion notes the impropriety of his Guard's tie that might give offense to the British in Paris. And there is the shamelessness of Fitzgerald's opening question: '"Tell me, did you and your wife sleep together before you were married?"' Hemingway's response is appropriately laconic: '"I don't know"' (151).

Later, the subject turned to literary matters, Fitzgerald reveals that he altered his stories to meet the editorial formulas of the

Saturday Evening Post, a form of whoring defended on the grounds that the changes were made only after the real stories had been written. Hemingway isn't convinced, and he sets off Fitzgerald's casual treatment of his talent with his own pure dedication to serious fiction:

> Since I had started to break down all my writing and get rid of all facility and try to make instead of describe, writing had been wonderful to do.

(156)

The madcap trip to Lyon to retrieve the Fitzgeralds' topless car, a deft piece of sustained farce, is more of the same: the wise, secure Hemingway set off against the bumbling, alcoholic Fitzgerald. Again, the point of the contrast is in the literary implication Hemingway is anxious to suggest. Whereas he is a rigorous craftsman who feels 'the death loneliness that comes at the end of every day that is wasted in your life,' around Fitzgerald there is just 'this silly comedy' (165–6). When, a day or two after the Lyon trip, Fitzgerald brings him a copy of *The Great Gatsby*, Hemingway is properly awed, but his admiration for the book is balanced by the condescension directed to its author:

> When I had finished the book I knew that no matter what Scott did, nor how he behaved, I must know it was like a sickness and be of any help I could to him and try to be a good friend.

(176)

The same view of Fitzgerald is attributed to Bumby in the deleted sketch that Hemingway had intended for inclusion in the book, the boy said to think only the best of Monsieur Fitzgerald, certain that his problems with drink and his wife will be surmounted.

The absurdist conclusion of the Fitzgerald recollection comes with Hemingway reassuring Fitzgerald in the chapter called 'A Matter of Measurements' that his penis is of adequate size (a story previously outlined for Harvey Breit in a 1954 letter; Fitzgerald's mistake, Hemingway said then, was that he gauged his penis from above, causing it to appear foreshortened). His wife's charge that he was inadequate, Hemingway explains to him, was meant 'to put you out of business' as a man and a writer (190). Fitzgerald remains doubtful even after a trip to the Louvre and the inspection of male statues. The scene breaks off with Fitzgerald leaving for the Ritz bar – and Hemingway, the diminishment of Fitzgerald now complete, leaping ahead in time to a passage of dialogue after World War II with a Ritz bartender who can't remember Fitzgerald. Georges recalls perfectly his first meeting with Hemingway but wonders, '"Papa, who was this Monsieur Fitzgerald that everyone asks me about?"' (191). Hemingway's response is to pledge – the bartender's forgetfulness reminiscent of the lack of memory of Karl and P.O.M. that supposedly inspires *Green Hills of Africa* – that he is 'going to write something about him in a book that I will write about the early days in Paris.' He will put Fitzgerald in the book 'exactly as I remember him the first time that I met him,' but the account in his book of remembering is neither so innocent nor so wholly dedicated to the historical past (193). Although Arnold Gingrich, among others, found the portrait of Fitzgerald astonishingly accurate ('. . . as I read it there Scott stood again alive, at his inimitably exasperating best and worst'), Hemingway wasn't so much looking back as ahead, trying to fix the lasting literary fate of his chief rival from the Paris days.[30]

Apparently, Hemingway's final plan was to place the 'A Matter of Measurements' chapter about Fitzgerald as the book's final sketch, and so conclude, as he had in *Green Hills of Africa*, with an explanation offered within the book for writing the memoirs. The plan, altered in the posthumous editorial changes, would have put the Schruns material before the three Fitzgerald chapters, thus also notably changing the feeling of the book's close by emphasizing the sardonic and comic intent of the memoirist – and underscoring all the more Fitzgerald's reduced status.

*   *   *

If getting the record straight, Hemingway fashion, is one strain in *A Moveable Feast*, another is the portrait of the artist, in love with work and wife, at the beginning of the famous career. Readers have generally found this side of the book the more appealing, yet equally elliptical in its treatment of things past and glancing in its characterization. What a book, Gertrude Stein had teased, 'would be the real story of Hemingway, not those he writes but the confessions of the real Ernest Hemingway.'[31] But real confessions wasn't what he provided in *A Moveable Feast*; his disclosures, whether by reflection or direct recollection, remain as selective and self-protective as they are in the other part of the memoir. It was all he chose to reveal about starting out, or, in the troubled time of composition, all he could recall.

The book's opening, with its echo of the celebrated opening of *A Farewell to Arms*, draws the reader into the harsh city at the turn of the season from fall to winter and the contrasting world of serious work and ideal love:

> Then there was bad weather. It would come in one day when the fall was over. We would have to shut the windows in the night against the rain and the cold wind would strip the leaves from the trees in the Place Contrescarpe. The leaves lay sodden in the rain and the wind drove the rain against the big green autobus at the terminal and the Café des Amateurs was crowded and the windows misted over from the heat and the smoke inside.
>
> (3)

Hemingway retreats from his chilly workroom on the top floor of a rundown hotel to a good café on the Place St-Michel. Here, in warm, clean and friendly surroundings, he drinks *café au lait* and then rum St James and works happily and well on a story set in Michigan. Since the day in Paris is wild and blowing, he makes it that way in the story – 'The Three-Day Blow' he obviously has in mind, though Kenneth Lynn has pointed out that the story wasn't in fact written for another two years. Even the arrival of a striking girl can't wholly break his concentration; the story seems to be writing itself and he has a hard time keeping up with it. It is a magic moment – precisely *not* the sort that had come to mind when he had read the forgotten Paris notebooks ('It was just as hard for me to write then as it is now') but precisely what he wished to imagine in the difficult time of work on *The Dangerous Summer* and *A Moveable Feast*:

> Then I went back to writing and I entered far into the story and was lost in it. I was writing it now and it was not writing itself and I did not look up nor know anything about the time nor think where I was nor order any more rum St James. I was tired of rum St James without thinking about it. Then the story was finished and I was very tired.
>
> (6)

Even when things weren't going well in those wonderous times there was no real cause for concern. He would merely sit in front of the fire in his workroom, drop the peel of a mandarine orange into the flames, and admonish himself not to worry:

> 'You have always written before and you will write now. All you have to do is write one true sentence. Write the truest sentence that you know.'

And it would work. He would write the one true sentence and he was launched. It was 'easy then because there was always one true sentence that I knew or had seen or had heard someone say' (12). Perhaps because of the hard struggle of writing in the present, writing in the reconstructed past took on all the more imagined ease. Among what appear to be late additions to the manuscript of *The Garden of Eden* is a passage in which writing is described as a torture likened to impotence:

> He had never in his life as a man been impotent, but in an hour standing at the armoire on top of which he wrote he learned what impotence was . . . He could not write more than a single sentence. And the sentences themselves were increasingly simple and completely dull.[32]

All such incapacity is lifted in *A Moveable Feast*. What remains is a romance of writing in which there is only the memory of good work and good luck:

> The blue-backed notebooks, the two pencils and the pencil sharpener (a pocket knife was too wasteful), the marble-topped tables, the smell of early morning, sweeping out and mopping, and luck were all you needed.
>
> (91)

The only trying thing while writing in cafés was the likelihood of interruption. In the 'Birth of a New School' sketch Hemingway tells of one annoying occasion in which he reacts with fervor ('"You rotten son of a bitch what are you doing in here off your filthy beat?"') to a would-be writer who speaks to him from the next table. (92). Still, he is going so well that even this can't throw him off. He keeps writing while the talk flows, getting back deeply into the story, paying attention to the speaker again only after he is finished

('I had not heard him for some time except as noise. I was ahead now and I could leave it and go on tomorrow' (93)). After the intruder is dismissed with the nastiest remark Hemingway can conjure up ('"Look, if you can't write why don't you learn to write criticism?"'), he decides he will avoid the café for the time being (95). The next morning he works at home on the dining-room table after, he pointedly notes, boiling the bottles, preparing the formula and feeding his infant son. The drudgery of domestic life disrupts his writing no more than unwanted café talk:

> . . . I worked better than I had ever done. In those days you did not really need anything, not even the rabbit's foot, but it was good to feel it in your pocket.
>
> (96)

As Hemingway chose to recall them, in those magic days 'work could cure almost anything' – a doctrine, he insisted from the vantage point of the present writing, he still believed in (21). The other cure was his love for Hadley, imagined back into existence in terms as idyllic as his portrayal of the ease of writing, and perhaps for a similar reason – as a response to the severe strains in his present marriage to Mary. The refashioning of Hadley into the great love of his life, completed with *A Moveable Feast*, had begun on the heels of the break-up of their marriage. In a letter written in November 1926, Hemingway had praised her as 'the best and truest and loveliest person that I have ever known.'[33] Some twenty years later, in a chatty letter written from Cuba in which she is Katherine Cat and he is Taty or Tatie, he professes his love for her, knowing her husband, Paul Mowrer, won't mind 'because knowing you he would know I would be crazy if I didn't and I have been crazy but never stay that way for very long.'[34] Just a few weeks before his death, worrying over the manuscript of *A Moveable Feast*, he had phoned Hadley from Ketchum, trying to recall names from the Paris days. The conversation was pleasant, the quality that had marked their relationship since they had gone their separate ways, but Hadley was struck by the tone of deep sadness that now attached to his voice.

In the memoir, Hadley is offered as the impossibly perfect mate for the young writer. She accepts the impoverished circumstances (as Hemingway, with considerable exaggeration, portrays them) of their life without complaint, and she is instantly ready to do what he wishes, go where he wishes – her sole purpose to selflessly accommodate herself to her husband. In the opening sketch, she is there when Hemingway finishes writing for the day, and she eagerly accepts his plan to leave Paris for the mountains now that bad weather has come. Hemingway gestures in the direction of her agreement ('we would go if my wife wanted to'), but there is never any question of that. Hadley, the true soulmate, even praises her husband for his thoughtfulness. '"Weren't you good to think of going, too,"' she tells him (8).

Thereafter, Hadley reappears in the sketches in the same fashion – a dimly seen yet always comforting and supportive presence after Hemingway has finished work for the day ('"How did it go, Tatie?"') or encountered one of his Paris acquaintances (38). She is there at the end of 'Miss Stein Instructs', an antidote to the melancholy that strikes Hemingway after Gertrude Stein's lesson on the homosexual behavior of males and females and his lonely walk back to the apartment on rue Cardinal Lemoine. At the end of 'Shakespeare and Company', when Hemingway proposes a walk in the city and then '"afterwards we'll read and then go to bed and make love,"' Hadley enthusiastically responds: '"What a lovely afternoon and evening"' (37–8). After the return from the trip to Lyon with Fitzgerald, Hemingway tells her that he has learned '"never to go on trips with anyone you do not love"' (175). With this suggestion of the trip they will soon make together to Spain for the bullfights, the two of them revel in the superiority of their love:

> 'Poor Scott,' I said.
> 'Poor everybody,' Hadley said. 'Rich feathercats with no money.'
> 'We're awfully lucky.'
> 'We'll have to be good and hold it.'
>
> (176)

But their luck, of course, wouldn't hold. As the relationship is recounted, Hemingway, in a chastened voice coming from outside the time frame of the sketches, hints at the failure to come, giving the book its slender line of narrative development. After saying on another occasion how fortunate they were, he adds that he foolishly hadn't knocked on wood. 'We're too lucky,' Hadley says at one point, and in the sketch about the horse races at Auteuil and Enghien, 'The End of an Avocation', Hemingway says directly: 'Racing never came between us, only people could do that' (55, 61). And he notes about the passion he developed for another kind of racing, bicycle racing, that it came later 'when the first part of Paris was broken up' (64). (Hemingway seems to have meant to include bicycle racing in the second book about Paris days, approaching it, as he had bullfighting in *Death in the Afternoon*, as a captivating activity in need of explanation for English readers. 'I must write the strange world of the six-day races,' he notes in *A Moveable Feast*, 'and the marvels of the road-racing in the mountains. French is the only language it has ever been written in properly and the terms are all French and that is what makes it hard to write . . . But that comes at another time in Paris' (65).)

A more suggestive moment pointing to failure ahead appears at the end of 'A False Spring', the best of the sketches dealing with Hadley and one that recalls the early stories portraying subtle strains in the marriage. Hemingway begins with the two of them spending a happy spring day at the track at Enghien, winning a great deal; then he jumps ahead to another successful day at a track and he and Hadley walking home through the city. On a bridge over the Seine they begin a rapid trading of remembered experiences centering on their friendship with 'Chink' Dorman-Smith. It is a moment of odd emotional hunger – 'Memory is hunger,' Hadley offers as an explanation – that leads to literal hunger and the splurge of a meal at Michaud's (57). Yet the hunger persists, and even after they are home and have made love, Hemingway feels it – a premonition, perhaps, of the hunger that will lead to Pauline and complexity and the end of the marriage. With Hadley asleep beside him, Hemingway, in a somber voice coming from the present, muses that

> Life had seemed so simple that morning when I had wakened . . .
> But Paris was a very old city and we were young and nothing was
> simple there, not even poverty, nor sudden money, nor the
> moonlight, nor right and wrong nor the breathing of someone
> who lay beside you in the moonlight.
>
> (57–8)

As it turns out, the issue of right and wrong in the break-up of the marriage isn't the memoirist's principal concern, nor are any of the actual details of what took place. From the Paris memories he turns in the final sketch to two winters spent in Schruns in Austria, the opening line introducing the story of disruption to follow: 'When there were the three of us instead of just the two . . .' (197). Yet before that cryptic reference is explained there is an account, one of the most effectively realized in the book, of the good life in the mountains: skiing above the village, abundant food and drink, frigid nights sleeping under feather quilts, forbidden poker games in the hotel dining-room, hard work on the revision of *The Sun Also Rises*. Hadley appears only as a background presence, skiing with her husband while a local girl looks after Bumby, knitting caps and sweaters and scarves with local wool. When the elaborately veiled explanation of the failure of the marriage comes at the end of the sketch, she nearly disappears from view. Hemingway abruptly turns back to the opening line of the sketch with the remark that, during the second winter in Schruns, 'new people came deep into our lives and nothing was ever the same again' (207). The pilot fish brings the rich, eager to warm themselves in the light of the up-and-coming young writer, and a fiesta concept of life ensues. Transformed for the purposes of the sketch from the wise figure who sees through everyone into an improbable innocent, Hemingway performs for the rich like a circus animal. But even before the appearance of the rich, Pauline ('another rich') has infiltrated the marriage, posing as Hadley's best friend (209). It seems ordinary enough at first, the friend a companion for the wife while the husband works, but 'all things truly wicked start from an innocence,' and soon the triangle that is created is dangerous and Hemingway finds himself living 'day to day as in a war' (210).

After a trip to New York to establish himself with Scribner's, he returns to Paris and Pauline rather than to Schruns and Hadley. When he eventually sees his wife at the train station in Schruns, he composes a still life, radiant in memory, of what he is putting aside:

> She was smiling, the sun on her lovely face tanned by the snow and sun, beautifully built, her hair red gold in the sun, grown out all winter awkwardly and beautifully, and Mr. Bumby standing with her, blond and chunky and with winter cheeks looking like a good Vorarlberg boy.
>
> (210)

Hadley is as loving and selfless as ever ('Oh Tatie, you're back and you made such a fine successful trip') and the 'lovely magic time' in the mountains is resumed (210–11). But with the return to Paris in the spring 'the other thing' with Pauline is resumed as well, and with that the marriage ends – and so too, as Hemingway puts it, the first chapter of his life in Paris. The city replaces the marriage in the lyric coda that ends the sketch as the place where, once, 'we were very poor and very happy' (211).

As mentioned earlier, the book's account of how the marriage ended may reveal more about the editorial hand exercised by Mary and Scribner's than about what Hemingway finally intended. Yet it is the version that stands, bearing with it several factual problems, among them Hemingway's side-stepping of personal guilt by heaping blame on his rich friends, Gerald and Sara Murphy, and on John Dos Passos as their pilot fish, and by the association of the three with Pauline's conspiracy. Pauline had visited Schruns during Christmas of 1925 after having first met Hemingway through Harold Loeb and his girl friend, Kitty Cannell. Dos Passos and the Murphys had come to Austria more than a year later, in March of 1926, at a time when Hemingway and Pauline probably were already lovers. Hemingway makes a stab at clarifying the time frame ('Before these rich had come we had already been infiltrated by another rich . . .'), but the book's linking of the rich Pauline with the rich Murphys remains a hazy leap of logic (209). Assigning Dos Passos a role in the break-up of the marriage was an especially gratuitous alteration of the record, Hemingway here settling the score for Dos Passos' protrayal of him as George Elbert Warner in his 1951 novel *Chosen Country*. In a letter at the time, prefiguring the assault to come in his memoir, he referred to a pack of dogs he kept in Cuba 'trained to attack one-eyed Portuguese bastards who wrote lies about their friends.'[35]

But getting things factually straight about the past, whether about the end of the marriage or his Paris contemporaries or his beginnings as a writer, wasn't the dominant impulse behind *A Moveable Feast*. In non-fiction as well as in fiction he wanted, as he said in *Death in the Afternoon*, to 'make all that come true again,' but true in the sense of faithful to his usual mixture of recollection and imagination grounded in the present, always making more than describing. He had discovered early on that there was no going back to the past as it actually had been. From Paris in 1923 he had written Bill Horne about a disappointing trip he and Hadley had taken back to the scene of his World War I exploits in Italy, advising him to look ahead because the past couldn't be recovered. It could only be found – found now – in the mind:

> Horney we've got to go on. We can't ever go back to old things or try and get the 'old kick' out of something or find things the way

we remembered them. We have them as we remember them and
they are fine and wonderful and we have to go on and have other
things because the old things are nowhere except in our minds
now.[36]

*   *   *

With the publication of *A Moveable Feast* the old lion seemed,
miraculously, to draw a fresh masterpiece out of his nearly depleted
fund of physical and creative energy. Marvin Mudrick joined with
many critics in finding the book 'proof of the strength he could still
muster', and added: 'The book is new, and stands with the best of
his early stories.'[37] Set against a background of Hemingway's later
work in both fiction and non-fiction, the book did seem engagingly
fresh, in large part, as Mudrick suggested, because it drew attention
back to the vivid, economical world of the early stories. The voice in
some of the sketches strongly recalls the early work; but the older,
embattled voice is there as well, speaking from the vantage point of
present struggles, concerned to 'stay sound and good in my head
until morning when I would start to work again' (77).
     The mingling of voices coming from different time frames gives *A
Moveable Feast* its uneven tone, sometimes joyous with work and
love and the sensual delights of Paris, sometimes darkly melancholy. The latter tone is most notable in the book's preoccupation
with death. There is the sadness of the seasons, the fall when 'part of
you died each year' and later the cold rains that 'killed the spring'
(45). There is the revelation of the true ending of the story 'Out of
Season' in which the fishing guide hanged himself, just as the
painter Pascin did and as Hemingway advises the tiresome Hal in
the sketch 'Birth of a New School': '"Go home. Get a job. Hang
yourself"' (94). In 'The man Who Was Marked for Death', Ernest
Walsh bears the sign of death like an ill-fated movie character, but
his appearance is more than a poet's pose. 'Death was not conning
with him,' Hemingway says. 'It was coming all right.' When Walsh
sets himself off from Hemingway as one who is '"marked for Life"',
Hemingway replies with grim irony: '"Give me time"' (127). During
their first meeting in the Dingo bar, Hemingway sees Fitzgerald's
face tighten in an alcoholic stupor into the appearance of a death
mask. In the Ritz bar conversation about Fitzgerald and other
remembered Paris types, Hemingway tells Georges that '"all those
people are dead"' (192).

The most haunting use of death comes in the final sketch set in Schruns, 'There is Never Any End to Paris'. Despite the joyous recreation of winters in the mountains before the marriage came apart, Hemingway drawing deeply and openly on memory ('I remember . . .'), he cannot remain free of death's presence. He recalls the avalanches that killed many during the first winter, and especially a corpse that had to be dug from the snow. The man had squatted down and made a box in front of him with his arms to create breathing space as the snow rose over him. When his body is recovered his neck is worn through, tendons and bone visible, from twisting his head from side to side under the snow. The motion apparently had caused snow to fill his air space, an action that raises a question of suicide:

> We could not decide whether he had done it on purpose or if he had been out of his head. He was refused burial in the consecrated ground by the local priest anyway, since there was no proof he was a Catholic.
>
> (204–5)

The weight of the present influences the book's structure as well as its tone. Overall design had been a problem with both the second African account and the report of the Ordóñez–Dominguín rivalry; in those trying efforts Hemingway had written at great length and occasionally with power, but an effective shape had eluded him. Works requiring extended development, fiction or non-fiction, had never been his strong suit, but with *Death in the Afternoon* and especially *Green Hills of Africa* he had found satisfying approaches. With *A Moveable Feast* he again found a form that could be sustained – the real triumph of the old lion's craft at the end. His greatest strength had always been for short narrative and a treatment of people more directed to capturing the veneer of personality than internal realms. For his non-fiction at this point, the brief, self-enclosed sketch – perhaps inspired by the discovery of the old material in the Paris trunks or the recollection that his early fiction had been dismissed as sketches – was an ideal form. It freed him from the need to build the account of Paris days into a connected whole, allowing him to rest with only a casual linking of the sketches and the single narrative line of his love for Hadley. It allowed him to slide over the differing aims and moods of the sketches. It enabled him, finally, to practice in non-fiction something of the fictional discipline of omission that he recalled in the book as 'my new theory', the aura of suggestion cast over the material that left the reader feeling more than was stated (75).

The practice of omission turned *A Moveable Feast* more toward the body of his fiction, the early stories especially, than the body of his non-fiction. As a result, when viewed in the light of his major non-fiction efforts in *Death in the Afternoon* and *Green Hills of Africa*, the book can seem a minor work – thin, driven by cross purposes, too given over to surface observations in its portrayal of both the young Hemingway and his Paris contemporaries. But comparisons are beside the point. In the Paris book he again turned his hand in non-fiction to something new – to a form of autobiography pursued through the fragmented, roundabout means of reflection. Once again he started with a familiar genre of fact writing and once again he shaped it, through the medium of fiction-like sketches, to his own special creation – a work suffused with temperament, the actual drawn deeply inside an imaginative construction, something made rather than recalled, and so possessed of continuing life. *A Moveable Feast* stands alone, as do his other non-fiction books. There are no proper comparisons.

As with *The Dangerous Summer*, what holds best in the mind are isolated pieces drawn from the work, moments of matchless Hemingway: a young woman's hair black as a crow's wing slanted across a rain-fresh face; eating *portugaises* and drinking cold white wine after writing a story; the virtuous feeling that follows a day of good work; Ford Madox Ford snubbing an imagined Hilaire Belloc; Scott Fitzgerald's face forever caught between handsome and pretty; Zelda Fitzgerald's hawk's eyes and her mind drifting from the table in anticipation of the night's party; skiing down a glacier above Schruns and the sense of dropping forever and forever; the changing moods inspired by Paris at the turn of the season. In this last, especially, there is the mingling of the old trademark responsiveness to life with the death-haunted sadness of the present, the divided emotion that so deeply colored the last work of non-fiction:

With so many trees in the city, you could see the spring coming each day until a night of warm wind would bring it suddenly in one morning. Sometimes the heavy cold rains would beat it back so that it would seem that it would never come and that you were losing a season out of your life. This was the only truly sad time in Paris because it was unnatural. You expected to be sad in the fall.

Part of you died each year when the leaves fell from the trees and their branches were bare against the wind and the cold, wintry light. But you knew there would always be the spring, as you knew the river would flow again after it was frozen. When the cold rains kept on and killed the spring, it was as though a young person had died for no reason.

(45)

With the Paris sketches Hemingway redeemed Harry's failure in 'The Snows of Kilimanjaro' in that he managed to get down a few things about the city and his life there that he cared about. Another aspect of the sadness given off by the book, however, is that there wasn't time for the second volume – and beyond that, time for all the fact work that might have been undertaken. 'There was so much to write,' Harry had said.[38]

Notes

The treasure trove of Hemingway material is the Ernest Hemingway Collection at the John Fitzgerald Kennedy Library, Boston. Letters to and from Hemingway cited below are located here and at the Firestone Library, Princeton University, and the Beinecke Rare Book and Manuscript Library, Yale University. Published letters are found in *Ernest Hemingway, Selected Letters, 1917–1961*, edited by Carlos Baker (New York: Scribner's, 1981). The editorial correspondence of Maxwell Perkins is in the Scribner Archives at the Firestone Library, Princeton University. The papers of Charles Fenton are at the Beinecke Library, Yale University. The original manuscript of *Death in the Afternoon* is at the Harry Ransom Humanities Research Center, University of Texas, that of *Green Hills of Africa* at the Alderman Library, University of Virginia. The manuscripts of *The Dangerous Summer* and of the sketches that make up *A Moveable Feast* are at the Kennedy Library. The manuscript of the second African book, usually referred to as the 'African Journal', was located at the Kennedy Library in 1988 but was not immediately opened to scholars. Hemingway's newspaper and magazine journalism has been collected in two volumes edited by William White, *By-Line: Ernest Hemingway* (New York: Scribner's, 1967) and *Dateline: Toronto* (New York: Scribner's, 1985).

INTRODUCTION: PERMANENT RECORDS

1. George Plimpton, 'Ernest Hemingway', in *Writers at Work: The Paris Review Interviews*, Second Series (New York: Viking, 1963), 233.
2. Hemingway expressed this conception of the non-fiction in *The Dangerous Summer* (New York: Scribner's, 1985), 82. The bullfighter in question in the passage used as the epigraph above is Antonio Ordóñez.
3. Robert O. Stephens, *Hemingway's Nonfiction* (Chapel Hill: University of North Carolina Press, 1968), 40.
4. Michael S. Reynolds, 'Unexplored Territory: The Next Ten Years of Hemingway Studies,' in *Ernest Hemingway, The Papers of a Writer*, Bernard Oldsey (ed.) (New York: Garland, 1981), 16.

CHAPTER 1: IN SPITE OF IT

1. Charles Fenton to Ernest Hemingway, 9 September 1951, Kennedy Library.
2. Charles Fenton to Mrs Paul Scott Mowrer, 26 February 1952, Yale University.

3.   Charles Fenton tö rnest Hemingway, 9 September 1951, Kennedy Library.
4.   Ernest Hemingway to Charles Fenton, 12 January 1951, *Selected Letters*, 719.
5.   Ernest Hemingway to Wallace Meyer, 21 February 1952, *Selected Letters*, 751.
6.   Ernest Hemingway to Charles Fenton, 22 January 1952, Kennedy Library.
7.   Charles Fenton to Ernest Hemingway, 14 June 1952, Kennedy Library.
8.   Ernest Hemingway to Charles Fenton, 18 June 1952, *Selected Letters*, 765.
9.   Ernest Hemingway to Charles Fenton, 26 June 1953, Kennedy Library.
10. Charles Fenton to Ernest Hemingway, 26 November 1953, Kennedy Library.
11. Ernest Hemingway to Carlos Baker, 16 January 1961, Kennedy Library.
12. Charles A. Fenton, *The Apprenticeship of Ernest Hemingway* (New York: Farrar, Straus & Cudahy, 1954), ix.
13. Quoted in Fenton, *The Apprenticeship of Ernest Hemingway*, 32. A 1925 copy of the style sheet is reproduced in *Ernest Hemingway, Cub Reporter*, Matthew J. Bruccoli (ed.) (Pittsburgh: University of Pittsburgh Press, 1970).
14. 'Back to His First Field', *Kansas City Times*, 26 November 1940, 1. The interview is reprinted in *Conversations With Ernest Hemingway*, Matthew J. Bruccoli (ed.) (Jackson: University Press of Mississippi, 1986), 21–4.
15. Fenton, *The Apprenticeship of Ernest Hemingway*, 37.
16. Ernest Hemingway, 'Rum-Running', in *Dateline: Toronto*, 41.
17. Ernest Hemingway, 'Tuna Fishing in Spain', in *Dateline: Toronto*, 92.
18. Ernest Hemingway, 'Tip the Postman Every Time?', in *Dateline: Toronto*, 106.
19. Quoted in Fenton, *The Apprenticeship of Ernest Hemingway*, 126.
20. Quoted in Scott Donaldson, 'Hemingway of *The Star*', in *Ernest Hemingway, The Papers of a Writer*, 95.
21. Quoted in Fenton, *The Apprenticeship of Ernest Hemingway*, 194. The young journalist who recalled the exchange, Walter Duranty, took note of more of it in a book he later wrote:

>   'All right,' I said, 'but what about your other idea of getting out of the newspaper game; how's that to be done?'
>   'Write a book,' he said simply.
>   'What book?' I asked.
>   'Any book, provided that it is your book, that's to say, the book that comes from you out of your consciousness and is not something that you are writing as you think you ought to write or as someone else wants you to write.'

Walter Duranty, *I Write as I Please* (New York: Simon & Schuster, 1935), 258.

22. Ernest Hemingway, 'Mussolini, Europe's Prize Bluffer', in *Dateline: Toronto*, 255.
23. Quoted in Fenton, *The Apprenticeship of Ernest Hemingway*, 222–3.
24. Ernest Hemingway to Gertrude Stein and Alice B. Toklas, 11 October 1923, *Selected Letters*, 93.
25. Mark Twain, *Roughing It* (New York: The Library of America, 1984), 746.
26. Ibid., 862.
27. Fenton, *The Apprenticeship of Ernest Hemingway*, 243.
28. Plimpton, *Writers at Work*, 225.
29. The letter is referred to in Peter Griffin, *Along with Youth: Hemingway, The Early Years* (New York: Oxford University Press, 1985), 81.
30. Elizabeth B. Moffett to Charles Fenton, 27 April 1952, Yale University.
31. E. H. Taylor to Charles Fenton, 4 April 1952, Yale University.
32. H. J. Haskell to Charles Fenton, 8 February 1952, Yale University.
33. John Selby to Charles Fenton, 27 February 1952, Yale University.
34. Marcel Wallenstein to Charles Fenton, 8 March 1952, Yale University.
35. J. N. Darling to Charles Fenton, 2 February 1952, Yale University.
36. Carlos Baker, *Ernest Hemingway, A Life Story* (New York: Scribner's, 1969), 37. Jeffrey Meyers, *Hemingway, A Biography* (New York: Harper & Row, 1985), 110.
37. Ernest Hemingway to Harvey Breit, 23 July 1956, *Selected Letters*, 867.
38. Maxwell Perkins to Ernest Hemingway, 20 December 1935, Kennedy Library.
39. William White, Introduction to *By-Line: Ernest Hemingway*, xi–xii. Jeffrey Meyers explores the literary uses Hemingway made of his reporting from the Greco-Turkish war in 'Hemingway's Second War: The Greco-Turkish Conflict, 1920–1922,' *Modern Fiction Studies*, 30 (Spring 1984), 25–36.
40. Ernest Hemingway, 'A.D. in Africa: A Tanganyika Letter,' in *By-Line: Ernest Hemingway*, 159.
41. In addition to Fenton's book, see Shelley Fisher Fishkin's chapter on Hemingway in *From Fact to Fiction: Journalism & Imaginative Writing in America* (Baltimore: Johns Hopkins University Press, 1985), 137–64.
42. Russell Baker, *Growing Up* (New York: New American Library, 1983), 254.
43. Ernest Hemingway to Gertrude Stein and Alice B. Toklas, 9 November 1923, *Selected Letters*, 101.
44. Gertrude Stein, *The Autobiography of Alice B. Toklas* (New York: Harcourt, Brace, 1933), 262.
45. Ernest Hemingway, 'Pamplona Letter', *the transatlantic review*, 2 (September 1924), 300.
46. Quoted in Fenton, *The Apprenticeship of Ernest Hemingway*, 262.
47. Plimpton, *Writers at Work*, 239.
48. Ernest Hemingway, 'Monologue to the Maestro: A High Seas Letter', in *By-Line: Ernest Hemingway*, 215–16.
49. Ernest Hemingway, *Death in the Afternoon* (New York: Scribner's, 1932), 2.
50. Quoted in Thomas Beer, *Stephen Crane* (New York: Knopf, 1923), 184. Nonetheless, Crane's novel *Active Service* has a reporter as protagonist.

51. Ernest Hemingway, *Death in the Afternoon*, 180.
52. Item 581, Hemingway Collection, Kennedy Library. Another passage from the story is quoted in Donaldson, Hemingway of *The Star*', 104.
53. Item 256, Hemingway Collection, Kennedy Library. At the top of the manuscript Hemingway wrote 'worthless sketch, discarded'. More of the sketch is reproduced in Donaldson, 'Hemingway of *The Star*', 91–2.
54. Item 270.5, Hemingway Collection, Kennedy Library. The passage is quoted in Donaldson, 'Hemingway of *The Star*', 104.
55. Ernest Hemingway, 'Fresh Air on an Inside Story', in *By-Line: Ernest Hemingway*, 296.
56. Quoted in Paul Zweig, *Walt Whitman* (New York: Basic Books, 1984), 7.
57. John O'Hara, 'Claude Emerson, Reporter', in *The Cape Cod Lighter* (New York: Random House, 1961), 76.
58. Saul Bellow, *The Dean's December* (New York: Harper & Row, 1982), 61.
59. Howard Good, *Acquainted With the Night: The Image of Journalists in American Fiction, 1890–1930* (Metuchen, NJ: Scarecrow Press, 1986), 87–106.
60. Arnold Samuelson, *With Hemingway: A Year in Key West and Cuba* (New York: Random House, 1984), 44, 178, 176, 177.
61. Ernest Hemingway, 'A Situation Report', in *By-Line: Ernest Hemingway*, 470, 471–2, 472.
62. Ernest Hemingway to Maxwell Perkins, 16 November 1933, *Selected Letters*, 400. The emphasis in the passage is Hemingway's.

CHAPTER 2: ALL THE DOPE

1. Ernest Hemingway, Note to 'A Natural History of the Dead', in *Winner Take Nothing* (New York: Scribner's, 1933), 137.
2. Richard B. Hovey, *Hemingway: The Inward Terrain* (Seattle: University of Washington Press, 1968), 109. Scott Donaldson, *By Force of Will: The Life of Ernest Hemingway* (New York: Viking, 1977), 90. Meyers, *Hemingway*, 228.
3. Michael S. Reynolds offers this view of Perkins' attitude in *Hemingway's Reading, 1910–1940* (Princeton: Princeton University Press, 1981), 33.
4. Ernest Hemingway, *Death in the Afternoon*, 86. Subsequent page references appear in the text.
5. Ernest Hemingway, *The Sun Also Rises* (New York: Scribner's, 1926), 130.
6. Ernest Hemingway to Maxwell Perkins, 15 December 1929, *Selected Letters*, 317.
7. Ernest Hemingway, 'Bullfighting, Sport and Industry', *Fortune*, **1** (March 1930), 83, 146.
8. Ernest Hemingway, 'Pamplona Letter', 300.
9. Ernest Hemingway to Maxwell Perkins, 15 April 1925, *Selected Letters*,

156. In a letter to John Dos Passos a week later, Hemingway reported that he had already received 'a commission to write a book on bull fighting with Flechtheim' that would have illustrations by Picasso and Juan Gris as well as photographs. The reference was to Alfred Flechtheim, founder of *Der Querschnitt*, the Berlin periodical that published some of Hemingway's early poetry and fiction, including 'The Undefeated'. Carlos Baker suggests in his biography that Hemingway might have had the agreement in mind when he wrote to Perkins, the idea being to find a more prestigious patron for the bullfight book. Hemingway received an advance from Flechtheim but did no work on the assignment. Ernest Hemingway to John Dos Passos, 22 April 1925, *Selected Letters*, 157–8.

10. T. E. Lawrence, Introduction to Charles M. Doughty, *Travels in Arabia Deserta* (New York: Boni & Liveright, 1921), xvii.

11. Maxwell Perkins to Ernest Hemingway, 22 November 1926, Scribner Archives, Princeton University.

12. Ernest Hemingway, 'Pamplona in July', in *By-Line: Ernest Hemingway*, 105, 108. Hadley later said of her own interest in bullfighting that 'I'm very proud, maybe ashamed to have liked it, loved it, from the beginning. Of course Ernest was there to explain it to me so that it made sense.' Quoted in Lawrence R. Broer, *Hemingway's Spanish Tragedy* (University, Alabama: University of Alabama Press, 1973), 2.

13. Ernest Hemingway to Edward J. O'Brien, 2 May 1924, *Selected Letters*, 117.

14. Ernest Hemingway, 'Pamplona Letter', 302.

15. Ernest Hemingway, 'On Writing', in *The Nick Adams Stories* (New York: Scribner's, 1972), 245.

16. Ernest Hemingway to Maxwell Perkins, 5–6 January 1932, *Selected Letters*, 351.

17. Ernest Hemingway to Maxwell Perkins, 12 August 1930, *Selected Letters*, 327.

18. Hemingway's revisions of the manuscript are examined by Robert W. Lewis in 'The Making of *Death in the Afternoon*', in *Ernest Hemingway, The Writer in Context*, James Nagel (ed.) (Madison: The University of Wisconsin Press, 1984), 31–52. Lewis concludes (p. 40) that one of the aims in revision was to make the book 'more than a mere handbook'.

19. Ernest Hemingway to Maxwell Perkins, 1 August 1931, Kennedy Library.

20. Ernest Hemingway to Maxwell Perkins, [no date] November 1931, Kennedy Library.

21. Ernest Hemingway to Maxwell Perkins, 9 December 1931, Kennedy Library.

22. Ernest Hemingway to Maxwell Perkins, 5–6 January 1932, *Selected Letters*, 351.

23. Maxwell Perkins to Ernest Hemingway, 25 January 1932, Scribner Archives, Princeton University.

24. Maxwell Perkins to Ernest Hemingway, 5 February 1932, Scribner Archives, Princeton University.

25. Dos Passos' remark is quoted in Townsend Ludington, *John Dos*

Passos (New York: Dutton, 1980), 304. Dos Passos' letter to Hemingway, in the Kennedy Library, is dated 14 January 1932, with the date crossed out. The letter is quoted in Virginia Spencer Carr, *Dos Passos, A Life* (Garden City, NY: Doubleday, 1984), 285.

26. Ernest Hemingway to John Dos Passos, 12 April 1932, *Selected Letters*, 356.

27. Ernest Hemingway to John Dos Passos, 30 May 1932, *Selected Letters*, 360.

28. Ernest Hemingway to Maxwell Perkins, 2 June 1932, Kennedy Library. 'Your notebook would be fun to publish,' the editor responded, 'but neither you nor I will have anything to do with that.' Maxwell Perkins to Ernest Hemingway, 11 June 1932, Kennedy Library. The letter is quoted in Susan F. Beegel, *Hemingway's Craft of Omission* (Ann Arbor: UMI Research Press, 1988), 67.

29. Ernest Hemingway to Maxwell Perkins, 5 April 1932, Kennedy Library. In a letter in January, Hemingway had told Perkins that if anything should happen to him before the book was finished the editor should publish it with only a few illustrations: 'No color plates – give Pauline the money they would cost. Pauline could pick the illustrations and write very short captions.' Ernest Hemingway to Maxwell Perkins, 5–6 January 1932, *Selected Letters*, 351.

30. Ernest Hemingway to Maxwell Perkins, 28 June 1932, *Selected Letters*, 361.

31. Quoted in A. Scott Berg, *Max Perkins, Editor of Genius* (New York: Dutton, 1978), 195.

32. Ernest Hemingway to Maxwell Perkins, 28 June 1932, *Selected Letters*, 362.

33. Ernest Hemingway to Alfred Dashiell, 7 February 1932, Scribner Archives, Princeton University.

34. Ernest Hemingway to Guy Hickok, 14 October 1932, *Selected Letters*, 372.

35. Maxwell Perkins to Ernest Hemingway, 3 November 1932, Scribner Archives, Princeton University.

36. Lawrence Stallings, 'Dissertation on Pride', in *Ernest Hemingway: The Critical Reception*, Robert O. Stephens (ed.) (New York: Burt Franklin, 1977), 109.

37. Max Eastman, 'Bull in the Afternoon', in *Hemingway, The Critical Heritage*, Jeffrey Meyers (ed.) (London: Routledge & Kegan Paul, 1982), 175, 176.

38. Quoted in Baker, *Ernest Hemingway*, 318.

39. Malcolm Cowley, 'A Farewell to Spain', *New Republic*, **73** (30 November 1932), 76.

40. Ernest Hemingway to Arnold Gingrich, 4 December 1932, *Selected Letters*, 378.

41. This passage and others from the discarded opening are reproduced in Beegel, *Hemingway's Craft of Omission*, 51–67. The material is found in Item 34, Hemingway Collection, Kennedy Library.

42. Carlos Baker, *Hemingway, The Writer as Artist*, 4th edn. (Princeton: Princeton University Press, 1972), 143.

43. Edmund Wilson, 'Hemingway: Gauge of Morale', in *The Wound and the Bow* (Cambridge, Mass.: Houghton Mifflin, 1941), 223, 227. Wilson first broached this view of the non-fiction in a discussion of *Green Hills of Africa*, 'Letter to the Russians about Hemingway', *New Republic*, 81 (11 December 1935), 137–8, and subsequently in 'Ernest Hemingway: Bourdon Gauge of Morale', *Atlantic*, 164 (July 1939), 36–46.

44. Ernest Hemingway to Maxwell Perkins, 6 December 1926, *Selected Letters*, 236.

45. F. O. Matthiessen, *American Renaissance* (New York: Oxford University Press, 1941), 170–1. Thoreau is quoted by Matthiessen on p. 85. The passage appears in *A Week on the Concord and Merrimack Rivers* (New York: The Library of America, 1985), 266.

46. In his fact book about Spain, *Homage to Catalonia*, George Orwell similarly advises the reader to skip, though to skip dense sections on political alignment in the Spanish Civil War in favor of the account of Orwell's personal involvement in the fighting. See *Homage to Catalonia* (London: Secker & Warburg, 1951), 47.

47. Carlos Baker, however, makes a case for Hemingway's indebtedness to Frank's sense of the tragic structure of the drama of the bullring in *Hemingway, The Writer as Artist*, 151.

48. Waldo Frank, *Virgin Spain* (London: Jonathan Cape, 1926), 236–7.

49. Ernest Hemingway to Alfred Dashiell, 7 February 1932, Scribner Archives, Princeton University.

50. Ernest Hemingway to Maxwell Perkins, 28 June 1932, *Selected Letters*, 362.

51. Quoted in Allen Josephs, '*Death in the Afternoon*: A Reconsideration', *The Hemingway Review*, 2 (Fall 1982), 10.

52. John McCormick and Mario Sevilla Mascareñas, *The Complete Aficionado* (Cleveland: World, 1967), 236.

53. Angel Capellán, *Hemingway and the Hispanic World* (Ann Arbor: UMI Research Press, 1985), 154.

54. James A. Michener, *Iberia* (New York: Random House, 1968), 642. James A. Michener, Introduction to Ernest Hemingway, *The Dangerous Summer* (New York: Scribner's, 1985), 12.

55. Lincoln Kirstein, 'The Canon of Death', in *Ernest Hemingway: The Man and His Work*, John K. M. McCaffery (ed.) (Cleveland: World, 1950), 60.

56. The remarks are Kenneth S. Lynn's in *Hemingway* (New York: Simon & Schuster, 1987), 396.

57. Geoffrey Brereton, 'Books in General', *New Statesman and Nation*, 39 (24 June 1950), 717.

CHAPTER 3: ONE CENTRAL NECESSITY

1. Quoted in Carr, *Dos Passos*, 311.

2. Ernest Hemingway to Arnold Gingrich, 4 December 1932, *Selected Letters*, 378.

3. Quoted in Baker, *Ernest Hemingway*, 240.

4. Arnold Gingrich to Ernest Hemingway, 20 June 1933, Kennedy Library.
5. Arnold Gingrich to Ernest Hemingway, 7 July 1933, Kennedy Library.
6. Ibid.
7. Arnold Gingrich to Ernest Hemingway, 2 December 1933, Kennedy Library.
8. Ernest Hemingway to Arnold Gingrich, 4 June 1935, Kennedy Library.
9. Arnold Gingrich to Ernest Hemingway, 2 December 1933, Kennedy Library.
10. Ernest Hemingway, 'A.D. in Africa: A Tanganyika Letter', 160, 161.
11. Ernest Hemingway, 'Notes on Dangerous Game: The Third Tanganyika Letter', in *By-Line: Ernest Hemingway*, 167–8, 168, 171.
12. Wilson, 'Letter to the Russians about Hemingway', 137.
13. Ernest Hemingway to Arnold Gingrich, 15 July 1934, *Selected Letters*, 409–10.
14. Ernest Hemingway to F. Scott Fitzgerald, 28 May 1934, *Selected Letters*, 408.
15. Ernest Hemingway to Maxwell Perkins, 20 November 1934, Kennedy Library.
16. Ernest Hemingway, *Green Hills of Africa* (New York: Scribner's, 1935), 149. Subsequent page references appear in the text.
17. Ernest Hemingway to Maxwell Perkins, 20 June 1934, Kennedy Library.
18. Maxwell Perkins to Ernest Hemingway, 8 February 1935, Scribner Archives, Princeton University.
19. Maxwell Perkins to Ernest Hemingway, 4 April 1935, Scribner Archives, Princeton University.
20. Quoted in Berg, *Max Perkins*, 283.
21. Maxwell Perkins to Ernest Hemingway, 2 April 1935, Kennedy Library.
22. Ernest Hemingway to Maxwell Perkins, 2 July 1935, Kennedy Library.
23. Quoted in Berg, *Max Perkins*, 284, 285.
24. John Chamberlain, 'Books of the Times'; Charles G. Poore, 'Ernest Hemingway's Story of His African Safari'; Carl Van Doren, 'Ernest Hemingway, Singing in Africa', in *Ernest Hemingway: The Critical Reception*, 150, 153, 155.
25. Wilson, 'Letter to the Russians about Hemingway', 138, 137. Later, the last remark was slightly revised to read that Hemingway 'has produced what must be one of the only books ever written which make Africa and its animals seem dull.' Wilson, *The Wound and the Bow*, 228.
26. Quoted in Richard Ellmann, *James Joyce* (New York: Oxford University Press, 1959), 708. Nora Joyce is quoted by Ellmann in *Four Dubliners* (New York: George Braziller, 1987), 69.
27. Ernest Hemingway, *The Sun Also Rises*, 10.
28. Ernest Hemingway to Maxwell Perkins, 20 November 1934, Kennedy Library.
29. Daniel W. Streeter, *Denatured Africa* (Garden City, NY: Garden City Publishing Company, 1926), 175. Michael Reynolds in *Hemingway's*

Reading doesn't list the work among Hemingway's books but does include Streeter's 1929 book *Arctic Rodeo*.

30. Streeter, *Denatured Africa*, viii.
31. Ernest Hemingway to Maxwell Perkins, 20 November 1935, Kennedy Library.
32. Maxwell Perkins to Ernest Hemingway, 8 November 1934, Scribner Archives, Princeton University. The emphasis is Perkins'.
33. Hemingway also kept a diary during the safari. In a book inventory he made in 1940 prior to leaving Key West for Cuba he listed 'Diary of E.H. (in Africa)'. See Reynolds, *Hemingway's Reading*, 57. The diary is among the Hemingway materials in Cuba.
34. Ernest Hemingway to Maxwell Perkins, 17 January 1934, Kennedy Library.
35. Charles P. Curtis, Jr, and Richard C. Curtis, *Hunting in Africa East and West* (Boston: Houghton Mifflin, 1925), 114. The book comes in two parts, the first – roughly the first three-quarters – written by Charles Curtis and about the safari in East Africa, the second written by his brother, Richard, about a brief hunt for sable in Angola in West Africa. The latter bears a faint resemblance to Hemingway's book in its concentration on the sable hunt. Richard and his father each kill one, the son's with horns slightly less admirable than the father's, bringing the remark: 'Everything was as it should be.' No rivalry here. A few days remaining before a steamer returns them to England, the hunting party is tempted to try for kudu but decides against it since 'it would have been a dreadful anticlimax after all our luck to miss a kudu' (pp. 275, 281). Near the end of *Green Hills of Africa* Hemingway mentions that he had heard and read that the Masai subsisted on the blood of their cattle mixed with milk, the blood drawn off by shooting an arrow into a neck vein at close range. This exotic bit of information appears in the Curtises' book.
36. Maxwell Perkins to Ernest Hemingway, 4 April 1935, Kennedy Library. Maxwell Perkins to Ernest Hemingway, 2 April 1935, Kennedy Library.
37. Quoted in Bernice Kert, *The Hemingway Women* (New York: Norton, 1983), 260.
38. Wilson, 'Letter to the Russians about Hemingway', 138. The emphasis is Wilson's.
39. Van Doren, 'Ernest Hemingway, Singing in Africa', 155.
40. Wilson, 'Letter to the Russians about Hemingway', 137.
41. Lionel Trilling, 'Hemingway and His Critics', in *Ernest Hemingway*, Harold Bloom (ed.) (New York: Chelsea House, 1985), 7. Trilling goes on to explain the Wilsonian contrast by maintaining that while Hemingway the 'artist' is conscious, innocent, disinterested and truthful, Hemingway the 'man' is self-conscious, naive, has a personal axe to grind and falsifies. The non-fiction, stemming from the 'man', would appear to have little to recommend it. Trilling refers in his article, originally published in *Partisan Review* in 1939, to Wilson's 1935 article, 'Letter to the Russians about Hemingway'.
42. Leo Gurko, *Ernest Hemingway and the Pursuit of Heroism* (New York:

43.   William Kennedy, 'The last Olé', *New York Times Book Review* (9 June 1985), 32.

44.   The passage appears on p. 86 of the holograph manuscript. It is quoted, in slightly different form, in Baker, *Ernest Hemingway*, 263.

45.   Ernest Hemingway to Ivan Kashkin, 12 January 1936, *Selected Letters*, 431.

CHAPTER 4: A FIRST CLASS LIFE

1.   Phillip Knightley, *The First Casualty* (New York: Harcourt, Brace, 1975), 212, 214. For a different estimate of Hemingway's work see William Braasch Watson, 'Hemingway's Spanish Civil War Dispatches', *The Hemingway Review*, **7** (Spring 1988), 4–13. This special issue of the journal reprints the dispatches Hemingway wrote for the North American Newspaper Alliance. Watson concludes (p. 7) about the quality of Hemingway's work: 'Some, quite frankly, were poorly done. They are trivial or incoherent or just simply perfunctory. Some were done well enough, but they were so full of topographical and place-name details that they were more appropriate for general staff colleges than for newspaper audiences. Some provided superb examples of his powers of observation, his fact-finding abilities, his responsiveness to human suffering and human excellence alike. Some were masterpieces of characterization, of analysis, of description, or of just plain factual reporting. A half-dozen or so of these dispatches can stand up to the best reporting from the Spanish Civil War.'

2.   Meyers, *Hemingway*, 325.

3.   Quoted in White, Introduction to *By-Line: Ernest Hemingway*, xiii.

4.   Ernest Hemingway, 'Voyage to Victory'; Ernest Hemingway, 'How We Came to Paris', in *By-Line: Ernest Hemingway*, 340, 376.

5.   Ernest Hemingway, 'The Snows of Kilimanjaro', in *The Short Stories of Ernest Hemingway* (New York: Scribner's, 1953), 59.

6.   Ernest Hemingway to Bernard Berenson, 14 October 1952, *Selected Letters*, 792–3.

7.   Quoted in Mary Hemingway, *How It Was* (New York: Knopf, 1976), 312.

8.   Mary Hemingway, *How It Was*, 321.

9.   Ernest Hemingway, 'Safari', *Look*, **18** (26 January 1954), 20.

10. Quoted in Denis Brian, *The True Gen* (New York: Grove Press, 1988), 291.

11. Ernest Hemingway to Harvey Breit, 3 January 1954, *Selected Letters*, 825.

12. Ernest Hemingway, 'The Christmas Gift', in *By-Line: Ernest Hemingway*, 440.

13. Ernest Hemingway to Bernard Berenson, 24 September 1954, *Selected Letters*, 838.

14. Ernest Hemingway to General Charles T. Lanham, 10 November 1954, *Selected Letters*, 839.

15. Ernest Hemingway to Wallace Meyer, 5 December 1955, *Selected Letters*, 852.
16. Quoted in Ray Cave, 'Introduction to an African Journal', *Sports Illustrated*, **35** (20 December 1971), 41.
17. Ernest Hemingway, 'A Situation Report', 470.
18. Philip Young and Charles W. Mann, *The Hemingway Manuscripts: An Inventory* (University Park: Pennsylvania State University Press, 1969), 6.
19. Quoted in Ray Cave, 'Introduction to an African Journal', 40.
20. Mary Hemingway, *How It Was*, 532, 535.
21. Ernest Hemingway, 'African Journal', *Sports Illustrated*, **35** (20 December 1971), 2. The first two parts of the series were subtitled 'Miss Mary's Lion', the third part 'Imperiled Flanks'.
22. Ibid., 8.
23. Ernest Hemingway to General Charles T. Lanham, 10 November 1954, *Selected Letters*, 839.
24. Ernest Hemingway, 'African Journal', 13, 11.
25. Ernest Hemingway, 'African Journal', *Sports Illustrated*, **36** (3 January 1972), 13.
26. Ibid., 16.
27. Ibid., 19.
28. Ernest Hemingway, 'African Journal', *Sports Illustrated*, **36** (10 January 1972), 4, 5, 7, 11.
29. Baker, *Ernest Hemingway*, 526.
30. Ernest Hemingway, *Green Hills of Africa*, 282.
31. Ernest Hemingway, 'African Journal', *Sports Illustrated*, **35** (20 December 1971), 13.
32. Graham Greene, *The Human Factor* (New York: Simon & Schuster, 1978), 139. The remark, voiced by the novel's protagonist, Maurice Castle, appears in the context of an assertion that American knowledge of Africa comes only through novelists like Hemingway. Hemingway's safari lasted three months, not one.

CHAPTER 5: *THIS ABOUT THE BULLS*

1. Ernest Hemingway, *The Dangerous Summer*, 56.
2. Quoted in Baker, *Ernest Hemingway*, 544.
3. Mary Hemingway, *How It Was*, 461.
4. Ernest Hemingway to L. H. Brague, Jr, 22 February 1959, *Selected Letters*, 893.
5. Ernest Hemingway to Maxwell Perkins, 14 October 1932, Kennedy Library.
6. Maxwell Perkins to Ernest Hemingway, 3 November 1932, Scribner Archives, Princeton University.
7. Ernest Hemingway to Maxwell Perkins, 23 October 1946, Princeton University.
8. The magazine, in an editorial note accompanying the first installment, said Hemingway had agreed to write a '5,000-word news article'.

Carlos Baker has the figure as 10 000 words in his biography, the same figure mentioned by Hemingway in a letter.

9. José Luis Castillo-Puche, *Hemingway in Spain* (Garden City, NY: Doubleday, 1974), 318–19.

10. Ernest Hemingway to Charles Scribner, Jr, 31 March–1 April 1960, *Selected Letters*, 901–2.

11. Ernest Hemingway to Gianfranco Ivancich, 30 May 1960, *Selected Letters*, 903.

12. Ernest Hemingway to Bill Lang, 3 January 1960, Kennedy Library. *Life* quoted from the letter in an editorial note accompanying the first installment of 'The Dangerous Summer'.

13. Ed Thompson to Ernest Hemingway, 14 April 1960, Kennedy Library.

14. Quoted in A. E. Hotchner, *Papa Hemingway* (New York: Random House, 1966), 242.

15. Ernest Hemingway to Charles Scribner, Jr, 6 July 1960, *Selected Letters*, 905.

16. Quoted in Mary Hemingway, *How It Was*, 490.

17. Ernest Hemingway to Mary Hemingway, 25 September 1960, *Selected Letters*, 907.

18. Quoted in Hotchner, *Papa Hemingway*, 263.

19. Bill Lang to Ernest Hemingway, 20 September 1960, Kennedy Library.

20. Ed Thompson to Ernest Hemingway, 10 November 1960, Kennedy Library.

21. Baker and Scribner are quoted in Edwin McDowell, 'New Hemingway Book on Matadors', *New York Times* (2 February 1985), C 13.

22. James Michener in his introduction to *The Dangerous Summer* gives different figures. He says the manuscript originally had 120 000 words and the edited version submitted to *Life* about 70 000.

23. A. E. Hotchner, letter to author, 27 May 1986.

24. Ernest Hemingway to Charles Scribner, Jr, 6 July 1960, *Selected Letters*, 906.

25. Ernest Hemingway to Ed Thompson, 2 June 1960, Kennedy Library.

26. Michael Pietsch, telephone conversation with author, 13 March 1986, and letter to author, 7 April 1986.

27. Ernest Hemingway, 'The Dangerous Summer', *Life*, **49** (5 September 1960), 86.

28. Ibid., 87.

29. Castillo-Puche, *Hemingway in Spain*, 321.

30. Ernest Hemingway, *The Dangerous Summer*, 82. Subsequent page references appear in the text.

31. Michener, Introduction to *The Dangerous Summer*, 37.

32. Ernest Hemingway, *Death in the Afternoon*, 238.

33. Ernest Hemingway, 'The Dangerous Summer', *Life*, **49** (19 September 1960), 95. The magazine called the three installments, in order, 'The Dangerous Summer', 'The Pride of the Devil', 'An Appointment with Disaster', with 'The Dangerous Summer' as the overall title.

34. Ibid., 96.

35. Capellán, *Hemingway and the Hispanic World*, 149.

36. Michener, Introduction to *The Dangerous Summer*, 16.

37. Quoted in Meyers, *Hemingway*, 526.
38. Eric Sevareid, 'Mano a Mano', *Esquire*, 52 (November 1959), 44. The article troubled Hemingway, who thought remarks of his, quoted by Sevareid, would make *Life*'s editors think he was giving away material they had paid for. He asked Hotchner to explain to Ed Thompson that Sevareid was 'just the usual character who comes to lunch and stuffs his pocket with your ideas instead of your silver.' Quoted in Hotchner, *Papa Hemingway*, 237.
39. Castillo-Puche, *Hemingway in Spain*, 317, 318.
40. Ernest Hemingway to Ed Thompson, 31 March 1960, Kennedy Library.
41. Ernest Hemingway to Edward J. O'Brien, 2 May 1924, *Selected Letters*, 117.
42. Kennedy, 'The Last Olé', 35.
43. In a 1963 letter to Kenneth Burke, Malcolm Cowley expressed bewilderment at Hemingway's inability in his last years to carry any of his work through publication. 'Apparently,' he wrote, 'Mr Papa had been writing steadily for all those years when he didn't publish anything. Possibly some of what he wrote is quite good . . . but he didn't get anything in final shape for publication; he just went on writing, like Mark Twain in his last ten years. We know why Mark Twain didn't publish; he thought that what he was writing would alienate his public; but what made Ernest start things, nearly finish them, then start something else? It's an absolute puzzle to me.' The letter appears in *The Selected Correspondence of Kenneth Burke and Malcolm Cowley*, Paul Jay (ed.) (New York: Viking, 1988), 346. For Burke's contorted answer to Cowley's question see his letter printed on pp. 346–7.
44. Ernest Hemingway, *Death in the Afternoon*, 2.

CHAPTER 6: HOW THINGS TRULY WERE

1.   Ernest Hemingway to L. H. Brague, Jr, 6 February 1961, *Selected Letters*, 917.
2.   Mary Hemingway, 'The Making of a Book: A Chronicle and a Memoir', *New York Times Book Review* (10 May 1964), 27.
3.   Ernest Hemingway, 'Pamplona Letter', 301.
4.   Ernest Hemingway to Janet Flanner, 8 April 1933, *Selected Letters*, 388.
5.   Ernest Hemingway to Maxwell Perkins, 26 July 1933, *Selected Letters*, 396.
6.   Ernest Hemingway to Malcolm Cowley, 17 October 1945, *Selected Letters*, 603.
7.   Ernest Hemingway, 'The Snows of Kilimanjaro', 70, 71.
8.   Ernest Hemingway, 'African Journal', *Sports Illustrated*, **36** (3 January 1972), 3.
9.   Ernest Hemingway, 'A Paris Letter', in *By-Line: Ernest Hemingway*, 155, 158.
10. Carlos Baker notes in his critical study that no listing of the exact

contents of the trunks was ever made. For doubt about the trunks' existence see Jacqueline Tavernier-Courbin, 'The Mystery of the Ritz Hotel Papers', in *Ernest Hemingway, The Papers of a Writer*, 117–31. She concludes (p. 129) that 'at this point, the evidence in favor of the story as told by Hemingway and, especially, Mary is not overwhelmingly convincing, and there is a possibility that the whole thing was a figment of Hemingway's imagination.' See as well the same author's article 'The Manuscripts of *A Moveable Feast*', *Hemingway Notes*, **1** (Spring 1981), 9–15.

11.   Quoted in Baker, *Ernest Hemingway*, 537.

12.   Ernest Hemingway to Harvey Breit, 16 June 1957, Kennedy Library.

13.   Ernest Hemingway, *Green Hills of Africa*, 70.

14.   Mary Hemingway, 'The Making of a Book: A Chronicle and a Memoir', 27. Carlos Baker points out that, as with many of Mary's remarks about the making of *A Moveable Feast*, this one is questionable. The work isn't a biography, and the term 'remate' in jai alai refers to a kill-shot, one that cannot be played by an opponent. Baker, *Hemingway, The Writer as Artist*, n. 375–6. Gerry Brenner, however, suggests that Mary had the term right, Hemingway intending his acid portraits of contemporaries as 'kill-shots they are literally unable to return'. Brenner, *Concealments in Hemingway's Works* (Columbus: Ohio State University Press, 1983), 218.

15.   Ernest Hemingway to General Charles T. Lanham, 18 September 1958, Kennedy Library.

16.   Ernest Hemingway to L. H. Brague, Jr, 22 February 1959, *Selected Letters*, 893.

17.   Quoted in Hotchner, *Papa Hemingway*, 285–6.

18.   Earl Rovit and Gerry Brenner, for example, say this: 'Mary Hemingway's "Note" in the front matter of *A Moveable Feast* . . . declares that Hemingway "finished the book in the spring of 1960," implying that the published book reproduces that "finished" text. We now know better. We know . . . that she made significant cuts and alterations, that to Hemingway's "finished" typescript she added material he had not written or had chosen to leave out, that the ending was one she doctored from his rejected drafts.' *Ernest Hemingway*, rev. edn. (Boston: Twayne, 1986), 155–6. See also Gerry Brenner, 'Are We Going to Hemingway's *Feast*?', *American Literature*, **54** (December 1982), 529, and Tavernier-Courbin, 'The Manuscripts of *A Moveable Feast*', 9.

19.   Quoted in Tavernier-Courbin, 'The Manuscripts of *A Moveable Feast*', 13. See also Brenner, 'Are We Going to Hemingway's *Feast*?, 530.

20.   Mary Hemingway, 'The Making of a Book: A Chronicle and a Memoir', 27.

21.   Quoted in Kert, *The Hemingway Women*, 484–5.

22.   See Brenner, 'Are We Going to Hemingway's *Feast*?', 543.

23.   Frank Kermode [review of *A Moveable Feast*], in *Hemingway, The Critical Heritage*, 471. Meyers, *Hemingway*, 537.

24.   Cyril Connolly, *Enemies of Promise* (London: André Deutsch, 1973), 66.

25. Ernest Hemingway, *Death in the Afternoon*, 100.
26. Ernest Hemingway to Harvey Breit, 18 August 1954, *Selected Letters*, 834. Hemingway's remark about Loeb is quoted in Baker, *Ernest Hemingway*, 552.
27. Ernest Hemingway to Charles Fenton, 29 July 1952, *Selected Letters*, 776.
28. Ernest Hemingway, *A Moveable Feast* (New York: Scribner's, 1964), 54–55, 202, 203, 206. Subsequent page references appear in the text.
29. Ernest Hemingway to Charles Fenton, 29 July 1952, *Selected Letters*, 777.
30. Arnold Gingrich, 'Scott, Ernest and Whoever,' *Esquire*, **66** (December 1966), 188. Edmund Wilson was equally struck by the surface accuracy of Hemingway's treatment of both Ford and Fitzgerald: 'In his book of reminiscences of Paris he reproduces for one who has known them the hoarse British gasps of Ford Madox Ford, the exasperating nonsense of Scott Fitzgerald so faithfully that one can hear them speaking . . .' 'An Effort at Self-Revelation,' *The New Yorker*, **46** (2 January 1971), 60.
31. Gertrude Stein, *The Autobiography of Alice B. Toklas*, 265–6.
32. Quoted in Barbara Probst Solomon, 'Where's Papa?', *New Republic*, **196** (9 March 1987), 32. The article discusses differences between the published version of *The Garden of Eden* and Hemingway's manuscripts.
33. Ernest Hemingway to Hadley Hemingway, 18 November 1926, *Selected Letters*, 228.
34. Ernest Hemingway to Hadley Mowrer, 25 November 1943, *Selected Letters*, 556.
35. Quoted in Carr, *Dos Passos*, 499.
36. Ernest Hemingway to William D. Horne, 17–18 July 1923, *Selected Letters*, 85.
37. Marvin Mudrick [review of *A Moveable Feast*], in *Hemingway, The Critical Heritage*, 509.
38. Ernest Hemingway, 'The Snows of Kilimanjaro', 66.

Works Consulted

BY HEMINGWAY

The Sun Also Rises. New York: Scribner's, 1926.

Death in the Afternoon. New York: Scribner's, 1932.

Green Hills of Africa. New York: Scribner's, 1935.

The Short Stories of Ernest Hemingway. New York: Scribner's, 1953.

'The Dangerous Summer'. *Life*, 49, 5 September 1960, 77–109; 12 September 1960, 60–82; 19 September 1960, 74–96.

A Moveable Feast. New York: Scribner's, 1964.

By-Line: Ernest Hemingway, Selected Articles and Dispatches of Four Decades. William White (ed.). New York: Scribner's, 1967.

Ernest Hemingway: Cub Reporter. Matthew J. Bruccoli (ed.). Pittsburgh: University of Pittsburgh Press, 1970.

Ernest Hemingway's Apprenticeship. Matthew J. Bruccoli (ed.). Washington, DC: NCR Microcard Editions, 1971.

'African Journal'. Ray Cave (ed.). *Sports Illustrated*, 35, 20 December 1971, 41–70; 3 January 1972, 26–46; 10 January 1972, 22–50.

The Nick Adams Stories. New York: Scribner's, 1972.

The Enduring Hemingway: An Anthology of a Lifetime in Literature. Charles Scribner, Jr (ed.). New York: Scribner's, 1974.

Ernest Hemingway: Selected Letters, 1917–1961. Carlos Baker (ed.). New York: Scribner's, 1981.

The Dangerous Summer. New York: Scribner's, 1985.

Dateline: Toronto. Hemingway's Complete Toronto Star Dispatches, 1920–1924. William White (ed.). New York: Scribner's, 1985.

ABOUT HEMINGWAY

Baker, Carlos. *Ernest Hemingway, A Life Story*. New York: Scribner's, 1969.

Baker, Carlos. *Hemingway, The Writer as Artist*, 4th edn. Princeton: Princeton University Press, 1972.

Beegel, Susan F. 'The Death of El Espartero: A Historic Matador Links "The Undefeated" and *Death in the Afternoon*'. *Hemingway Review*, 5, Spring 1986, 12–23.

Beegel, Susan F. *Hemingway's Craft of Omission: Four Manuscript Examples*. Ann Arbor: UMI Research Press, 1988.

Berg, A. Scott. *Max Perkins, Editor of Genius*. New York: Dutton, 1978.

Brenner, Gerry. 'Are We Going to Hemingway's *Feast*?' *American Literature*, 54, December 1982, 528–44.

Brenner, Gerry. *Concealments in Hemingway's Works*. Columbus: Ohio State University Press, 1983.

Brereton, Geoffrey. 'Books in General'. *New Statesman and Nation*, 39, 24 June 1950, 716–17.

Broer, Lawrence R. *Hemingway's Spanish Tragedy*. University, Alabama: University of Alabama Press, 1973.

Bruccoli, Matthew J. (ed.). *Conversations with Ernest Hemingway*. Jackson: University Press of Mississippi, 1986.

Bruccoli, Matthew J. (ed.). *Scott and Ernest: The Authority of Failure and the Authority of Success*. New York: Random House, 1978.

Brian, Denis. *The True Gen*. New York: Grove Press, 1988.

Capellán, Angel. *Hemingway and the Hispanic World*. Ann Arbor: UMI Research Press, 1985.

Castillo-Puche, José Luis. *Hemingway in Spain*. Garden City, NY: Doubleday, 1974.

Cave, Ray. 'Introduction to An African Journal'. *Sport Illustrated*, 35, 20 December 1971, 40–1.

Cowley, Malcolm. 'A Farewell to Spain', *New Republic*, 73, 30 November 1932, 76–7.

Donaldson, Scott. 'Hemingway of *The Star*'. In *Ernest Hemingway, The Papers of a Writer*. Bernard Oldsey (ed.). New York: Garland, 1981, 89–107.

Donaldson, Scott. *By Force of Will: The Life of Ernest Hemingway*. New York: Viking, 1977.

Fenton, Charles. *The Apprenticeship of Ernest Hemingway*. New York: Farrar, Straus & Cudahy, 1954.

Fishkin, Shelley Fisher. *From Fact to Fiction: Journalism & Imaginative Writing in America*. Baltimore: Johns Hopkins University Press, 1985.

Fuentes, Norberto. *Hemingway in Cuba*. Secaucus, NJ: Lyle Stuart, 1984.

Gingrich, Arnold. 'Scott, Ernest and Whoever'. *Esquire*, 66, December 1966, 186–8.

Griffin, Peter. *Along with Youth: Hemingway, The Early Years*. New York: Oxford University Press, 1985.

Gurko, Leo. *Ernest Hemingway and the Pursuit of Heroism*. New York: Crowell, 1968.

Hemingway, Mary Welsh. *How It Was*. New York: Knopf, 1976.

Hemingway, Mary Welsh. 'The Making of a Book: A Chronicle and a Memoir'. *New York Times Book Review*, 10 May 1964, 26–7.

Hotchner, A. E. *Papa Hemingway*. New York: Random House, 1966.

Hovey, Richard B. *Hemingway: The Inward Terrain*. Seattle: University of Washington Press, 1968.

Joost, Nicholas. *Ernest Hemingway and the Little Magazines*. Barre, Mass.: Barre Publishers, 1968.

Josephs, Allen. '*Death in the Afternoon*: A Reconsideration'. *Hemingway Review*, 2, Fall 1982, 2–16.

Kennedy, William. 'The Last Olé'. *New York Times Book Review*, 9 June 1985, 1, 32.

Kert, Bernice. *The Hemingway Women*. New York: Norton, 1983.

Kirstein, Lincoln. 'The Canon of Death'. In *Ernest Hemingway: The Man and His Work*. John K. M. McCaffery (ed.). Cleveland: World, 1950.

Knightley, Phillip. *The First Casualty*. New York: Harcourt, Brace, 1975.

Kobler, J. F. *Ernest Hemingway, Journalist and Artist*. Ann Arbor: UMI Research Press, 1986.

Lewis, Robert W. 'The Making of *Death in the Afternoon*'. In *Ernest Hemingway, The Writer in Context*. James Nagel (ed.). Madison: University of Wisconsin Press, 1984, 31–52.

Lynn, Kenneth S. *Hemingway*. New York: Simon & Schuster, 1987.

McDowell, Edwin. 'New Hemingway Book on Matadors'. *New York Times*, 2 February 1985, C 13.

Meyers, Jeffrey (ed.). *Hemingway, The Critical Heritage*. London: Routledge & Kegan Paul, 1982.

Meyers, Jeffrey. 'Hemingway's Second War: The Greco-Turkish Conflict, 1920–1922'. *Modern Fiction Studies*, 30, Spring 1984, 25–36.

Meyers, Jeffrey. *Hemingway, A Biography*. New York: Harper & Row, 1985.

Michener, James A. Introduction to *The Dangerous Summer*. New York: Scribner's, 1985, 3–40.

Philips, Steven R. 'Hemingway and the Bullfight: The Archetypes of Tragedy'. *Arizona Quarterly*, 29, Spring 1973, 37–56.

Plimpton, George. 'Ernest Hemingway'. *Writers at Work: The Paris Review Interviews*, Second Series. New York: Viking, 1963, 219–39.

Raeburn, John. *Fame Became of Him*. Bloomington: Indiana University Press, 1984.

Reynolds, Michael S. *Hemingway's Reading, 1910–1940*. Princeton: Princeton University Press, 1981.

Reynolds, Michael S. *The Young Hemingway*. New York: Basil Blackwell, 1986.

Rovit, Earl and Gerry Brenner. *Ernest Hemingway*, Revised edn. Boston: Twayne, 1986.

Samuelson, Arnold. *With Hemingway: A Year in Key West and Cuba*. New York: Random House, 1984.

Solomon, Barbara Probst. 'Where's Papa?' *New Republic*, 196, 9 March 1987, 30–4.

Stephens, Robert O. *Hemingway's Nonfiction*. Chapel Hill: University of North Carolina Press, 1968.

Stephens, Robert O. (ed.). *Ernest Hemingway: The Critical Reception*. New York: Burt Franklin, 1977.

Tavernier-Courbin, Jacqueline. 'The Manuscripts of *A Moveable Feast*'. *Hemingway Notes*, 1, Spring 1981, 9–15.

Tavernier-Courbin, Jacqueline. 'The Mystery of the Ritz Hotel Papers'. In *Ernest Hemingway, The Papers of a Writer*. Bernard Oldsey (ed.). New York: Garland, 1981, 109–31.

Trilling, Lionel. 'Hemingway and His Critics'. In *Ernest Hemingway*. Harold Bloom (ed.). New York: Chelsea House, 1985, 7–15.

Watson, William Braasch. 'Hemingway's Spanish Civil War Dispatches'. *Hemingway Review*, 7, Spring 1988, 4–13.

Wilson, Edmund. 'Letter to the Russians about Hemingway'. *New Republic*, 81, 11 December 1935, 137–8.

Wilson, Edmund. 'Ernest Hemingway: Bourdon Gauge of Morale'. *Atlantic*, 164, July 1939, 36–46.

Wilson, Edmund. *The Wound and the Bow*. Cambridge, Mass.: Houghton Mifflin, 1941.

Wilson, Edmund, 'An Effort at Self-Revelation'. *The New Yorker*, 46, 2 January 1971, 60.

Young, Philip. *Ernest Hemingway: A Reconsideration*. University Park: Pennsylvania State University Press, 1966.

Young, Philip and Charles W. Mann. *The Hemingway Manuscripts: An Inventory*. University Park: Pennsylvania State University Press, 1969.

Index